BLOOD and FIRE

BLOOD and FIRE

Revival Movements That Transformed
Culture and Society

Nigel Scotland

CASCADE Books • Eugene, Oregon

BLOOD AND FIRE
Revival Movements That Transformed Culture and Society

Copyright © 2022 Nigel Scotland. All rights reserved. Except for brief quotations in critical publications or reviews, no part of this book may be reproduced in any manner without prior written permission from the publisher. Write: Permissions, Wipf and Stock Publishers, 199 W. 8th Ave., Suite 3, Eugene, OR 97401.

Cascade Books
An Imprint of Wipf and Stock Publishers
199 W. 8th Ave., Suite 3
Eugene, OR 97401

www.wipfandstock.com

PAPERBACK ISBN: 978-1-6667-3732-5
HARDCOVER ISBN: 978-1-6667-9662-9
EBOOK ISBN: 978-1-6667-9663-6

Cataloguing-in-Publication data:

Names: Scotland, Nigel [author].

Title: Blood and fire : revival movements that transformed culture and society / Nigel Scotland.

Description: Eugene, OR: Cascade Books, 2022 | Includes bibliographical references and index.

Identifiers: ISBN 978-1-6667-3732-5 (paperback) | ISBN 978-1-6667-9662-9 (hardcover) | ISBN 978-1-6667-9663-6 (ebook)

Subjects: LCSH: Revivals—History | Revivals—United States—History—18th century | Revivals—United States—History—19th century | Revivals—United States—History—20th century | Revivals—Great Britain—History—18th century | Revivals—Great Britain—History—19th century | Revivals—Great Britain—History—20th century

Classification: BV3770 S36 2022 (print) | call number (ebook)

08/11/22

Barry Kissell
dear friend

Contents

Preface | vii

1. Introducing Revivals | 1
2. The Revival in Northampton, Massachusetts | 16
3. Revival in Cambuslang, 1742–43 | 34
4. The Methodist Revival in England, 1738–91 | 51
5. The Revival in the Southern Colonies of America | 72
6. The Primitive Methodist Revival, 1811–51 | 92
7. Revival in Upper New York State, 1824–32 | 115
8. The Welsh Revival of 1904 | 138
9. The Azusa Street Revival | 161
10. The Lowestoft Revival | 182
11. The Hebridean Revival | 202
12. Inspirational Revivals | 221

Also by Nigel Scotland | 235
Bibliography | 237
Index | 245

Preface

REVIVALS ARE THE HIGH point of Christian experience. They are times when the presence of Christ powerfully transforms the lives of individuals, churches, and their surrounding societies and culture. Revivals are a repetition of the Day of Pentecost releasing the Holy Spirit to empower the church to know Christ more deeply and to make him known to people and nations. It is therefore vital that Christian people should know something of the world's great revivals and be inspired by them. As we read what the Lord accomplished in past times, it encourages us to have faith that he will do the same again in the present and future. The accounts of revival also challenge us to a deeper level of commitment both to Christ and to those around us.

No revivals are perfect because they happen in communities of fallible people like ourselves. Inevitably there will be mistaken emphases and errors of judgment but revivals nevertheless represent the high moments of God's gracious and powerful coming. As such they inspire us to reach out for his transforming presence both now and in the future. The ten great revivals recounted in the chapters of this book will be an inspirational experience. They will challenge us to deepen our faith in Christ, raise the level of our expectancy, increase our hopes and vision for the future, and, most of all, cause us to pray for revival in our own lives, churches, and nation.

I am grateful for the help I have received with this project along the way from Emily Callihan, Rachel Saunders, Caleb Shupe, and Robin

Parry at Cascade Books. I am particularly indebted to Brian Palmer for his very thorough proofreading and attention to detail.

Nigel Scotland

1

Introducing Revivals

THE TERM *REVIVAL* COMES from the verb "to revive." It speaks of resuscitation and giving new life into someone who has stopped breathing. It signifies bringing something that was dead or dying back to life. We often hear talk of businesses having a revival in their fortunes. So, the word revival is frequently used to refer to new life being breathed or coming back into a church or community which has been in a low, indifferent, or dying state. Christian revivals therefore necessarily nearly always arise out of a time or situation when the spiritual life of the church or Christian community is at a low ebb.

Since the beginning of the Christian church on the day of Pentecost there have been times in every century when godly men and women have been raised up to bring a revival of the empowering presence of Jesus into the lives of people and churches. And this is a book which focuses on ten such revivals which occurred in more recent times. They all took place in either Britain or America, and they all made a powerful and positive impact, not just on the churches but on daily life, society, and culture. Revivals are moves of God which will increase our faith in him and inspire and encourage us with fresh hope and renewed vision for the future.

This book begins with the revival which took place in Northampton, Massachusetts in 1735. People felt the whole town was full of the presence of God. The Congregational minister, Jonathan Edwards, believed that at least one person in every home came to faith in Christ. Next in time is the revival at Cambuslang, close to the city of Glasgow in Scotland. This began in 1742 and centered round the preaching of William McCulloch, the Church of Scotland parish minister, and the visits made by the dramatic preacher and Church of England priest, George Whitefield.

Whitefield preached to more people than anyone else before him in history. Crowds from all parts of the country were reliably assessed at 30,000 or more gathered, and hundreds committed their lives to Christ. At the very same time, revival spread over large parts of the whole of England under the gifted leadership of John and Charles Wesley. Beginning in 1738, following John Wesley's conversion, it endured to the time of his death in 1791. Four hundred thousand came to faith in Christ, many of them joining the newly formed Methodist societies. The revival changed the face of the nation and a number of historians believe it saved England from a bloody revolution such as occurred in France.

In the nineteenth century three revivals are considered. The Second Great Awakening in the Southern American Colonies of Kentucky and Tennessee extended from 1801–10 and featured huge camp meetings and fervent preachers such as James McGready and Barton Stone. Between 20,000 and 30,000 were estimated to have been present at the six-day meeting at Cane Ridge. Just as the American revival was plateauing the Primitive Methodist Revival began in the northwest of England in Staffordshire in 1811 under the leadership of Hugh Bourne and William Clowes. It spread across much of rural England and powerfully impacted the life and culture of agricultural and mine-working communities. Then in the 1820s a whole succession of small-town gatherings brought revival to upper New York State. Fired by the preaching and leadership of Charles Finney, it was noted for its interdenominationalism and numbers of people coming to faith in Christ simply by entering the towns where the revival was taking place but without even attending any of the meetings. These revivals were noted for their powerful impact on the poor, their vigorous worship often accompanied by emotional phenomena and their social impact which included temperance, opposition to slavery, educational improvement, and with the passing of time the emergence and support of trade unions.

The last four chapters consider the Welsh Revival of 1904–5, the Azusa Street Revival in Los Angeles in 1906–9, the Lowestoft Revival of 1921, and the Hebrides Revival of 1949. The movement in Wales began when Evan Roberts, a former mine worker and then-Bible college student, left his studies and started to hold meetings for revival. They were marked by testimony and singing. By the end of 1905, church membership in the country had grown by more than 100,000. The revival at Azusa Street was particularly significant because it marked the beginning of the modern worldwide Pentecostal movement. It focused on receiving a second fresh experience of the Holy Spirit accompanied by speaking in tongues, similar to the day of Pentecost. The central figure, William Seymour, was a black preacher, and the revival was marked by healings and wonderfully by the presence of large numbers of people coming together from both black and white communities. The revival in the East Anglian fishing town of Lowestoft began when the Baptist Church invited Douglas Brown to hold a series of special meetings. The news of his powerful preaching soon spread, and two Anglican churches became fully involved in the work. Townspeople, fishermen, and a large number of seasonal fish-workers from Scotland had deep experiences of the presence of Christ. The Hebridean revival was born of sustained prayer and flourished under the leadership and solid biblical preaching of Duncan Campbell. Scores of men and women both young and old committed their lives to Christ, and there were many testimonies of transformed behavior.

The Characteristics of Revival

All genuine revivals can be readily recognized by a number of characteristics. These will now be highlighted as they will enhance our understanding of the revivals which are examined in the chapters that follow.

Revivals Are a Sovereign Work of God

Revivals, of course, involve human beings, but they are not primarily or solely born of human effort and organization. They may feature special advertising, campaigning, and music, but without the power and presence of God there can be no genuine revival. In 1832, William Sprague, an American Presbyterian minister, published what has since been recognized as an important book entitled *Lectures on the Revivals of Religion*. In it he stated, "In every revival we are to distinctly recognize the sovereignty of God."[1] Max Warren, the General Secretary of a Church of England Missionary Society, wrote a piece just over a century later entitled *Revival: An Inquiry*. He agreed and stated that the element of

---

1. Sprague, *Lectures on Revivals*, 105.

surprise and God's sovereignty are always present in the birth of a revival. "There is," he wrote, "a divine mystery about revivals. God's sovereignty is in them."[2] Jonathan Edwards, who was at the center of the great New England revival, described it as a "surprising work of God."[3] It was nothing he had engineered by his preaching or pastoral care or brought into being by his own endeavors. J. H. Armstrong shared his view. Revivals, he wrote,

> are God-given and cannot be staged. Humans, who long for revivals to come, cannot bring them through their own energy or wills. We cannot bring revival any more than we can breathe life into one dead sinner. We can, and we must, pray to God to work, but we cannot bring life! The author of revival is God, and God alone.[4]

Iain Murray made the very same emphasis, stating, "Revival is always a sovereign work of God brought about solely in conjunction with the biblically appointed means of prayer, fasting and preaching."[5]

Revivals Replicate New Testament Christianity

A number of historians have rightly reminded us that any God-given revival must replicate the Christianity of the New Testament. Vance Havner, for example, defined revival as a "work of God's Spirit among His own people." "What we call revival," he continued, "is simply New Testament Christianity, the saints back to normal."[6] This is a guideline which apostles constantly urged on the early churches for which they were responsible. They were to teach and live out the doctrines and practices which were in line with their teaching and instructions. Writing to the Philippians, the apostle Paul was forthright that "whatever you have learned or received or seen in me—put into practice."[7]

Piggin, in his book *Firestorm of the Lord*, made exactly this point, writing that revivals "will always be a repeat of what happens in the

---

2. Warren, *Revival*, 15.
3. Edwards, *Narrative of Surprising Conversions*, 17.
4. Armstrong, "Revival?," 11.
5. Murray, *Revival and Revivalism*, 21.
6. Havner, *Hearts Afire*, 103–4.
7. Phil 4:9.

Book of Acts."[8] If this is not the case, they will not be genuine revivals. "Whenever the Holy Spirit moves the Church to such awakenings," Piggin continued, "he will always do it in such a way as to focus on Jesus and his gospel."[9] Murray also made the important point that "unless this work of the Spirit which is prominent in the book of Acts is in evidence, individuals are not going to turn from 'attitudes of indifference' or 'cold religious formality.'"[10] Importantly the apostle Paul expressed his astonishment that the churches in Galatia had so quickly begun to turn away to "a different gospel."[11] When he wrote to the church at Thessalonica Paul urged them "to stand firm and hold to the teachings we passed on to you whether by word of mouth or by letter."[12]

Revivals Renew the Church

Any genuine revival will of course include a reviving of the church. Only so will there be a community able to sustain those who become believers in the revival. We see this principle enshrined in the prophecy uttered by the Old Testament prophet Ezekiel. He saw the people of God in his day as being "like a valley of dry bones" but then suddenly rising up to become an invigorated army as the Holy Spirit breathed new life into them.[13] Unsurprisingly J. H. Armstrong asserted, "Revival, by definition, is the life principle of the church." "It is," he continued, "the power that brings life to dead sinners."[14] Max Warren also focused on the importance of revival renewing church.[15] "Revival then," he stated, "is a renewing, a reformation of the church for action."[16] As he perceived it, such renewing could include theology, liturgy, music, and other aspects of worship. It might, on occasion, also embrace the reviving of social conscience. Jesus

---

8. Piggin, *Firestorm of the Lord*, 102.
9. Piggin, *Firestorm of the Lord*, 102.
10. Piggin, *Firestorm of the Lord*, 16.
11. Gal 1:6.
12. 2 Thess 2:15.
13. Ezek 37:1–10.
14. Armstrong, "Revival?," 10.
15. Warren, *Revival*, 15.
16. Warren, *Revival*, 2.

was clear that he had come to build a church and that the gates of hell would not prevail against it.[17]

Piggin outlined some of the ways in which churches are renewed in times of revival. The great doctrines of the faith become real to their people. They begin to be concerned about their behavior and are "resensitized" to the corruption in their own hearts. They also find a renewed energy to pursue holiness in their daily living and are possessed by a new vision of the glory of God. They begin to wait on God and pray strenuously that their minister will have a message which satisfies their new spiritual hunger. J. I. Packer wrote similarly that when God sends revival to a church five things should happen: there would be a greatly enhanced sense of God's presence, a heightened responsiveness to God's word, an increased sensitivity to sin, an unprecedented sense of personal liberation, and an unparalleled fruitfulness in a person's testimony for Christ.[18]

Jonathan Edwards, in his *Narrative of Many Surprising Conversions*, which was published in 1736, chronicled the ways in which his church and congregation in Northampton, Massachusetts was revived. The young people started to get together in small groups to discuss issues of the Christian concern. In another place, Edwards noted that "the minds of people were wonderfully taken from the world." His congregation began to take worship seriously. He reported, "We have six hundred and twenty communicants which includes almost all our adult population." The Bible became for many of them a new book, and public praise in the church's worship was "greatly enlivened."[19]

Ian Randall demonstrated that the Welsh Revival of 1904–5 made a significant impact on the life and worship of many churches both within Wales and outside the Principality.[20] He underlined the fact that following the revival there were "significant increases in Baptist membership across England in 1905."[21]

Worship and fresh outbursts of song are and have been a recurring feature of revivals. It was so during the great Wesleyan revival in the eighteenth century. Charles Wesley is reported to have written some 6,500 hymns. John Wesley published *Wesley's Hymns*, which he described in

17. Matt 16:18.
18. Packer, *God in Our Midst*, 26–35.
19. Edwards, *Narrative of Many Surprising Conversions*, 13–19.
20. Randall, "'Breath of Revival,'" 196–205.
21. Randall, "'Breath of Revival,'" 205.

the introduction as "a little body of practical divinity."[22] The Second Great Awakening in America was marked by singing, and huge numbers of Isaac Watts's hymns were sold. Dwight L. Moody's campaigns in America and England were marked by powerful singing. Ira Sankey, his musical partner and worship leader, published *Sankey's Sacred Songs and Solos*. By 1900, 80 million copies worldwide had been sold. It is therefore clear from all of this that genuine revivals always renew the life, worship, and practice of Jesus' followers.

Revivals Are an Enduring Work of God

We would expect that any move of God's spirit that could be considered a revival must have lasting impact. Indeed, Jesus underlined the importance of his followers enduring with him to the end of their days.[23] In the New Testament the Christian's life is compared to running a long-distance race and battling on to the finishing line.[24] The impact of genuine revivals will therefore be seen in transformed lives that will stay the passage of time. Significantly F. C. Booth wrote that "While revivals do not last, the effects of revival always endure."[25] William Sprague, in his *Lectures on Revival*, emphasized the fact on which we principally rely as evidence of the genuineness of a revival, "is its substantial and abiding fruit."[26] He wisely counselled that "the professions which may be made of devotedness to Christ" are equivocal and that "delusion and self-deception" often occur in these matters.[27] It is important, therefore, to suspend judgment "to see whether the individual can endure temptation; whether he is faithful in the discharge of all duty; whether he is a good soldier of Jesus Christ."[28] Some writers have referred to this testing of endurance as the "Gamaliel Principle," Gamaliel being a Pharisee who advised the Sanhedrin not to stop the apostles proclaiming Jesus' message on the ground that if it was of God it would endure.[29]

---

22. Scotland, *Apostles of the Spirit and Fire*, 139–62.
23. Matt 10:22; Mark 4:17; John 6:27.
24. Phil 3:14; Heb 12:1–2.
25. Booth, in Harrison, *Baker's Dictionary of Theology*, 460.
26. Sprague, *Lectures on Revivals*, 21.
27. Sprague, *Lectures on Revivals*, 21.
28. Sprague, *Lectures on Revivals*, 21.
29. Acts 5:39.

The early Methodist revival under the Wesleys began at a meeting in Aldersgate Street in 1738. There John Wesley had an overwhelming assurance of Jesus' forgiveness which stayed with him until the day of his death in 1791. It was this same experience that enabled his followers to sustain their faith in Christ to the end of their lives. In fact, Wesleyan Methodist membership rose continuously throughout the whole of Wesley's life. It brought perhaps as many as 400,000 men and women into a commitment to Christ.[30] Importantly the social consequences of the Methodist revival also had an enduring quality. Wesley's relentless attacks on the liquor traffic led to the founding of temperance societies in the nineteenth century. Wesley's constant support and encouragement of Sunday schools prompted Christians to promote a scheme for primary day school education. Wesley's unremitting attacks against slavery motivated William Wilberforce and others to found the *Abolition Society* in 1787 and carry the campaign forward into Parliament. Wesley's tireless outspoken attacks on the brutalities of the Industrial Revolution led to the passing of a series of Factory Acts and social reforms.[31] In these and a number of other significant avenues the Wesleyan revival evidenced an enduring impact on English society.

The Welsh Revival of 1904, according to Piggin, harvested 100,000 souls and brought about a massive decrease in the crime rate. Iain Murray wisely counseled that "in times when it seems as though almost whole communities are entering the Kingdom of God, time must elapse before a more balanced assessment can be made."[32] In the end, the genuineness and reality of a revival can only really be assessed with hindsight. We need to be mindful of Jesus' warning that many will do wonderful works in his name, but he never knew them.

Revivals Magnify Jesus Christ.

One of the primary and eternal functions of the Holy Spirit is to bear witness to Jesus. Shortly before his crucifixion Jesus spoke of the coming of his Spirit and declared him to be "another counsellor" who would

---

30. It is generally agreed that by the time of Wesley's death Methodist membership reached 100,000 but that the number who worshipped in Methodist meetings were probably four times that number.

31. Bready, *England Before and After Wesley*, 351–405.

32. Murray, *Revival and Revivalism*, 82.

bear testimony to him (John 15:26). Every genuine revival or movement of God's Spirit will therefore always meet this vital biblical test. Revivals enhance people's reverence, knowledge, and worship of Jesus, the Lord of heaven and earth. Martin Lloyd-Jones, a former minister of Westminster Chapel, put it starkly when he wrote, "the hallmark of the work of the Holy Spirit is that he presents the Lord Jesus Christ to us, and brings us to an ever-increasing intimacy with him, and an enjoyment of his glorious presence."[33]

It is therefore a truism that every genuine Christian revival will bring a renewed consciousness and love for Jesus expressed in worship, private spirituality, and daily duties. McDow and Reid put the matter simply, stating that "Revival is a fresh passion for God."[34] In the Great Awakening of 1734–35, Jonathan Edwards reported that the town of Northampton "seemed full of the presence of God."[35] Iain Murray underscored this point when he wrote:

> If revival consists in a larger giving of God's Spirit for the making known of Christ's glory, then it follows that a sense of God will always be evident at such times—evident not only in the conviction of sin but equally in the bewildered amazement of Christians at the consciousness of the Lord who is in their midst.[36]

Revivals Always Come through Biblically Appointed Means

A number of the early American writers were rightly and strongly of the view that genuine revivals can only be brought about by biblically appointed means. For them the only God-given, scripturally appointed instruments of revival were the faithful preaching of God's word, private and corporate prayer, especially joined with fasting, and the faithful fulfillment of parental and church duties. There were others who were happy to employ methods which, though not having exact scriptural precedents, were nevertheless, in their view, in keeping with biblical principles. Such, they maintained, were calls for public decisions for Christ, camp and protracted meetings, anxious benches, inquiry rooms, and after-meetings.

---

33. Lloyd-Jones, *Growing in the Spirit*, 54.
34. McDow and Reid, *Firefall*, 249.
35. Edwards, *Narrative of Many Surprising Conversions*, 14.
36. Murray, *Revival and Revivalism*, 30.

At times there were considerable debates between revival preachers and evangelists over some of these issues. All however were firmly agreed that no genuine revival could be born of methods which were manifestly contrary to the teaching and principles of Scripture. The use of hype and fervent rhetoric designed to stir the emotions and promote shouting and "religious exercises" such as "jerking," "shaking," and "barking" were to be avoided. Thus, William Sprague wrote:

> Suppose that for the simple, and honest, and faithful use of the sword of the Spirit there should be substituted a mass of machinery designed to produce its effect on animal passions: suppose the substance of religion instead of being made to consist in repentance, and faith and holiness, should consist of falling, and groaning, and shouting; we should say unhesitatingly that that could not be a genuine work of divine grace; or if there were some pure wheat, there must be a vast amount of chaff and stubble.[37]

Gardiner Spring (1785-1873), who ministered at Brick Church, New York City from 1810 until his death in 1873, shared Sprague's concern. He wrote that "Revivals are always spurious when they are got up by man's device, and not brought down by the Spirit of God."[38] Charles Spurgeon (1834-92), the greatest of Victorian preachers, also cautioned against certain forms of revivalism. "If you want to get up a revival, as the term is," he wrote, "you can do it just as you can grow strawberries in winter, by artificial heat. There are ways and means of doing that kind of thing, but the genuine work of God needs no such planning and scheming."[39] Although there were widespread occurrences of emotional phenomena during the Second Great Awakening of 1801-10, Iain Murray nevertheless underlined the fact that the majority of the preachers were united in the belief that prayer and preaching were "the great means" appointed by God. Murray added his own comment that "there are no greater means which may be employed at special times to secure supposedly greater results."[40]

It is plainly obvious that this is a biblical principle which must hold a top priority when examining anything that is claimed to be a genuine revival. If something is from God, it clearly cannot have been generated

---

37. Sprague, *Lectures on Revivals*, 17-18.
38. Spring, *Personal Reminiscences*; see also Murray, *Revival and Revivalism*, xv.
39. *Metropolitan Tabernacle Pulpit* 17, 499 in Murray, *Revival and Revivalism*, xv.
40. Murray, *Revival and Revivalism*, 127.

by what is plainly not of God. The New Testament Letters make frequent reference to the importance of integrity, of walking in the light, of being honest, and of not doing things in a covert manner.[41] The apostle Peter reminded the recipients of his second letter that they had not followed "cleverly invented stories" when they had been speaking of the power of Jesus Christ.[42] Writing to the Thessalonians, Paul emphasized that their appeal did "not spring from error or impure motives," and nor did they attempt to trick them.[43] He continued by underlining the fact that he and his fellow apostles spoke "as men approved by God to be entrusted with the gospel."[44] Writing to his younger colleague Timothy, Paul urged him to do his best to present himself as "one approved, a workman who does not need to be ashamed and who correctly handles the word of truth."[45] The revivals of religion recounted in the book of Acts were not brought about by flamboyant preachers who stirred people's emotions with clever rhetoric, laced with fervent worship. Equally, it is argued that new revivals are not likely to be generated by these sorts of excess.

Revivals Release the Gifts and Fruit of the Holy Spirit

It is clear from the narrative of the day of Pentecost and the subsequent chapters of the book of Acts that revivals are frequently associated with the release and positive use of the gifts of the Holy Spirit. At the same time, there will also be a marked increase in the fruits or character of the Holy Spirit, and most obviously the fruit of love. The apostle Paul in his First Letter to the Corinthians has a lengthy section in chapters 12 and 14 on the value and practice of the gifts of the Holy Spirit, and yet sandwiched in between them is his famous discourse about the supreme importance of the fruit of love. Jesus cautioned that though men and women could perform miraculous signs and wonders, or utter startlingly correct prophesies, it was no necessary proof that they were his genuine followers.[46] The test must always be "by their fruit you will

---

41. See for example the account of Ananias and Sapphira in Acts 1:1–5.
42. 2 Pet 1:16.
43. 1 Thess 2:3–4.
44. 1 Thess 2:4.
45. 2 Tim 2:15.
46. Matt 7:23.

recognize them,"[47] the fruit of the Spirit being godly lives of sacrificial love care and service.[48]

Whilst therefore the widespread use of spiritual gifts is of itself no guarantee of a genuine move of the Spirit of God, many revivals have nevertheless witnessed a renewed and right use of the charismata. Billy Graham, the American evangelist, was once asked what would be the result if the Holy Spirit were to be poured out on us in a spiritual revival? He wisely responded:

> There will be increased evidence of both the gifts and the fruit of the Spirit. . . . Believers will learn what it means to minister to one another and build each other up through the gifts the Holy Spirit has given. . . . No longer will the world say that the church is powerless and silent. . . . Our lives will be marked by the fruit only He can bring.[49]

All great revivals have witnessed the fruit of changed lives with people demonstrating acts of love and compassion. Others have sought forgiveness, been reconciled to their neighbors, repaid long-standing debts, and overcome drunkenness and habits of laziness.

Revivals Often Include the Conversion of Large Numbers of People

In the great majority of revivals from the day of Pentecost to the present time, large numbers of people have been converted and added to the churches. In many cases these conversions have been sudden. This is a pattern which we see in the revivals which are chronicled in the book of Acts. Following the outpouring of the Spirit in Jerusalem in Acts 2, Philip preached to crowds in Samaria "with evil spirits coming out of many" and "many paralytics and cripples" being healed.[50] Later, at Antioch, Luke records that "a great number of people were brought to the Lord" through the ministry of Barnabas.[51] Then, in Acts 15, there is a report of the word of God spreading through the whole region of Pisidia.[52] This pattern of

47. Matt 7:16.
48. Gal 5:22–23.
49. Graham, *Holy Spirit*, 217.
50. Acts 8:6–8.
51. Acts 11:24.
52. Acts 13:49.

large numbers being converted finds a resonance with the Old Testament picture of revival in Joel's prediction of "God's spirit being poured out on all people."[53] In all of the revivals which are considered in the following chapters of this book large numbers of people came to faith in Christ.

Care, however, is needed when it comes to this particular issue, the reason being that there is always the danger of falling away. Many of those who professed faith at the meetings held in Toronto in 1994 subsequently drifted from their earlier commitment. William Sprague was aware of this same problem and warned in his lectures that we are too much inclined to assess a revival by the number of professed converts. "There is," he declared, "scarcely a more uncertain test than this." He continued, "we confidently maintain that the mere fact that many profess to be converted does not prove a revival genuine." For suppose, he continued, that every one of these individuals, or far the larger part of them, should finally fall away, "this surely we should say, would prove the work spurious."[54] Lyman Beecher (1775–1836) had earlier shared Sprague's concern and warned against "the hasty recognition of persons as converted upon their own judgement, without interrogation or evidence."[55] Before leaving this point, it needs to be said that genuine revivals can and do occur where only relatively small numbers are involved. It is perfectly possible, as has already been noted, for a genuine revival to take place in a single church, college, or mission station.

Revivals Transform the Communities in Which They Occur

Revivals that are worthy of the name will always transform the communities in which they are located. This is an aspect which has often been overlooked by historians and students of revival. It is one which Piggin rightly stressed in *Firestorm of the Lord*, contending that "revival is not for the church only, but for the transformation of the community in which the church is located."[56] There is an emphasis, particularly in the Old Testament, which underscores this point. It is explicit in the familiar revival sermon text of 2 Chronicles 7:14 which speaks of the "healing of

---

53. Joel 2:28.

54. Sprague, *Lectures on Revivals*, 14.

55. Letter to N. S. S. Beman, January 1827, *Letters of the Rev. Dr Beecher*, 83, in Murray, *Revival and Revivalism*, 215.

56. Piggin, *Firestorm of the Lord*, 11.

the land." It is a theme emphasized in the prophecies of Amos and Micah who challenged the injustices of their day.

All the great revivals have made a profoundly positive social impact. The Great Awakening in New England and that in the Southern Colonies resulted in improved education, better morals, and, to some extent, encouraged the colonists to stand up against the injustices of British rule. Wesley's preaching in England during the same period changed the face of the British nation. The Second Great Awakening in the Southern Colonies brought further educational advances, birthed a number of reform societies, and raised the level of public opinion against slavery. In more recent times Billy Graham's 1959 campaign in Australia witnessed a reversal in Australia's crime level, slowed the number of illegitimate conceptions in a permissive age, and reduced the per capita consumption of liquor.[57]

Sprague put particular emphasis on this aspect of revival. In his lecture IX entitled "The Results of Revival," he stressed their role "in elevating the intellectual, spiritual and social condition of men." In revival times people's minds, he suggested, "come into contact with the higher orders of being"[58] and "the intellect and the heart get warm together."[59] Sprague saw revivals as favorably impacting culture because they birth in individuals "moral feelings and good habits." For the same reason, revivals also drive away vice and encourage industry. "Revivals," Sprague further asserted, "have an important supporting influence on our benevolent institutions."[60] He went on to point out that "all our great benevolent institutions—our Missionary, Bible, Tract and Education, Temperance, and all kindred societies—have flourished as a result of revivals."[61] The evangelical revival under the Wesleys, which impacted both William Wilberforce and later the Seventh Earl of Shaftesbury, birthed a widespread movement of social reform.[62] Ford K. Brown, in his *Fathers of the Victorians*, listed more than 300 charity and self-help societies founded in England between Wesley's conversion in 1738 and 1844. When Shaftesbury died in 1885, his funeral service in Westminster Abbey was attended by representatives of more than 500 different

---

57. Piggin, "Billy Graham in Australia, 1959," 2–33.
58. Sprague, *Lectures on Revivals*, 262.
59. Sprague, *Lectures on Revivals*, 263.
60. Sprague, *Lectures on Revivals*, 272.
61. Sprague, *Lectures on Revivals*, 274.
62. See Brown, *Fathers of the Victorians*, 317–63,

improvement societies.[63] A great many of these had been founded in the wake of revival.

Clearly, in summary, any significant work of God which could be designated as a "revival' will demonstrate these characteristics. They must reflect the values and practice of New Testament Christianity. They may well witness the conversion of large numbers of people whose new-found faith will mature and stand the test of time. Such revivals will come from a divine intervention or a sovereign move of God's Spirit. They will also magnify and raise people's devotion and esteem for Jesus Christ. Additionally, they will exhibit the gifts and fruit of the Holy Spirit working together to transform the surrounding community and the culture in which they occur.

Keeping these characteristics in mind, we are now hopefully better equipped and more able to be inspired by the ten great revival movements of God's Spirit which form the following chapters of this book. They will bring us to new revelations of the Lord's love, profound insights into his ways, and a deeper awareness of his concern and compassion for the world and its peoples. There is great encouragement here for all the people of God because what God has done in the past he can do again in the present with even greater intensity. Most important of all, we can and should be challenged to pray and seek revival in our own personal lives. As once was prayed so we can and should pray now, "O Lord send revival and begin in me."

---

63. Bradley, *Call to Seriousness*, 135.

2

The Revival in Northampton, Massachusetts

In September 1620, 102 passengers set sail from England for the American colonies on the ship called the *Mayflower*. Having been harshly persecuted for their Puritan faith they were now searching for freedom. After a stormy crossing they finally reached land in early November and founded the first New England settlement at Plymouth. This was absorbed shortly afterwards into the larger Massachusetts Bay Company. From this beginning, along with Virginia, which had earlier been founded in 1607, British North America gradually began to emerge in the seventeenth century with the founding of a number of other independent colonies stretching down the continent's east coast. Each one had their own charter and governor and largely fostered one religious tradition. In most instances this was that of their founding fathers. Thus, Georgia was dominated by the Church of England and was overseen by the Bishop of London's commissary. Maryland had been founded as a settlement for Roman Catholics and Pennsylvania as a refuge for Quakers. In the case of Massachusetts, Congregationalism, which centered on the independence of the local church, was the dominant faith.

Generally speaking, the first and second generation of colonial settlers maintained the fervor of their founding fathers. But by the beginning of the eighteenth century, Christian faith in the colonies was becoming progressively nominal. In Pennsylvania, for example, Quaker children could retain their membership of the Society of Friends without having to give personal testimony to having received "inner light." The same was also true of the Congregationalists in Massachusetts. A synod had met at Boston in 1662 and ruled that parishioners could be considered as church members without having to give an open public witness of their faith in Christ. Such was also the case in the town of Northampton, which is the focus of this chapter.

The settlement began in 1654, and the community grew steadily until the year 1735, when its population numbered about 1,000 souls. It was then that revival first came and profoundly touched and transformed almost every household. Generally referred to as "The Great Awakening," it was at its height between 1735 and 1736 and was rekindled in 1740-42.

Jonathan Edwards

Edwards was born on October 5th, 1703, the son of Timothy Edwards, a minister at East Windsor, Connecticut, which was then a frontier town. He was the only boy among ten sisters! He had a deep experience of God's presence when he was about five years of age during an awakening in his father's parish. He was gifted academically and gained entrance to Yale College in 1716, at just under the age of thirteen, and graduated in 1720. Following this he served for a short period as an assistant minister in New York City during which time he had a powerful conversion experience. He returned to Yale and completed his MA in 1723. While he was working in New York he wrote out *Thirty-Four Resolutions,* by which, like many other Puritans, he planned to govern his personal and social life. He resolved to continually mortify worldly pleasures and to overcome his weakness of character which included uncontrolled temper and sexual imaginations.

In 1726, he moved to Northampton to become assistant minister to his grandfather, Solomon Stoddard. He was a diligent and dedicated pastor from whom Edwards gained valuable experience. Stoddard had seen a series of small "harvests" among his people during his long ministry. Stoddard died at the beginning of 1727, and Edwards took on the sole charge of the church. Later, in July of the same year, Edwards married Sarah, the daughter of the Reverend James Pierpont of New Haven. She proved to be a remarkable wife and coworker who enabled Edwards to devote himself fully to both his pastoral ministries as well as his studies and writing.

Jonathan Edwards, engraved by R. Babson and J. Andrews. Public domain.

For the next five years Edwards worked as a faithful, prayerful, and godly pastor without seeing any obvious change in the spiritual life of his people. He did all he could to encourage them by prayers and solid biblical preaching. The word "revival" implies the reviving or recovering something that was dead or in serious decline. Northampton was no exception. Jonathan Edwards (1703–58), who was minister of both church and parish, wrote that "the greater part seemed at that time to be insensible to the things of religion,"[1] and again that "it seemed to be a time of extraordinary dullness of religion."[2] Edwards was particularly concerned about the young people. He wrote, "Licentiousness for some years prevailed among the youth of the town; many of them were addicted to night walking, and frequenting the tavern, and lewd practices, wherein some, by their example exceedingly corrupted others." In the same vein, Edwards further elaborated that "it was their manner very often to get together, in conventions of both sexes for mirth and jollity, which they called frolics, and they would spend the greater part of the night in them."[3] At this very time traditional Christian beliefs were beginning to be challenged and undermined by the impact of Enlightenment thinking. The writings of men such as John Locke and John Tolland contributed to the growth of a rational Christianity which was skeptical of both the divine revelation of Scripture and religious experience.

Signs of a Coming Change

A year or so before the awakening took place Edwards observed signs that things were beginning to change.[4] In his sermons he quite often reminded his hearers of the contrast between those who were damned on account of their sins and the blessings of those who were regenerate.[5] About the beginning of 1733, Edwards began to notice that the young were being brought under conviction by his preaching. This was further increased after the sudden death in April 1734 of a young man "in the bloom of his youth" who was violently seized with pleurisy. This was followed by the death of a young married woman who was in considerable distress about the salvation of her soul. She died, Edwards wrote, "very full of comfort" at the same time "warning and counselling others" and this "much affected many young people." At this time there was also "a remarkable religious concern" in the village of Pascommuck, which was about three miles from Northampton and was part of Edward's responsibility. A number of inhabitants were "savingly wrought upon." Towards the end of the year, in December, a woman, "one of the greatest company

---

1. Edwards, *Narrative of Many Surprising Conversions*, 9.
2. Edwards, *Narrative of Many Surprising Conversions*, 9.
3. Edwards, *Narrative of Many Surprising Conversions*, 9.
4. Edwards, *Narrative of Many Surprising Conversions*, 9.
5. Edwards, *Narrative of Many Surprising Conversions*, 9.

keepers of the town," was converted. Contrary to Edwards's expectations this had a powerful impact on the whole community. "The news of it," he wrote, "seemed to be almost like a flash of lightning upon the hearts of the young people all over the town, and upon many others."[6]

The Town in Revival

Shortly after this a great and earnest concern about the things of religion was universal throughout the town and upon many others. Edwards recalled, "The minds of the people were wonderfully taken from the world" and yet people "did not neglect their worldly business."[7] By the summer of 1735, Northampton was in a state of revival. Edwards related, "the town seemed full of the presence of God"[8] and it was "a time of joy in families on account of salvation being brought to them." He recalled that "even at weddings there was now no discourse of anything but religion." Many of those who had difficulties and questions "now had their doubts removed by a more satisfying experience, and more clear discoveries of God's love."[9] Visitors who came to the town went away "with their consciences smitten and awakened, and went home with wounded hearts, and with impressions that never wore off till they had hopefully a saving issue." "There were many instances of people who came from abroad on visits, on business, who had not long been here, before, to all appearances, they were savingly wrought upon."[10]

"Halfway members" in the congregation came under conviction of sin and their need of the new birth while fully covenanted members found new heights of devotion and spiritual renewal. Edwards reported that "public praises were greatly enlivened" and "our congregation excelled all that I ever knew . . . they were wont to sing with unusual elevation of heart and voice." This transformation was particularly visible in the large numbers who came to take part in communion services. Edwards recorded, "We have about six hundred and twenty communicants which include almost all our adult persons."[11] There was also a marked

---

6. Edwards, *Narrative of Many Surprising Conversions*, 12.
7. Edwards, *Narrative of Many Surprising Conversions*, 13.
8. Edwards, *Narrative of Many Surprising Conversions*, 13.
9. Edwards, *Narrative of Many Surprising Conversions*, 14.
10. Edwards, *Narrative of Many Surprising Conversions*, 15.
11. Edwards, *Narrative of Many Surprising Conversions*, 14.

improvement in the demeanor of the young persons, with Edwards writing, "Those of our young people who were formerly loose are generally to all appearances become true lovers of God and Christ and spiritual in their dispositions." Edwards wrote, "the bulk of our young people have been greatly affected" as were "old men" and "little children." A careless person," he noted, "could scarcely be found in the whole neighbourhood." Any such people were spoken of as "a strange thing." In sum, Edwards calculated that "three hundred souls were savingly brought to Christ in Northampton in the space of six months. "There were," he reported, "upwards of fifty persons converted in the town who were over forty years of age; more than twenty of them over fifty; about ten of them above sixty; and two of them above seventy years of age."[12]

Regarding the precise time or moment when converts were first touched by God's grace Edwards noted there was considerable variation. In some instances, the very time was clearly apparent, but in others it was difficult to put a precise time on it.[13] Edwards highlighted this contrast in another paragraph: "In some, converting light is like a glorious brightness suddenly shining upon a person, and all around him; they are in a remarkable manner brought out of darkness into marvellous light. In many others it has been like the dawning of the day."[14] In the town of Northampton as a whole there were very few houses into which salvation did not come in one or more instances.[15] And, he added, "there are several negroes [sic] who from what was seen in them then, and what is discernible in them since, appear to have been truly born again in the late remarkable season."[16] There was, Edwards recalled, earnest application to reading and prayer, meditation and public worship. Far more people resorted to Edwards's house than had been the case in times past to the tavern. New converts in Northampton frequently found that "texts of Scripture were brought to their minds," many of which were particularly suited to their needs or circumstances. Such verses impacted them quite powerfully and left them with great light and comfort.[17]

---

12. Edwards, *Narrative of Many Surprising Conversions*, 20.
13. Edwards, *Narrative of Many Surprising Conversions*, 40.
14. Edwards, *Narrative of Many Surprising Conversions*, 41.
15. Edwards, *Narrative of Many Surprising Conversions*, 20.
16. Edwards, *Narrative of Many Surprising Conversions*, 20.
17. Edwards, *Narrative of Many Surprising Conversions*, 41.

Edwards observed that no discourses have been more remarkably blessed than those in which the doctrine of God's absolute sovereignty regarding the salvation of sinners has been asserted. He continued, "I never found so much immediate saving fruit, in any measure, of any discourses I have offered my congregation, as some from these words, Rom iii, 19, 'That every mouth may be stopped'; endeavouring to show from thence, that it would be just with God for ever to reject and cast off mere natural men."[18] Edwards found that for many people "Christ is distinctly made the object of the mind, in his all-sufficiency and willingness to save sinners."[19]

Many of those who came to faith in Christ in Northampton frequently spoke of religious things seeming new to them and that they found "preaching is a new thing." "It seemed," Edwards noted, "as if they never heard preaching before." Others declared that they found "the Bible to be a new book." They found "new chapters, new psalms, new histories, because they see them in a new light."[20] At a later point in his *Narrative of Surprising Conversions,* Edwards returned to this theme of writing that "While God was so remarkably present amongst us by his Spirit, there was no book so delightful as the Bible, especially the Book of Psalms, the Prophecy of Isaiah, and the New Testament."[21] Edwards observed that when people received these gracious revelations of Christ, their affections, by which he meant their feelings and senses, "were in some cases deeply moved." This caused some of them "to break forth into laughter, and tears often at the same time issuing like a flood and intermingling with loud weeping." Sometimes they were not able to forbear crying out in a loud voice, expressing their great admiration."[22]

As one would expect in any genuine revival the awakening in Northampton resulted in a great love among the people. "Our converts," Edwards wrote, "appeared remarkably united in dear affection to one another and many expressed that spirit of love which they felt toward all mankind; and particularly to those who had been least friendly towards them." There were many who confessed to having caused hurts and injuries and others who put an end to their differences.[23] Such was

---

18. Edwards, *Narrative of Many Surprising Conversions*, 41.
19. Edwards, *Narrative of Many Surprising Conversions*, 34.
20. Edwards, *Narrative of Many Surprising Conversions*, 34.
21. Edwards, *Narrative of Many Surprising Conversions*, 47.
22. Edwards, *Narrative of Many Surprising Conversions*, 37–38.
23. Edwards, *Narrative of Many Surprising Conversions*, 47.

the love among people that "there was an exceeding great desire for the conversion of others."[24]

The revival impacted the social life and culture of the town and the surrounding area. Where the Spirit was poured out it was noted that "people of the looser sort" quit their practices and that "people had done with their old quarrels, backbitings, and inter meddlings with other men's matters. . . . The tavern was soon left empty, and persons kept very much at home; none went abroad unless on necessary business, or on some religious account, and every day seemed in many respects like a Sabbath day."[25] Edwards summed it up by writing that "the apostolic times seemed to have returned upon us; such a display has been the power of the Spirit."[26]

The Revival Spreads

Neighboring towns and villages soon began to be impacted by what was happening in Northampton. In March 1735, Edwards reported that the nearby town of South Hadley had been "seized with deep concern regarding the things of religion."[27] About the same time "it soon spread into other parts" of Suffield. In Sunderland, it "soon overspread the town" and it also filled the town of Deerfield, where there was "glorious work." In the second week of April 1835, Edwards reported that the whole town of Hatfield "seemed to be seized as it were at once with concern about the things of religion; and the work of God was great there." There was also "a very general awakening in West-Springfield and Long Meadow." The Rev. Mr. Bull of Westfield informed Edwards that "there had been a great alteration there, and that more had been done in a week than in seven years before." In Northfield there was for a short time "a very general concern." Edwards recalled that in all these places "God brought saving blessings with him, and his word attended with his Spirit (as we have all reason to think) returned not void."[28]

24. Edwards, *Narrative of Many Surprising Conversions*, 47.
25. Edwards, *Narrative of Many Surprising Conversions*, 24.
26. Edwards, *Distinguishing Marks*, 77.
27. Edwards, *Narrative of Many Surprising Conversions*, 15.
28. All the references in the paragraph are from Edwards, *Narrative of Many Surprising Conversions*, 16.

Edwards recorded that "this remarkable pouring out of the Spirit of God, which thus extended from one end to the other of this county, was not confined to it, but many places in Connecticut have partaken in the same mercy."[29] He cited the case of the town of Windsor, under the Rev. Mr. Marsh, where there was "a very great ingathering of souls to Christ." At East Windsor, where Edwards's father was the pastor, "there was a general awakening of the people." At Coventry there was "a wonderful work of God under the ministry of the Rev. Mr Meacham." There were similar reports from the Rev. Mr. Wheelock about his town of Lebanon and from the Rev. Mr. Chauncey regarding the ingathering of souls in his pastoral care in the town of Durham. Edwards noted that at Stratford, under the ministry of Mr. Gould, many of the young people had been impacted. There was also a considerable revival at Newhaven and in parts of Guildford and at Tolland, Hebron, and Bolton. In addition to these places, "there was no small infusion of the Spirit of God in the north in the parish of Preston." Edwards added that the minister, the Rev. Mr. Lord, had been up to Northampton to see the work of God, and on returning to Preston had given an account of what he had seen to his people, and "they were greatly affected by it."[30]

Edwards continued his account of the spread of the awakening, stating that "this shower of divine blessing has been yet more extensive" and that "there was no small degree of it in some parts of the Jerseys." He reported that the Rev. William Tennent had told him of "a very great awakening of many in a place called the Mountains under the minister, the Rev. Mr Cross; and of a very considerable revival of religion under the ministry of his brother, the Rev. Gilbert Tennent." Edwards summed up the spread of revival in the following paragraph.

> This seems to have been a very extraordinary dispensation of providence; God has in many respects gone out of, and much beyond, his usual ordinary way. The work in this town, and others about us, affecting all sorts, sober and vicious, high and low, rich and poor, wise and unwise. It reached the most considerable families and persons, to all appearances, as much as others. In former stirrings of this nature, the bulk of the young people have been greatly affected; but old men and little children have been so now. Many of the last have, of their own accord, formed themselves

---

29. Edwards, *Narrative of Many Surprising Conversions*, 17.

30. All the details in the above paragraph are taken from Edwards, *Narrative of Many Surprising Conversions*, 17–18.

into religious societies in different parts of the town. A loose careless person could scarcely be found in the whole neighbourhood; and if there was anyone that seemed to remain senseless or unconcerned, it would be spoken of as a strange thing.[31]

One of the great means by which the revival spread was publicity, with Edwards writing, "There is no one thing that I know of which God has made such a means of promoting his work amongst us, as the news of others' conversions.... This," he continued, "has been owned in awakening sinners, engaging them earnestly to seek the same blessing, and in quickening the saints.[32] Edwards published his *Narrative of Many Surprising Conversions* so that those who read it might see for themselves "how manifold God's works have been amongst us." He sent a copy of it to the Rev. Dr. Colman of Boston and requested him to send it to Rev. Dr. Isaac Watts and the Rev. Dr. John Guyse in England. The latter gentleman read sections of it to his congregation and it met with a very encouraging response on their part.[33]

The Plateauing of the First Phase of the Revival

When the work appeared to be at its greatest height in May 1835, a man who was a resident of the town became disturbed in his mind and "harried with violent temptations to cut his own throat." Fortunately, he failed, but as Edwards reported, he "continued a considerable time [to be] overwhelmed with melancholy." Eventually "the light of God's presence lifted him and he was greatly delivered."[34] It was about the time of this attempted suicide that Edwards began to be aware that the Spirit of God "was gradually withdrawing from us, and after a time Satan seemed to be more on the loose, and raged in a dreadful manner.[35] A second instance of this appeared when another man succeeded in putting an end to his life by cutting his own throat. Edwards described him: "A gentleman of more than common understanding, of strict morals, religious behaviour, and a useful and honourable person in the town" but, he added, was "from a family that are exceedingly prone to the disease of melancholy."

31. Edwards, *Narrative of Many Surprising Conversions*, 19.
32. Edwards, *Narrative of Many Surprising Conversions*, 40.
33. Edwards, *Narrative of Many Surprising Conversions*, 74
34. Edwards, *Narrative of Many Surprising Conversions*, 69.
35. Edwards, *Narrative of Many Surprising Conversions*, 70.

Following this tragic incident many in Northampton and other nearby towns had similar strong impulses to do what this gentleman had done. Edwards noted that "they were obliged with all their might to resist it, and yet no reason suggested to them why they should do it."[36]

After these occurrences, instances of conversion were rare in comparison to what they had been. Although the revival was clearly waning in both the town and the county "religion remained the main subject of conversation." Edwards was able to report that those people who had been converted retained "a new sense of things" and new apprehensions of God and Jesus Christ and of the great things of the gospel.[37] Some, he recalled, who were very rough in their temper and manners "seemed to be remarkably softened and sweetened."[38] There was still a great deal of conversation on religious matters in the town on the part of both young and old and "a religious disposition" was maintained among the people which was manifested in the holding of frequent private meetings for worship in peoples' homes and in keeping of sabbath-nights.[39]

After several years in which the revival was diminished in intensity Edwards observed a visible upturn in the spring of 1740. There was an increased seriousness and a greater degree of religious conversation. More people began to seek his advice on matters of salvation. Then, in the middle of October, George Whitefield arrived in the town and preached four sermons in the meeting house and gave a lecture at Edwards's home. In his record of these years, entitled *An Account of the Revival in Northampton in 1740–1742*, Edwards noted that Whitefield's sermons "were suitable to the circumstances of the town." Whitefield issued "a just reproof for our backslidings' and urged a return to God from whom we had departed."[40]

The revival first appeared among those to whom Whitefield addressed his sermons. They were those who had been earlier converted and those who trusted they were in a state of salvation.[41] Edwards also observed that in a very short time "there appeared an awakening and deep concern among some young persons that looked upon themselves as in a

---

36. Edwards, *Narrative of Many Surprising Conversions*, 70.
37. Edwards, *Narrative of Many Surprising Conversions*, 71.
38. Edwards, *Narrative of Many Surprising Conversions*, 72.
39. Edwards, *Narrative of Many Surprising Conversions*, 72.
40. Edwards, *Account of the Revival*, 149.
41. Edwards, *Account of the Revival*, 149.

Christless state." Within a month or six weeks there was "a considerable work among those that were very young." By the spring of 1741, "an eagerness of spirit about the things of religion was become very general among young people and children. Many of them appeared to be overcome with a sense of the glory and greatness of divine things and were distressed about their state before God. At meetings numbers of them cried out and fell to the ground, some "continuing thus for hours."[42] Children going home from meetings were observed crying aloud through the streets."[43]

In the middle of the summer Edwards called together a meeting of young people from the ages of sixteen to twenty-six who were communicants. It proved to be "a most happy meeting marked by love and joy with many fainting under these affections." Similar meetings followed, and Edwards noted that "about this time people began to cry out loud in the meetings by themselves for prayer and sometimes joined in fasting.[44]

The months of August and September proved to be the most remarkable both in "the conviction and conversion of sinners" and in "the extraordinary external effects of these things." "It was," Edwards recorded, "a very frequent thing to see a house full of outcries, faintings, convulsions, and such like, both with distress and also with admiration and joy." Edwards went on to point out that it was not the custom to hold meetings all night in Northampton as happened elsewhere, but it was "now often the case that some of those who attended the evening meetings were so affected, and their bodies so overcome, that they could not go home but were obliged to stay all night where they were."[45] Great numbers, Edwards had reason to hope, were savingly brought home to Christ. There was a remarkable outpouring of the Spirit on the children, more even than had occurred during the first phase of the revival in 1735–36. Many of all ages who had been impacted by the Holy Spirit in earlier times and had drifted away and gone after the world "now passed under a remarkable new work of the Spirit of God as if they had been subject of a second conversion."[46]

In February 1742, Edwards had to be away from Northampton and invited the Rev. Samuel Buell to use his pulpit. Buell therefore preached

---

42. Edwards, *Account of the Revival*, 150.
43. Edwards, *Account of the Revival*, 150.
44. Edwards, *Account of the Revival*, 151.
45. Edwards, *Account of the Revival*, 151.
46. Edwards, *Account of the Revival*, 152.

almost every day in the meeting house. He in fact spent almost the whole time "in religious exercises with the people, either in public or private, the people continually thronging him."[47] Under Buell's labors there were "very extraordinary effects." The people were exceedingly moved, many of them crying out in great numbers in the meeting house, and a large part of the congregation commonly stayed for hours after the public services ended. Edwards, who returned after two weeks away, found that the whole town "seemed to be in a great and continual commotion, day and night, and there was indeed a very great revival of religion." Buell continued about three weeks after Edwards's return "there being still great appearances attending his labours."[48] There were some instances of some people lying in a sort of trance, "remaining perhaps twenty-four hours motionless, and with their senses locked up; but in the meantime, under strong imaginations, as though they went to heaven and had there a vision of glorious and delightful objects."[49]

In the following month of March 1742, Edwards invited the people of the town to join in a solemn public renewal of their covenant with God. This took place during public worship on the 16th of March, 1742. The covenant was a lengthy document and began with the words,

> Acknowledging God's goodness to us, a sinful, unworthy people, in the blessed manifestations and fruits of his gracious presence in this town, both formerly and lately, and particularly in the very late spiritual revival . . . we do this day present ourselves before the Lord, to renounce our evil ways . . . and with one accord to renew our engagements to seek and serve God.

There then followed a whole series of commitments, many of which had to do with the treatment of, and attitude towards, others in the community. These included "endeavouring to render to everyone his due," making full restitution to anyone who had been wronged, not allowing back-biting, and being careful to avoid doing anything from a spirit of revenge. Those who were in their youth pledged never to allow themselves to indulge "in any diversions or pastime, in meetings, or companies of young people" which were not "most agreeable to God's will." The final

---

47. Edwards, *Account of the Revival*, 153.
48. Edwards, *Account of the Revival*, 153.
49. Edwards, *Account of the Revival*, 157–58.

part of the covenant was a pledge to surrender all to God and beg for his strength to keep these solemn vows."[50]

A month or two after the making of this covenant Edwards noticed a change in the intensity of the religious life of the community. In the beginning of the summer of 1742, he observed that "there seemed to be abatement of the liveliness of the people's affections in religion." He commented further that "in general, people's engagedness in religion, and the liveliness of their affection have been on the decline." In particular, some of the young people had lost "their vigour in religion." On a more positive note, Edwards was also able to state that there were still many "that walk as becometh saints" and "a considerable number that seem to be near to God."[51]

Summary of the Revival Years, 1735–42

William Cooper, in his preface to Edwards's *The Distinguishing Marks of the Spirit of God*, which was published in 1741, recounted that "some of the greatest sinners have appeared to be turned into real saints; drunkards have become temperate; fornicators and adulterers of a chaste conversation; swearers and profane persons have learned to fear that glorious and fearful Name, THE LORD THEIR GOD; and carnal worldlings have been made to seek first the kingdom of God."[52] Again he recalled, "Many things not becoming the profession of the gospel are in a measure reformed. Taverns, dancing-schools, and such meetings as have always proved unfriendly to serious godliness, are much less frequented. Many have reduced their dress and apparel, to make them look more like the followers of humble Jesus."[53] Cooper reported Edwards's observation that there was still more talk of religion in people's homes than he had ever known in the past and that there were increasing numbers of Christian meetings in private homes.[54]

Clearly there were some who drifted away from the faith and fell into error of various kinds as the revival diminished in its intensity, but, as Edwards pointed out, "it is no sign that a work is not from the Spirit of God that many who seem to be the subjects of it are guilty of great

---

50. Edwards, *Account of the Revival*, 157–58.
51. Edwards, *Account of the Revival*, 158.
52. Edwards, *Distinguishing Marks*, 80.
53. Cooper, "Mr. Cooper's Preface to the Reader," 82.
54. Cooper, "Mr. Cooper's Preface to the Reader," 82.

imprudences and irregularities." Indeed, he wrote, "A thousand imprudences will not prove a work not to be of the Spirit of God."[55] Edwards reminded his readers of "the great irregularities" of the church at Corinth and "the strange confusion" they ran into over the Lord's Supper and their lack of adequate discipline. He was clear that if we investigate church history, we will not find any great revival or general work of the Spirit of God which has not been accompanied by some error or scandalous behavior.

As Edwards looked back over all the revival years from 1735–42, he was of the view that the work in the years 1740 and 1741 "seemed to be much more pure, having less of a corrupt mixture than in the former great outpouring of the Spirit in 1735 and 1736." People were "now better guarded, and their affections were not only stronger but attended with greater solemnity, and a greater humility and self-distrust, and a greater engagedness after holy living and perseverance; and there were fewer errors in conduct."[56]

Learning from Northampton

It is the case that where there is light, shadows follow. Such is understandably the case in revival movements among frail, fallen human beings. As noted earlier in this chapter, during the revival several people suffered from strong impressions of the mind to engage in acts of self-harm, including the urge to commit suicide.[57] Some of them reported that it was as if someone was urging them, "Cut your throat, now is a good opportunity. Now! Now! So, they were obliged to fight with all their might to resist it, and yet no reason suggested to them why they should do it."[58] Edwards also noted that some of those who "had very great raptures of joy" and "had been extraordinarily filled (as the vulgar phrase is) and have their bodies overcome" proved to be far less Christian in their conduct than some of the others who had no great outward manifestations of the Spirit in their lives.

These incidents underline the need to test and measure everything, including religious experience by the yardstick of Scripture and rational common sense. In particular, the disturbing suicidal impulses

---

55. Edwards, *Distinguishing Marks*, 101.
56. Edwards, *Account of the Revival*, 158.
57. Edwards, *Narrative of Many Surprising Conversions*, 70.
58. Edwards, Preface to *Distinguishing Marks*, 70.

experienced by some members of Edwards's congregation demonstrate the importance of the renewing of the mind, as the apostle Paul urged in both his letters to the Romans and Philippians. It is clear that Edwards, ever the wise pastor and leader, was sufficiently aware of these issues and did his utmost to handle them well. He warned in his *Distinguishing Marks of a Work of the Spirit of God*, "Some true friends of the work of God's Spirit have erred in giving too much heed to impulses and strong impressions on their minds."[59]

The character of the revival in Northampton was first and foremost a sovereign work of God. There were, as Edwards so well charted, "many surprising conversions." The work was such that all sections of the town were impacted. The "professors," that is, those who already professed the faith in some measure, were renewed in the depth and vitality of their faith, which included singing, prayer, attention to sermons, and teaching. Young people and children were brought to a saving faith in large numbers. Their affections were powerfully touched, and they banded together, often of their own accord, and held meetings for prayer and reading Scripture. People from all sections of the town's community came under the influence and power of God's presence and became committed followers of Christ. Included in their number were those who formerly had idled in the tavern and spent time in dancing and other pursuits which Edwards called "frolicks."

The revival spread beyond the confines of Northampton, and the inhabitants of the fourteen other towns and villages in the county shared in the same outpouring of God's Spirit. Edwards reported that at times the town was so full of the presence of God that visitors who were just passing through went away knowing the presence of Christ in their lives.

Edwards's role in the revival was that of the wise and godly pastor. He was present in Northampton throughout the whole of the nine-year period of the awakening. When necessity required him to leave the town, he made sure that a wise and trusted friend such as Buell was able to be present to give pastoral care and teaching. Edwards made it his duty to be present at all the meetings which took place when he was resident in the parish. This enabled him to assess and scrutinize what was taking place. He also organized many small gatherings for teaching and instruction both in the meeting house and in his own home. He was time conscious and made sure that meetings did not continue late into the night.

---

59. Edwards, *Distinguishing Marks*, 137.

Edwards constantly urged that everything was to be tested in the light of scriptural principles. He studied revival in early Christian times and in the more recent past and applied the lessons he drew from the past to the religious life on Northampton.

Edwards recounted the revival in detail, highlighting both its positive and dysfunctional aspects. His publication of *The Distinguishing Marks of a Work of the Spirit of God* was evidence of Edwards's deep thought and theological reflection on the revival. The book provided a solid set of biblical criteria and wisdom by which any work of God may be assessed. In this work Edwards also demonstrated that there are a number of issues and experiences that may on the surface appear extraordinary or dysfunctional but are nevertheless insufficient to take the view that a particular outpouring is not a work of God.

One of Edwards's practices during the revival was to make sure that he was satisfied with his people's spiritual state and to signify it to them. Edwards was frequently criticized for this but the pastor in him recognized that there was always the possibility that individuals could be led astray in what were, in effect, spurious experiences. Edwards, however, made it clear that he judged "qualifications and declared experiences rather than persons." He wrote, "I have thought it my duty as a pastor, to assist and instruct persons in applying scripture-rules and characters to their own case."[60]

Edwards did not hold center-stage in the revival all the time. It often happens that the central figure or human instrument who is used to initiate revival overworks to the point of exhaustion. Edwards does not appear to have fallen into that trap. He welcomed others from time to time to teach and have the use of his pulpit. Among them were George Whitefield, whom he welcomed to preach in 1740, and his neighbor Samuel Buell, whom he left in charge during a period of absence.

There were several reports spread around the country that many people in Northampton were in fear that the revival was a sign of the end times and that the world was about to come to an end. Such reports, Edwards was quick to make clear, were manifestly false.[61] He pointed out that the glory of the end of the age will be a time when gifts of the Spirit will have passed away with only perfect love remaining.[62] Edwards the

---

60. Edwards, *Narrative of Many Surprising Conversions*, 39.
61. Edwards, *Narrative of Many Surprising Conversions*, 53.
62. Edwards, *Distinguishing Marks*, 139–40.

wise pastor was always aware of the value of good, accurate publicity. His many letters and recountings of the revival did much to make it widely known in other American colonies, as well as in parts of England.

Edwards had guided his church and the town through a truly remarkable revival, but tensions arose between him and leading members in the congregation. A major sticking point was Edwards's refusal to give the Lord's Supper to Halfway Covenant members, a practice that Solomon Stoddard had allowed. The issue was further complicated by the fact that members of the town council had to be communicant members of the Congregational Church. A hostile parish majority convened a church meeting which resulted in his dismissal on June 22nd, 1750. Edwards spent his remaining years first at Stockbridge, and then very briefly at Princeton, where he died in 1758, just as he was beginning a new post at Princeton as President of the Presbyterian College of New Jersey. Edwards's wide-ranging theological writings have been much discussed,[63] but those on the Great Awakening, which have never been out of print, demonstrate its many genuine aspects from which valuable lessons can still be learned.

---

63. See for example Noll, *Old Religion in a New World*, 205–8.

3

Revival in Cambuslang, 1742–43

On April 29th, 1742, the presbytery of Hamilton ordained William McCulloch (1691–1771) minister of Cambuslang, a parish on the south side of the river Clyde about five miles from Glasgow. It was a small village with a population of about 900. Most of the inhabitants were employed in farming, but some earned their keep as weavers while others labored as colliers, a work which was "laborious, hazardous and disagreeable."[1]

William was born in 1691 at Wigtown. Little is known of his early years. He received his early education from his father who was the village school master. When he was about thirteen years of age William was captivated by the preaching of the parish minister, Mr. Ker, and became a communicant member of the church. His father recognized his son was academically bright and sent him to the universities of Edinburgh and Glasgow where he developed a great love for the Scriptures and became fluent in both Hebrew and Greek. This, according to his son Robert, made him "determined to consecrate all his talents to the work of the ministry."[2] He was licensed as a lay preacher in 1722 and lived with the Hamilton family at Aikenhead. In 1725, William was honored by being chosen to give the annual sermon by a probationer. His address entitled "A Sermon against The Idolatrous Worship of the Church of Rome" took place in the New-Church of Glasgow. Consisting of forty-eight pages and printed by Robert Sanders of Glasgow, it began by focusing on the Popish Pretender,

1. *Old Statistical Account*, 7.252–57 in Fawcett, *Cambuslang Revival*, 33.
2. Macfarlan, *Revivals of the Eighteenth Century*, 34.

sitting under the Pope's nose at Rome. It was, however, moderate in tone but warned of the dangers of idolatrous worship.

Once settled in Cambuslang he proved to be a popular preacher and an able and faithful minister. His son, in a foreword to a volume of his father's sermons, wrote of him:

> He commonly rose about five in the morning, and excepting about two or three hours, which allowed for relaxation; he was closely employed in study till eight o'clock in the evening. His ordinary practice was to write out and commit to memory two sermons every week. He spent much time in secret prayer, waiting with humble patience for a favorable return. He greatly encouraged Christians to meet for social prayer, and particularly to intercede that God would revive his work everywhere. He was often employed in reading and meditating on the Scriptures.[3]

McCulloch had a big heart for the poor, but, noted for his humility, he was careful not to publish details of his endeavors to others. Among his many charitable acts on behalf of the poor he printed 3,000 copies of a scheme to teach reading to young children and purchased quantities of Bibles which he gave away to those who needed them. Five years after his ordination McCulloch married Janet Dinwoodie, the daughter of a Glasgow merchant named William Hamilton. She, it seems, provided encouragement and solid support for his ministry.

Prelude to the Revival

Towards the close of 1740 and at the beginning of 1741, McCulloch began the practice of reading to his congregation accounts of George Whitefield's revivalist open-air preaching to the miners of Kingswood near Bristol and in the American colonies. His people's hearts were touched and the congregations began to increase in size. The Cambuslang kirk soon became too small to cope so McCulloch began holding services in the open fields when the weather was fine. A natural amphitheater alongside the church provided an ideal location. Thus, it happened that about a year before the revival began in earnest crowded congregations were coming together on Sunday evenings to listen to McCulloch's preaching. His constant theme was the biblical necessity of regeneration. Macfarlan commented,

---

3. McCulloch, *Some Account of Mr McCulloch of Cambuslang*, in Macfarlan, *Revivals of the Eighteenth Century*, 35–36.

> In this retired and romantic spot Mr McCulloch for about a year before "the work" began, preached to crowded congregations, and on the Sabbath evenings, after sermon, detailed to the listening multitudes the astonishing effects produced by the ministrations of Mr Whitefield in England and America; and urged, with great energy, the doctrine of regeneration and newness of life.[4]

Philip, one of Whitefield's early biographers, noted that McCulloch's sermons had begun to impact his hearers in considerable numbers well before Whitefield had arrived on the scene. Indeed "some were so violently agitated . . . as to fall down under visible paroxysms of bodily agony."[5] This soon led to numbers of them praying for a revival of religion.[6]

An eyewitness account, attested by McCulloch, observed that this heightened spiritual concern led to "good fruits appearing both in Cambuslang and the surrounding countryside. . . . There is," he wrote,

> a visible reformation of the lives of some who were formerly notorious sinners, particularly in the laying aside cursing and swearing, and drinking to excess, among persons addicted to these practices;—remorse for acts of injustice and the violation of relative duties, confessed to the persons wronged, joined to new endeavours after a conscientious discharge of the duties previously neglected;—restitution, which has more than once been distinctly and particularly inculcated in public, since this work began;—forgiving injuries;—desirable evidence of fervent love for one another, to all men, and even to those who speak evil of them.[7]

Macfarlan also recorded the fact that people had become much more affectionate toward their ministers, were diligent in family worship, and were keen to establish new meetings for prayer. Twelve such societies had recently been formed within the parish of Cambuslang. Together with these positive transformations, "there was an ardent love of the Holy Scriptures" and a "resolve to learn to read" on the part of young and old. McCulloch attached his name to this printed account, stating, "I have perused the following short narrative and can attest the facts contained in it."[8]

4. Macfarlan, *Revivals of the Eighteenth Century*, 39.
5. Philip, *Life and Times of George Whitefield*, 294.
6. Fawcett, *Cambuslang Revival*, 104.
7. Macfarlan, *Revivals of the Eighteenth Century*, 49.
8. Macfarlan, *Revivals of the Eighteenth Century*, 52.

During the winter of 1741 and on into January and February 1742, there was increasing expectancy of, and much praying for, revival. After McCulloch's lecture on the 18th of February, about fifty men and women, most of whom were distressed about their state before God, went to the dining room of the manse. There he exhorted and prayed with them.[9] After this eventful night large crowds from near and far began to stream into Cambuslang and sermons and teaching became necessary every day. News of these events reached John Willison, the minister of Dundee, who made his way south to check out what was happening. He gave this testimony on April 15th, 1742,

> Having resided several days in Mr McCulloch's house, I had occasion to converse with many who had been under convictions there. I spoke with many who had got relief from soul trouble, and in whom the gracious work of the Spirit of God appeared. . . . I conversed with some who had been very wicked and scandalous, but who were now wonderfully changed. . . . I look upon the work at Cambuslang as a singular and marvellous outpouring of the Holy Spirit; and I pray that it may be a happy forerunner of a general revival of the Lord's work.[10]

Among those who heard news of the awakening in Cambuslang was the Rev. George Whitefield, who wrote to McCulloch on March 22, "I rejoice to hear of the great work begun in Scotland and doubt not its continuance."[11]

Whitefield's Arrival in Cambuslang

Whitefield had embarked for Scotland a second time on the *Mary Ann* on May 29th and arrived on June 3rd, 1742. Onboard ship he wrote, "I spent most of my time in secret prayer." Unsurprisingly, as soon as he went ashore he felt "the Holy Spirit filling his soul." Many people came to him weeping and blessing him, and great numbers followed his coach as he travelled to Edinburgh.[12] He spent the next four weeks ministering in and around Edinburgh and Glasgow and revisiting places and churches where he had ministered during his first preaching tour, which had

---

9. See McCulloch's Sermons, 2.101, in Fawcett, *Cambuslang Revival*, 108.
10. Macfarlan, *Revivals of the Eighteenth Century*, 53–54.
11. *Glasgow Weekly History* 17, p. 1, in Fawcett, *Cambuslang Revival*, 111.
12. "Letter to Mr A__," 4 June 1742, in Whitefield, *Works*, 1:399.

extended from July to October 1741. As he was leaving on that occasion he wrote in a letter, "I scarce know how to leave Scotland. I shall think it my duty to pay the inhabitants another visit as soon as possible."[13]

And so it proved. Word continued to reach Whitefield about the awakening in Cambuslang from the moment he set foot on Scottish soil. On June 8th, he wrote encouragingly to McCulloch, "I believe you will both see and hear of far greater things than these. I trust that not one corner of poor Scotland will be left un-watered by the dew of God's heavenly blessing."[14] A month later, on July 6th, Whitefield left Glasgow for Cambuslang, arriving at noon the same day.[15] His intention was to be a part of the move of God that was taking place, but more specifically he had been invited by McCulloch to assist in serving communion at the tables.

On his arrival in the town Whitefield preached "to a vast body of people, and at six in the evening, and afterwards at nine, to a vast body of people." "Such a commotion," he wrote, "surely was never heard of, especially about eleven o'clock at night. It far out-did all that I ever saw in America."[16] For about an hour and a half there was "such weeping," with many uttering agonized cries, many falling into deep distress, and the people slain by scores. Many were carried to shelter like wounded soldiers taken off the battlefield. After Whitefield had finished speaking, McCulloch preached till past one o'clock in the morning. Even then he found it an uphill task to persuade the people to depart to their homes. Throughout the whole of the night the voice of praise and prayer could be heard in the fields.[17] On the day following, July 7th, he preached several times and the level of the commotions increased.[18] On Saturday, July 10th, Whitefield preached to more than 20,000 people and then on the sabbath he assisted with the sacrament and wrote that "there were undoubtedly twenty thousand people present." Two tents had already been set up for Lord's Supper, which was planned for Sunday, July 11th, and was to be administered in the fields.[19]

13. "Letter to Mr J_C_," 27 October 1741, in Whitefield, *Works*, 1:337.

14. "Letter to Mr McCulloch," 7 July 1742, in Whitefield, *Works*, 1:403.

15. "Letter to Mrs Whitefield," 7 July 1742, in Whitefield, *Works*, 1:405.

16. Macfarlan, *Revivals of the Eighteenth Century*, 63. Duncan Macfarlan (1771–1857) copied this from William McCulloch's original accounts of the revival.

17. Information and quotations in this paragraph are taken from "Letter to Mrs Whitefield," 7 July 1742, Whitefield, *Works*, 1:405.

18. "Letter to Mrs Whitefield," 7 July 1742, in Whitefield, *Works*, 1:405.

19. "Letter to Mr J_C_," 15 July 1742, in Whitefield, *Works*, 1:409.

Revival in Cambuslang, 1742-43

George Whitefield preaching at Moorfields, 1742. Engraving from the *Illustrated London News*, July 22, 1865. Public domain.

When the communion began, Whitefield served at one of the tables. The presence of God came on him with such power that the people began to press in on him. In view of the impending crush, he was compelled to go and preach in one of the tents while other ministers continued to serve the remainder of the communicants. Preaching continued throughout the day with one sermon immediately following another. This meant that those who had received the Lord's Supper were able to go and listen. In the evening, when the sacrament was over, Whitefield preached at the request of the ministers to the entire gathering. He did so for an hour and a half, and many of those who listened either cried out, wept, or wrung their hands.[20] "Some were swooning and others crying out over a pierced Saviour." On the Monday following, Whitefield preached again to nearly as many and wrote to John Cennick that "such a universal stir I never saw before."[21] McCulloch wrote in a letter the following Wednesday, "It is not quite five months since the work began, and during that time, I have reason to believe that upwards of five hundred souls have been awakened, brought deep under deep conviction of sin, and a feeling

20. "Letter to Mr J_C_," 15 July 1742, in Whitefield, *Works*, 1:409.
21. "Letter to Mr J_C_," 15 July 1742, in Whitefield, *Works*, 1:409.

sense of their lost condition. Most of these have also, I trust, been savingly brought home too God."[22] Very significantly McCulloch went on to state, "I do not include in this number, such as have been awakened by Mr Whitefield's sermons; because I cannot pretend to compute them."[23] McCulloch continued, "The meetings were very great. On the Sabbath it was reckoned that there could not be fewer than thirty thousand present; but Mr Whitefield who has been accustomed to large meetings, estimated them at twenty thousand."[24]

The fact that the Cambuslang revival had its central focus at a sacramental meeting may well have been due, at least in part, to the Presbyterian practice. Their custom of sharing the Lord's Supper annually meant that communicants treated the matter with great seriousness. They came to the Lord's Table with reverence and awe, having carefully prepared themselves. In order to be admitted, participants were required to obtain a small metal token from their minister, and these were not readily given out.[25] Many of those who took part at Cambuslang traveled considerable distances and arrived with great expectancy. A gentleman from Kilmarnock who was present recorded his impressions in the following lines.

> Persons from all parts flocked to see, and many from many parts went home convinced, and converted to God. A brae, or hill, near the manse at Cambuslang, seemed to be formed by Providence, for containing a large congregation. People sat unwearied till two in the morning, to hear sermons, disregarding the weather. You could scarce walk a yard, but must tread on some, either rejoicing in God for mercies received, or crying out for more . . . The communion-table was in the field; three tents, at a proper distance, all surrounded with a multitude of hearers; above twenty ministers (among whom was good old Mr Bonner) attending to preach and assist, all enlivened by one another.[26]

Such was the joy and the overwhelming presence of God in the sacrament that both the ministers and the people resolved to have another in imitation of Hezekiah's Passover.[27] The proposal to do this was made by Alexander Webster of Edinburgh and supported by McCulloch.

22. Macfarlan, *Revivals of the Eighteenth Century*, 61.
23. Macfarlan, *Revivals of the Eighteenth Century*, 61.
24. Macfarlan, *Revivals of the Eighteenth Century*, 65.
25. Fawcett, *Cambuslang Revival*, 118.
26. "Report by a Gentleman from Kilmarnock," cited in Gillies, *Memoirs*, 12
27. Gillies, *Memoirs*, 124.

Whitefield readily agreed and wrote in a letter, "In less than a month, we are to have another sacrament at Cambuslang, a thing not practised before in Scotland."[28] James Robe, the parish minister from Kilsyth, observed that it had not been known for the Lord's Supper to be held twice in a summer anywhere in Scotland before the revival.[29] Whitefield, however, had from the time of his conversion and membership in the Oxford Holy Club greatly valued the sacrament, which he took whenever the opportunity arose. He immediately seconded the proposal for another sacrament at Cambuslang. There is no doubt that his encouragement contributed to the decision to hold it.[30]

The Second Communion

The day chosen for the second Lord's Supper was August 15th. Whitefield reported that he found himself opposed on every side and that the Erskines and the seceders of the Associate Presbytery were holding a fast against him and denouncing his preaching as an instrument of delusion and an agent of the devil.[31] They had evidently reached the conclusion that their stance against the Church of Scotland was right and were therefore of the view that any blessing that appeared to come upon it could not be of God. Whitefield by this stage was undeterred by these arrows from their bows and remained in Cambuslang and the vicinity until the end of August. McCulloch wrote of this second communion that "it did indeed much exceed the former, not only in the number of ministers, people and communicants, but which is the main thing, in a much greater measure of the power and special presence of God, in the experience of multitude attending."[32]

McCulloch described the "vast concourse of people" who came out not just from Glasgow "but from many places at a considerable distance." He described the moving scenes of the second gathering for the Lord's Supper, stating that "the voice of prayer and praise could be heard all night" and that it was supposed that between 30,000 and 40,000 people

---

28. *Christian Monthly History*, November, 1743, 28, cited in Fawcett, *Cambuslang Revival*, 118.

29. *Christian Monthly History*, November, 1743, 28, cited in Fawcett, *Cambuslang Revival*, 118.

30. Robe, *Faithful Narrative*, 222.

31. "Letter to Howell Harris," 26 August 1742, in Whitefield, *Works*, 1:426.

32. Macfarlan, *Revivals of the Eighteenth Century*, 72.

were assembled, of whom 3,000 communicated. Significantly, the *Glasgow Weekly History* estimated the crowd to have been "upwards of 30,000."[33] The very large collections which were taken would also seem to endorse the estimated numbers present. The first Communion sabbath brought in £117.12s and the second £194.2s which can be compared with the normal sabbath day offerings of between £3 and £12. The money which was given from February—December 1741 was £146.13.9d compared with £1,445.17.9d for the same period in 1742.[34] Numbers of people to whom Whitefield served the bread and wine had an overwhelming sense of God's presence. James Robe recorded the testimony of Mr L. M,. a twenty-eight-year-old man who attended the sacrament at Cambuslang:

> I went to the sacrament at Cambuslang and being at the table the Rev. Mr Whitefield expressed these words, "O dear Redeemer, seal these lambs of thine to the day of redemption." At which words my breath was near stopping, and the blood gushed at my nose. He said, "Be not afraid, for God shall put thy tears in a bottle." These words were put into my heart, "A new heart I will give you, and a right spirit I will put into you & co." I sat afterwards at the table overjoyed with love for my dear redeemer.[35]

Whitefield stated that there were three tents and that "the ministers were enlarged, and great grace was among the people." He himself preached on the Lord's Day morning, served five tables, and preached at about ten at night to a great company in the churchyard, and though it was raining there was "a considerable awakening."[36] Another communicant informed James Robe that while Whitefield was serving the tables at the second sacrament "he appeared to be so filled with the love of God as to be in a kind of ecstasy or transport."[37] McCulloch reported that Whitefield's sermons were attended with "much power" and that there was "a very great but decent weeping." He also stated that "the lowest estimate I hear . . . has been upwards of thirty thousand."[38]

Many ministers and clergy came to Cambuslang from across Scotland and others were present from England and Ireland. Prominent

---

33. *Glasgow Weekly History* 39, pp. 1–2, cited in Fawcett, *Cambuslang Revival*, 119.
34. Fawcett, *Cambuslang Revival*, 119.
35. Robe, *Faithful Narrative*, 85–86.
36. "Letter to Mr A__," 27 August 1742, in Whitefield, *Works*, 1:429.
37. Robe, *Faithful Narrative*, 225.
38. Macfarlan, *Revivals of the Eighteenth Century*, 73.

among them were Alexander Webster from Edinburgh, John Gillies from Glasgow, and James Robe from Kilsyth, where an awakening similar to that at Cambuslang took place in its wake. Also present were several people of rank and distinction. Many of these individuals carried the presence of God's Spirit with them to the places from which they had come. In this way Whitefield's seemingly prophetic words to McCulloch that the revival would spread across the land were more than fulfilled. The second communion at Cambuslang is generally taken to be the high point of the revival in Scotland. Indeed, Whitefield wrote in a letter written from Cambuslang on August 27th, 1742,

> This day fortnight I came to this place to assist at the sacrament, with several ministers of the Church of Scotland. Such a Passover has not been heard of. The voice of prayer and praise was heard all night. It was supposed that between thirty and forty thousand people were assembled, and three thousand communicated. The minsters were enlarged, and great grace was among the people. I preached once on Saturday, once on Lord's day morning. I served five tables and preached at ten at night to a great number in the churchyard, though it rained much. There was a great awakening. On Monday at seven in the morning, the Rev. Mr Webster preached and there was very great commotion; and also in the third sermon, when I preached.[39]

Such was the impact of Cambuslang that some of those who participated in the revival saw it as the Spirit of God being poured out in the last days and began in consequence to think in terms of the imminent return of Christ. John Erskine (1721–1803) who was later to become the minister of the Old Greyfriars Church, Edinburgh, was so taken by what he had witnessed and experienced that he published a small treatise entitled *The Signs of the Times Considered, or the High Probability that the Present Appearances in New England, and the West of Scotland, Are a Prelude of the Glorious Things Promised to the Church in the Latter Ages*.[40] Avoiding the trap of speculating about dates or times, Erskine gave it as his view that the work of God now carrying on would in all probability spread and increase. "Blessed be God," he wrote, "our eyes see and ears hear such glorious things as these. The Lord has indeed done marvellous things."[41]

---

39. Macfarlan, *Revivals of the Eighteenth Century*, 76.
40. Erskine, *Signs of the Times Considered*, 34.
41. Erskine, *Signs of the Times Considered*, 33.

From Cambuslang to Kilsyth and Beyond

One of the prominent features of the revival in Cambuslang was its spread to Kilsyth and beyond. Indeed, as Whitefield had declared, it reached all parts of the country. James Robe (1688–1753), the parish minister at Kilsyth, was a frequent attender and helper in the ministry at Cambuslang. He did his best to encourage his people to attend the meetings but with little success. However, on Sunday May 16 he preached with unusual power and "some strong and stout men" cried out "in distress."[42] By July, Robe believed that about 200 of his parishioners had been awakened.[43] It soon became clear that, as at Cambuslang, a quickening of spiritual life preceded the revival at Kilsyth. Significantly, Whitefield once again proved to be the catalyst which God used to kindle the flames. On Tuesday June 15, he preached there to 10,000 and wrote, "such commotion, I believe you never saw. O what cries of agony were there!"[44] The first sacrament of the Lord's Supper was held at Kilsyth on July 11th, 1742, the same day as that which took place at Cambuslang. Robe attended the second Communion there on August 15th, and McCulloch suggested to him that he consider a second occasion at Kilsyth. Initially he was apprehensive but was eventually persuaded by one of his elders for whom he had great respect. The date was set for Sunday October 3rd. Although the days were shortening, large crowds came across, many having travelled a considerable distance. There were twenty-two servings and about 1,500 communicants.

Whitefield was an enthusiastic participant and wrote in a letter dated October 6th that "we have seen Jesus exalted to the glory of his name in Scotland." He went on to relate that "last Sabbath-day and Monday, very great things, greater than ever, were seen in Kilsyth."[45] During this period Whitefield preached twice every day with great power. The following week he wrote again that "the work is still increasing in Scotland, especially at Kilsyth" and that in consequence he would be spending a further three weeks in the country before setting out to London.[46]

---

42. Macfarlan, *Revivals of the Eighteenth Century*, 239; Fawcett, *Cambuslang Revival*, 129.

43. Fawcett, *Cambuslang Revival*, 129.

44. Tyerman, *Life of the Rev George Whitefield*, 2:5.

45. "Letter to Mr E__ C__," 6 October 1742, in Whitefield, *Works*, 1:446.

46. "Letter to John Wesley," 11 October 1742, in Whitefield, *Works*, 1:449.

Macfarlan, in his *Revivals of the Eighteenth Century Particularly at Cambuslang*, which was based on manuscripts prepared by William McCulloch, charted the spread of the revival from Cambuslang and Kilsyth to parishes and towns across the nation. It moved to Dundee and southern Perthshire, where it centered on Muthil, a few miles from the town of Auchterarder.[47] William Halley, the parish minister at Muthil, reported fifty people had been awakened in his parish in just three months between March and the beginning of July 1742.[48] The Lord's Supper was administered on the third Sunday in July and many were brought to Christ. From that time onward "unusual power" attended Halley's preaching. Each week crowds came to the manse for spiritual counsel after evening worship was concluded. Formerly there had been two praying societies in the parish. but within in a year there were eighteen. In a letter dated September 29th, 1742, Halley wrote, "The work here is still advancing," "many are deeply affected," and there is "a general sound of weeping throughout the congregation, which sometimes rises till I have to stop."[49] McCulloch left eyewitness accounts of the spread of revival to the presbyteries of Hamilton, Irvine, and Paisley, the cities of Glasgow and Edinburgh, the town of Dundee, and a host of other parishes.[50]

Inspiration from Cambuslang

Critics

As is the case in all revivals, Cambuslang inevitably had its critics. On July 15th, 1742, those who had left the established church and formed the Associate Presbytery held a public fast on account of the "awful work upon the bodies and spirits of men going on at Cambuslang." Ralph Erskine, one of their leaders, opined, "We have seen convulsions instead of convictions," but Robe responded that "they are greatly mistaken who imagine that all those who have been observably awakened, have come under faintings, tremblings, and other bodily distresses. These have been

---

47. Fawcett, *Cambuslang Revival*, 132. Fawcett details many of the places to which the revival extended. See 124-25 and 136-42.

48. Macfarlan, *Revivals of the Eighteenth Century*, 342-47; Fawcett, *Cambuslang Revival*, 133.

49. Macfarlan, *Revivals of the Eighteenth Century*, 245.

50. See Macfarlan, *Revivals of the Eighteenth Century*, 213-63.

by far the fewest number."[51] Robe made a further observation that in 1742 "conversions carried on in a calm, silent and quiet manner are the more numerous."[52] In another response, John Currie, the parish minister of Kinglassie, pointed out to the Associate brethren that "he himself had heard such loud outcryings in their seceding meeting house in Dunfermline that the sermon could not be heard."[53]

There is, as Fawcett and others have pointed out, a close link between spirituality and sensuality. This is known in some cases to have resulted in sexual improprieties. There were indeed situations in the Cambuslang revival which might well have raised suspicions, such as men and women spending the whole night out in the fields praying and singing. Yet there were no reports of any such scandals at Cambuslang. The records of the Presbytery of Hamilton from 1741–50 have been scrutinized with care. During the entire period there were eighty-three cases of presbyterial discipline for sexual offenses. Twenty-five came from Hamilton, sixteen from Avendale, and thirteen from East Monkland, but only one case was from Cambuslang. The worst that could be said about the general tone of behavior during the revival was that a number of "idle boys—apprentices from Glasgow" left their workplaces and came to see what was happening. They wandered about the fields, some of them causing distractions while the meetings were taking place.[54]

The revival which took place in both Cambuslang and Kilsyth was notable for a number of positive reasons. First, as has been noted, for some months there had been a quickening of spiritual life in both towns and parishes with many gatherings for earnest and prevailing prayer and a reviving of personal religion.

Second, in both parishes the central focus of the move of God was the gatherings for corporate communion with open-air preaching. These were occasions of great solemnity which were added to by their infrequency and by the serious preparation of the clergy. The majority of those who sat at the tables to receive the bread and wine did so with great expectancy of experiencing the presence of God. James Robe, for example, noted that "some people came to the Lord's table at Kilsyth under much

---

51. Philip, *Life and Times of George Whitefield*, 304.
52. Philip, *Life and Times of George Whitefield*, 304.
53. Currie, *New Testimony*, 15
54. Fawcett, *Cambuslang Revival*, 144.

terror."[55] The revival which took place at the same time at Muthil appears to have broken out following the administration of the Lord's Supper. William Halley, the parish minister, reported that at the sacrament "many were brought to the Conqueror's Feet."[56] One result of the revival, and Whitefield's part in it, was a growing desire to have more frequent communion services. This was made plain in 1749 when John Erskine (1721–1803) published *An Attempt to Promote the Frequent Dispensing of the Lord's Supper* in which he argued that four times a year would have much greater spiritual benefit than the church's annual sacramental service.[57]

Third, many ministers from other places took part both in preaching and in serving at the sacramental meetings. At the time of the second Lord's Supper at Kilsyth on October 3rd, Robe was assisted by John McLaurin of Glasgow, Thomas Gillespie of Carnock, and William McCulloch from Cambuslang. In most instances preaching went on continuously throughout the course of an entire day. This meant that those wanting to receive communion in one of the tents could receive teaching both beforehand and afterwards. Much of the preaching was done in the open air and in the fields where the tents had been set up. It was noted to be thoroughly biblical and grounded in the core doctrines of the faith.

One of the reasons why so many journeyed to Cambuslang was the limited range of mid-eighteenth-century attractions. People were therefore happy to travel long distances to listen to powerful preaching from men such as McCulloch, Whitefield, Robe, and others. This was seen for instance when twenty-seven members of Halley's parish walked nearly thirty miles from Muthil to the second Communion at Kilsyth.[58] The drawing power of Whitefield's preaching in the revivals at Cambuslang and Kilsyth should not be underestimated. His influence was well assessed by one of the ministers in the city of Aberdeen.

> I shall acquaint you freely of what I think of the Rev. Mr Whitefield.... He is I believe, justly esteemed by all who are personally acquainted with him, an eminent instrument of reviving, in these declining times, a just sense and concern for the great things of religion . . .the Lord raised up this eminent instrument, from

---

55. Robe, *Faithful Narrative*, 104.
56. Fawcett, *Cambuslang Revival*, 133.
57. Erskine, *Attempt to Promote*, 4.
58. Fawcett, *Cambuslang Revival*, 134.

a quarter, whence we could not have expected it, to call us to return to him; from whom it is plain, we have deeply revolted.[59]

Gillies observed the importance of Whitefield's personal interactions. He is "calm and serene under all he meets with, yea his joy in tribulation, is to me surprising."[60] Whitefield did indeed do his best to keep the doors of friendship open with the Associate Presbytery. He wrote to Ebenezer Erskine in June 1742, assuring him that he loved and respected them and applauded their zeal for God. He went on to say that he felt no resentment in his heart towards them and "would gladly sit down and hear you or your brethren preach."[61]

By extending the hand of friendship across the denominational spectrum and working with ministers from the established Church of Scotland Whitefield strengthened the hand of Scottish evangelicals. His visits north of the border revealed his remarkably wide sympathies. Thomas Somerville (1740–1830), minister of Jedburgh, paid great tribute to his conversation and preaching, contending that he was a major cause in ending "narrow prejudices . . . and the more rapid progress of a catholic spirit."[62]

Fourth, the revival was marked by the preaching of a literal hell, often with depictions of punishment.[63] Critics urged that this promoted unnecessary fear and contributed to outbursts of shaking and cries. That said, there were, as Fawcett noted, "many who were melted down by the love of Christ."[64]

Fifth, the revival proved to be portable. The gatherings in both Cambuslang and Kilsyth were attended by ministers and clergy from many places across the country. They then traveled home and carried the Spirit of God with them to their parishes and meeting houses much in the way that the Old Testament prophet Elisha had carried away the mantle of his master Elijah.

Sixth, the revival spread by writing and publicity. McCulloch and Robe, much like Whitefield, were constant correspondents, writing letters to ministers and people in many parts of Scotland, the British Isles,

---

59. Gillies, *Memoirs*, 88, 90.
60. Gillies, *Memoirs*, 90.
61. "Letter to Ebenezer Erskine," 10 June 1742, in Whitefield, *Works*, 1:402.
62. Fawcett, *Cambuslang Revival*, 218.
63. Fawcett, *Cambuslang Revival*, 154.
64. Fawcett, *Cambuslang Revival*, 154.

and beyond.⁶⁵ This played a major part in widening the revival and its impact. There was also a growing correspondence with ministers in the New England colonies. McCulloch wrote that James Robe, who produced a *Monthly History* charting the revival, "became eminently the herald of the day."⁶⁶ The publication at Glasgow in 1742 of his *A Faithful Narrative of the Extraordinary Work of the Spirit of God*⁶⁷ also played a part in spreading news of the awakening in Cambuslang and Kilsyth. In his preface Robe stated that it was his hope that his narrative would awaken the godly and allay prejudice and fear in others. Many of those who came to the meetings were able to record and pass on truths they had learned from the preaching.

Seventh, the revival in both Cambuslang and Kilsyth had many positive social outcomes. The evidence suggests that most of those who professed conversion remained steadfast in the faith. McCulloch, writing in April 1751, stated that he had a list before him of about 400 people who had been awakened at Cambuslang and who were still living as "becometh the gospel."⁶⁸ A similar endorsement was found at Kilsyth in the same year, with more than a hundred who had come to Christ in 1742 still continuing in the faith. Again, at Kilsyth Robe observed that "many former feuds and animosities in his parish had now been in great measure laid aside." He noted also that the summer of 1742 "was the most peaceable among neighbours that could ever be remembered."⁶⁹ Similar benefits were witnessed at Cambuslang, where there were numerous instances of injuries being forgiven and "evidences of love to one another."⁷⁰ In general, the defenders of revival were quick to point out the ways in which it had changed the quality of people's lives. Drunkards, swearers, whoremongers, and liars had put away their past and were demonstrating their Christian commitment in transformed living.⁷¹ Writing nearly a decade after the revival, McCulloch stated, "Such as were accustomed to frequent taverns, to drink and play cards till late, or it may be morning hours, have, for these nine years past, avoided any occasions of the

---

65. Fawcett, *Cambuslang Revival*, 137.
66. MacFarlan, *Revivals of the Eighteenth Century*, 237.
67. Robe, *Faithful Narrative*, Preface.
68. McCulloch, *Sermons*, 8, cited in Fawcett, *Cambuslang Revival*, 168.
69. Robe, *Faithful Narrative*, 15.
70. Robe, *Faithful Narrative*, 16.
71. Macfarlan, *Revivals of the Eighteenth Century*, 99-100.

kind, and kept home, spending their evenings in Christian conference, in matters profitable to their families and in secret and family devotions."[72]

Eighth, the revival was, as Arnold Dallimore contended, a revival in the way that Jonathan Edwards understood the term. It was not, he argued, humanly planned, although the sacramental meetings took a good measure of negotiating, organization, and discussion. It was, however, an inspirational revival born of much prayer, and there was no attempt at sensationalism or showmanship. Those who professed conversion were examined by one or more of the ministers.[73] The evidence is that the great majority persevered in their newfound faith. The revival was watched over by wise and able pastors, and it was deeply rooted in Scripture and grounded in creedal doctrines. Lives were changed, relationships restored, and wrongs and injustices righted. Above all, the name of Jesus Christ was honored and lifted up.

---

72. Macfarlan, *Revivals of the Eighteenth Century*, 99–100.
73. Dallimore, *George Whitefield*, 2:135–36.

4

The Methodist Revival in England, 1738–91

ON THE EVENING OF May 24th, 1738, a disillusioned Church of England clergyman who had just returned from the American colony of Georgia made his way to a society meeting at Aldersgate on the outskirts of London. What took place on that occasion proved to be momentous. Not only was his life profoundly changed, but the face of the English nation was also transformed. John Wesley recorded his conversion in the following words:

> In the evening I went very unwillingly to a society in Aldersgate Street where one was reading Luther's preface to the Epistle to the Romans. About a quarter before nine, while he was describing the changes which God works in the heart through faith in Christ, I felt my heart strangely warmed. I felt I did trust in Christ alone, for salvation; and an assurance was given me that He had taken away my sins, even mine, and saved me from the law of sin and death.[1]

So began what was to become the greatest revival in English history. It had a particularly powerful impact in London, Bristol, and the Southwest, and in Yorkshire and the Northeast. But as Wesley trained helpers and coworkers who preached in the open air there was hardly a county or aspect of social and political life that remained untouched by this powerful awakening.

---

1. Wesley, *Journal*, 26 April, 1738.

Remarkably, this was a revival that didn't, like so many revivals, simply fade away after a year or two—it was sustained with a growing, vibrant tenacity.

The key ingredient in Wesley's experience was assurance. Conversion was no longer an intellectual assent to an objective set of doctrines; it was primarily a subjective experience of the presence of Christ in the believer's inner being. It was, in Wesley's own words, "a heart-warming experience" of the Christ who stood behind those doctrines. There are some who feel that Wesley had "a first conversion" in 1725 while studying the writings of William Law.[2] He had written, "But meeting now with Mr Law's Christian Perfection and Serious Call . . . the light flowed in so mightily into my soul, that everything appeared in a new light. I cried to God for help and was persuaded that I should be accepted of him and that I was even then in a state of salvation."[3] Against this view however, is the fact on his return to England Wesley had confessed himself unconverted, stating, "I went to America to convert the Indians but Oh who is there to convert me?" Regardless of how we interpret Wesley's experiences, the fact is that the 24th of May, 1738, was a major turning point in his life. From that day forward the seed of one of the world's great revivals had been sown.

Social Context

The word *revival*, as has been noted, generally signifies something that was dead or dying being brought back to life. There can be little doubting that both the English church and nation were not in a healthy state. The Church of England was dominated by Latitudinarianism which asserted intellectual reason by itself was sufficient to bring a person to faith in Christ. Clergy of all denominations were expressing doubts about the doctrine of the Trinity This was the age of the hunting, shooting, and fishing clergy. J. R. Green described the clergy as "the idlest and most lifeless in Europe,"[4] and Norman Sykes pointed out that half of all English clergy in the eighteenth century were absentees who lived away from their parishes."[5]

---

2. See Skevington Wood, *Burning Heart*, 68.
3. Davies, *Methodism*, 48.
4. Green, *Short History of the English People*, chap. 10, sec. 1.
5. Sykes, *Church and State*, 217.

John Wesley

John Wesley (1703-91) was one of nineteen children born to Samuel and Susannah Wesley. Samuel Wesley was a Tory high churchman and incumbent of the Lincolnshire parish of Epworth. Susannah was a remarkable lady who among other things started a church meeting in the rectory while Samuel was absent at convocation in 1712.[6] This may be one of the reasons Wesley was happy to endorse women preachers. When he was at the impressionable age of six, young John almost died in a fire at the rectory, which appeared to have been started by the ill will of some within the parish. He was, however, dramatically rescued from an upstairs window just seconds before the roof collapsed. This was seen by the bystanders and more particularly by his mother as "a sign of God's special interest in the boy."[7] He was indeed, in the words of the prophet Zechariah, "a brand plucked from the burning" (Zech 3:2). In consequence Susannah resolved to be, as she put it, "more particularly careful of the soul of this child which God had so mercifully provided for."[8] It comes as no surprise that Wesley grew up to believe that individuals were specially "chosen" for specific tasks. In later years Wesley regularly kept the anniversary of his rescue and distributed copies of his engraved portrait inscribed with the words, "Is not this a brand plucked from the burning?"

After education at Charterhouse School, John and his younger brother Charles (1707-88), who was later to be his co-leader in the revival, went up to Oxford University. John was made a deacon in September 1725 and ordained priest in September 1728. The following year he gathered a group of very devout young men together with the purpose of mutually encouraging one another in the Christian faith. Dubbed by its critics as "The Holy Club" its chief activities involved studying the classics and a book of divinity on Sundays. Charles Wesley, who came up to Oxford from Westminster School in 1727, had earlier collected a smaller group together who read devotional works.[9] They read and discussed works such as Hermann Francke's *Treatise Against the Fear of Man* and Henry Scougal's *The Life of God in the Soul of Man*, which led to Whitefield's conversion in 1735.[10] John Wesley drew up a set of General Rules

---

6. Rack, *Reasonable Enthusiast*, 53.
7. Rattenbury, *Wesley's Legacy to the World*, 29.
8. Semmel, *Methodist Revolution*, 165.
9. Rack, *Reasonable Enthusiast*, 85.
10. Scotland, *George Whitefield*, 24-25.

for self-examination which members began to use for themselves. This methodical and disciplined lifestyle led to their being called "Methodists."

In 1736, Wesley left Oxford for the new slave-free colony of Georgia, having been a fellow of Lincoln College from 1729–35. He had been invited by the governor, James Oglethorpe, to be his chaplain and his brother Charles as his secretary. Wesley soon came to the realization that his Christian faith was lacking. During the outbound voyage aboard the vessel *Simmonds* Wesley was deeply impressed by the calm behavior of a group of Moravian missionaries during a major storm. Soon after landing, Wesley met up with their leader, A. G. Spangenberg, who asked him several challenging questions. "Do you know Jesus Christ?" Wesley's reply was, "I know he is the Saviour of the world." "True," he replied, "but do you know He has saved you?" Wesley answered: "I hope he has died to save me." Spangenberg then added, "Do you know yourself?" Wesley replied, "I do" but afterwards recalled, "I fear they were vain words."[11] Once settled in the community Wesley caused friction by his rigid adherence to the formularies of the *Book of Common Prayer*. He refused to baptize infants except by total immersion and excluded those he judged to be unrepentant sinners from the communion services he held weekly. More trouble ensued when he became deeply involved with Sophy Hopkey and probably wanted to marry her. She, however, rejected him in favor of a Mr. Williamson. After her marriage, Wesley, driven by jealousy, found ways to repel her from the Lord's table, which naturally offended her husband and her uncle, Thomas Causton, who was a shopkeeper and a magistrate. Things came to a head when Causton had Wesley indicted by a grand jury for this and other charges of eccentric and oppressive conduct as a minister. Wesley was then forced to leave the county.[12]

Revival Begins

Whitefield and Wesley

The originator of the Methodist revival was neither John nor Charles Wesley but George Whitefield (1714–70). For quite some time the British public regarded him as the movement's leader. Born at the Bell Inn in the city of Gloucester, he had risen to the position of tapster in the family

---

11. Rack, *Reasonable Enthusiast*, 115.
12. Rack, *Reasonable Enthusiast*, 124.

hostelry. From there, with the help of friends, he found his way to Pembroke College as a servitor at the age of eighteen. In this new environment he joined the Methodists in 1735 and underwent an experience he afterwards described as "the new birth." He wrote, "I was delivered from the burden that had so heavily oppressed me. The Spirit of mourning was taken from me, and I knew what it was to rejoice in God my Saviour."[13] For some reason that isn't altogether clear, Martin Benson, the Bishop of Gloucester, took it upon himself to ordain Whitefield when he was below the canonical age of twenty-three, a step which may have caused him some regret. Whitefield proved to be a remarkable preacher, particularly in the open air. After his first sermon it was reported to the bishop that he had sent fifteen people mad. In truth, they had probably fallen under the Spirit and cried for mercy. The bishop, perhaps with a smile on his face, replied to the complainants that he hoped they would not recover before the next Sunday so that they might be spared a second dose!

In February 1738, Whitefield followed what he believed was God's call and went to Savannah in the colony of Georgia in order to explore and assess the situation. This despite Wesley having discouraged him. He arrived back in England in December in order to receive his ordination as priest, which took place on January 14th, 1739. After preaching in one or two London churches he journeyed to Bristol at the beginning of February. With a heart always open to the needs of the poor, Whitefield determined to visit the colliers of Kingswood and to show that God loved and cared about them. He arrived there on Sunday, February 25th, and preached to a crowd which "at a moderate computation were about ten thousand." He spoke for an hour with great power and was afterwards told "that all could hear me."[14] This was the first of several visits to this mining community. On Sunday, March 25th, he preached again to a crowd that "was computed to be upwards of twenty-three thousand people." "I was told afterwards," he wrote, "that those who stood farthest off could hear me very plainly."[15] It was this open-air field-preaching which set the revival in motion. Indeed, it became both the major vehicle of the revivals which took place in both Britain and the American colonies. Whitefield was a born orator. Not only did his powerful voice carry long distances and reach huge crowds, but it was also musical, captivating, and melodic.

---

13. Whitefield, *Short Account of God's Dealings*, 66.
14. Whitefield, *Journals*, Sunday 25 February, 1739.
15. Whitefield, *Journals*, Sunday 25 March, 1739.

On one occasion, David Garrick said that Whitefield could move a crowd to tears just by pronouncing the word "Mesopotamia." He thought it truly wonderful that Whitefield could cast such a spell over people by proclaiming the simplest truths of the Bible.[16] Following Kingswood, huge crowds gathered to hear him at Moorfields and Kennington Common. On Sunday, April 29th, he preached in the morning at Moorfields to "an exceeding great multitude and went on in the afternoon to Kennington Common, which was about two miles form London. He recorded that no less than thirty thousand people were supposed to be present." The vast crowd were quiet and attentive and joined in the Psalm and the Lord's Prayer. In Whitefield's words, "all agreed it was never seen on this wise before."[17] Truly remarkable is the fact that similar, and indeed even larger, crowds continued to come together to listen to Whitefield's sermons for the next thirty years right until the time of his death in 1770. By that time, he is calculated to have preached at least 18,000 times.[18]

Wesley Takes to the Fields

At the moment of his time in Kingswood Whitefield had his mind set on returning to Georgia. Thinking of what he had heard of John Wesley's change of heart and his newfound peace of mind, he wrote at the beginning of March urging him "in a most pressing manner to come to Bristol without delay" and share in the work and extend when he left the country.[19] Wesley was reluctant but finally arrived in Bristol on the 31st of March and met up with Whitefield. He wrote in his journal, "I could scarce reconcile myself at first to this strange way of preaching in the fields, of which he set me an example on Sunday; having been all my life (till very lately) so tenacious of every point relating to decency and order, that I should have thought it a sin, if it had not been done in a church."[20] The following day Wesley "submitted" as he put it "to be more vile, and proclaimed in the highways of the glad tidings of salvation."[21]

---

16. Haykin, *Revived Puritan*, 35–37.
17. Whitefield, *Journals*, 2 April, 1739.
18. See Scotland, *George Whitefield*, 214.
19. Wesley, *Journal*, 15 March, 1739.
20. Wesley, *Journal*, 31 March, 1739.
21. Wesley, *Journal*, 2 April, 1739.

The Methodist Revival in England, 1738–91

A crowd "of about three thousand people" hung on his every word as he preached "The Spirit of the Lord is upon me, because he has anointed me to preach the gospel to the poor; he has sent me to heal the broken hearted; to preach deliverance to the captives, and recovery of sight to the blind; to set at liberty them that are bruised, to proclaim the acceptable year of the Lord."[22]

John Wesley preaching at Epworth Market Cross. Source *United Methodist Insight*. Public domain.

22. Wesley, *Journal*, 2 April, 1739.

From this moment on, Wesley took to the outdoor world like a duck to the water and came to believe with Whitefield that field-preaching was a God-appointed means to bring about revival. On the 8th of April, he preached to "about fifteen hundred on the top of Hanham Mount in Kingswood, on Thursday, 14th June," at Blackheath to "twelve or fourteen thousand people," on Sunday, 17th June, "in Upper Moorfields, to I believe six or seven thousand people" and at five in the evening on Kennington Common, "to about fifteen thousand people."[23] From this point on, both Wesley and Whitefield constantly preached in the open air until the end of their days. Wesley rode on horseback until he was seventy-one, after which time he traveled by coach. Whitefield did much the same but often traveled by chaise, particularly in his later years. Both men preached without notes.[24] By his introducing Wesley and others to field-preaching Whitefield transformed the pietism of the Holy Club into a worldwide revival movement and at the very least should be considered a co-founder of Methodism. In these early days of the movement Wesley and Whitefield declared the world was their parish and preached in any parish they chose, Wesley maintaining that no binding mission restraints were laid down in the New Testament. Whatever the needs of mission dictated should be followed. Initially the two men worked together, preaching and establishing their converts into small groups known as societies. As the months and years went by however, they gradually drew apart over the doctrines of election and predestination, with Whitefield's followers becoming known as the Calvinistic Methodists and being organized separately. Both men proclaimed salvation by faith through the cross of Christ, though in practice Whitefield believed that only "the elect" could receive it. Whitefield came increasingly to see himself as "an awakener" rather than a pastor and organizer.[25] In later years this led him to transfer some of his societies over to Wesley's pastoral oversight and others to the Countess of Huntingdon's Connexion.

Organization and Pastoral Care

It seems almost a contradiction to speak of revival and organization in the same sentence, yet such was indeed the case in the Methodist revival.

---

23. Wesley, *Journal*, 8 April, 14 and 17 June, 1739.
24. See Rack, *Reasonable Enthusiast*, 141. See also Scotland, *George Whitefield*, 214.
25. Rack, *Reasonable Enthusiast*, 194.

In fact, it was the pastoral structures and organization that Wesley, and to a lesser extent Whitefield, put in place that both sustained and fueled the revival, making it the longest and most extensive in history. Just as the revival which broke out in Jerusalem on the day of Pentecost was nurtured and furthered by small groups meeting together in homes for prayer,[26] fellowship, and the breaking of bread, so Wesley and Whitefield established small groups, known as societies, on exactly the same principle.

Following the successes of his preaching in Bristol, Wesley quickly realized the need for a base. On May 9th, 1739, he took possession of a piece of ground near St. James churchyard, in the Horse Fair on which a building known as New Room was erected. It was of sufficient size to accommodate the two recently formed societies of Nicolas and Baldwin Street.[27] On July 20th, 1740, Wesley parted company with the Fetter Lane society which had become taken over by strange Moravian teachings. A few days later, Wesley established his headquarters at the old King's Foundery which he had purchased the previous November.[28] This building was superseded in 1777 by the erection of City Road Chapel in London's West End. By the 1740s it was clear that Wesley and Whitefield were going their separate ways. Whitefield soon established his headquarters at Moorfields alongside the north wall of the city of London. Whitefield's powerful preaching soon produced a trail of converts who he organized into societies. After 1741, Whitefield's Calvinistic Methodist societies developed around his four main centers of activity: London, Bristol, Gloucester, and Wales, where he worked in tandem with Howell Harris (1714–73), known as "the hammer and the axe" on account of his forthright, in-your-face manner. In later times, when Whitefield was in America, Harris acted as his second in command and oversaw his English societies. By 1742, there was a substantial network of "Whitefieldian Methodist Societies" and fifteen full-time preachers. In 1747, they numbered thirty societies, with over twenty-four preaching places, with over twenty full- and part-time preachers and exhorters in active service.[29]

In a similar way Wesley also extended his mission out from London and Bristol to the rest of the nation. Like Whitefield, his journeyings, which continued to the day of his death, took him into Wales, Scotland,

---

26. See Acts 2:42–47.
27. Wesley, *Journal*, May 1739. See also Rack, *Reasonable Enthusiast*, 212–13.
28. See Telford, *Life of John Wesley*, 130, 132–33, 136.
29. Jones et al., *Elect Methodists*, 59.

and Ireland. The first place in the north which Wesley visited was Newcastle-upon-Tyne. He went because of his earlier successes among the miners at Kingswood. He entered the town on foot with a companion singing the Hundredth Psalm, which soon attracted a crowd. When he had finished, the people "stood staring at him with the most profound astonishment." Wesley then introduced himself, announcing he would preach again at five in the evening. At the appointed time Wesley made his way to the hill to find it covered from top to bottom. "I never," he wrote, "saw so large a crowd of people together, either in Moorfields or Kennington Common."[30] Wesley's experience at Newcastle was one which came to be replicated many hundreds of times in the years that lay ahead. The same was also true for Whitefield, who drew huge crowds on both sides of the Atlantic until the day of his death in 1770.

Holiness and the Spirit

Both Wesley and Whitefield had experienced the witness of the Spirit in their lives, and both preached and witnessed the Holy Spirit coming in power on those who listened to their preaching. Wesley declared, "A Methodist is one who has the love of God shed abroad in their hearts by the Holy Ghost given unto him."[31] The distinguishing mark of a Methodist conversion was its stress on the assurance of the Holy Spirit, whose presence strangely warmed the heart. Wesley stated it as follows: "the testimony of the Spirit is an inward impression on the soul whereby the Spirit of God witnesses with my spirit that I am child of God; that Jesus has loved me and given himself for me; that all my sins are blotted out and I, even I, am reconciled to God."[32] Whitefield was also insistent that Christian believers should experience the witness of the Spirit in their lives. "Beg God," he wrote to a friend, "that you may feel his spirit working mightily in your soul and witnessing with your spirit that you are a child of God."[33]

Both Wesley and Whitefield had fashioned and nurtured their spirituality in the Oxford Holy Club, and it was therefore no surprise that the revival prompted them to stress the importance of holy living.

---

30. Southey, *Life of John Wesley*, 203.
31. Rattenbury, *Wesley's Legacy to the World*, 97.
32. Rattenbury, *Wesley's Legacy to the World*, 97.
33. Whitefield, "Letter to Mrs_," 10 November, 1739, in Whitefield, *Works*, 2:118.

Wesley was quite clear that his mission was "spreading scriptural holiness throughout the land."[34] Whitefield shared the same objective, disciplining his own life and urging his followers to join a society to pray and to worship corporately and privately.

Sustained Itinerant Preaching

A distinctive feature of the Methodist revival in England was the sustained preaching not only of Whitefield and the Wesleys but also of their helpers, lay preachers, and other leaders. Most revivals begin with anointed and powerful preaching, the fervency of which then gradually slows, finally leveling off into the administration and routines of church order. In contrast, the structure which Whitefield and the Wesleys put in place did the reverse. It both created, sustained, and thrust the revival forward. The lynchpin of all Methodist societies (Wesley didn't call them churches) were the class meetings. These were small groups consisting of twelve or thirteen members with a trained and appointed leader. They were designed to enable each person to rekindle the Holy Spirit's presence in their lives. This was achieved by everyone being required to testify to their experience of Christ, share lessons learned, and recount prayers answered. Vitality was enhanced by fervent singing, outbursts of praise, and sometimes shouts of joy and exaltation. Wesley recounted his own personal experience of such meetings after having attended one on New Years Day, 1739. "About three in the morning," he recorded, "as we were continuing instant in prayer, the power of God came mightily upon us, and many fell to the ground. As soon as we recovered a little from that awe and amazement at the presence of His majesty, we broke out with one voice, 'We praise Thee, O God; we acknowledge Thee to be the Lord.'"[35]

Methodist societies, with their class meetings, also provided stopping places for traveling leaders such as the Wesleys, Whitefield, and their helpers. They could spread the news that a preacher was coming to their locality, provide support at the designated venue, and offer a base and hospitality when it was needed. For their part, the traveling preachers were able to stir up the Spirit in the people, check on the local leaders, and give training, encouragement, and instruction. All this created a powerful support network which sustained and enabled the Wesleys,

---

34. Wood, "John Wesley's Mission," 8.
35. Telford, *Life of John Wesley*, 117.

Whitefield, Harris, and others to continue traveling back and forth, preaching and exhorting across the British Isles to the end of their days. It was preaching, particularly in the open air, that extended and sustained the revival for the greater part of the eighteenth century.

Revival Preaching

From the very beginning the preaching of both Whitefield and Wesley had remarkable effects on their hearers. People experienced instantaneous conversion and, particularly in the early days, often shook or fell to the ground. Others also wept, cried aloud, shouted out for forgiveness, and lifted their hands in praise as the following instances make plain. Between April 2nd and July 29th, Whitefield recounted in his journal nineteen occasions on which he had preached to very large crowds at Kennington Common. He calculated that the total number of hearers was in excess of 300,000. On Sunday, September 9th, 1739, Wesley wrote in his journal, "I declared to about ten thousand, in Moorfields, what they must do to be saved." Later in the day his mother went with him at five, to Kennington, where there were estimated to be 20,000 people. He wrote, "I again insisted on that foundation of all our hope, 'Believe on the Lord Jesus, and thou shalt be saved.'"[36]

On Tuesday, September 20th, 1742, Wesley was at Trezuthan Downs and preached to 2,000–3,000 people on the "highway" of the Lord, the way of holiness. He reached Gwennap a little before six and found the plain covered from end to end. It was supposed there were 10,000 people, to whom "I preached Christ our wisdom, righteousness, sanctification, and redemption." "I could not conclude," he wrote, "till it was so dark we could scarcely see one another." There was deepest attention on all sides, no one speaking, stirring, or scarcely looking aside. "Surely here, though in a temple not made with hands, was God worshiped in 'the beauty of holiness.'"[37]

On Sunday, September 2nd, 1750, Wesley preached in a meadow at Tiverton "that was full from side to side, and many stood in the gardens and orchard ground."[38] In September 1766, Wesley was in Cornwall and preached at Redruth to one of the largest congregations he had ever seen

---

36. Wesley, *Journal*, 9 September, 1739.
37. Wesley, *Journal*, 20 September, 1742.
38. Wesley, *Journal*, 2 September, 1750.

there, but which was small compared to the one encountered the same evening at Gwennap amphitheatre.[39] On Tuesday, 30th April, 1776, Wesley preached at Colne in Yorkshire "to a multitude of people, all drinking in the Word. I scarce ever saw a congregation wherein men, women and children, thirty years ago, no Methodist could show his head."[40]

It frequently happened that both Whitefield and the Wesleys encountered the mob during their sermons. At Mighton Car, for example, a huge multitude, rich and poor, horse and foot, with several coaches, were soon gathered together, to whom Wesley cried with a loud voice, "What shall it profit a man, if he shall gain the whole world, and lose his own soul?" Some of "the thousands" who had gathered attended to his words with seriousness, but others did not. "Clods and stones flew about on every side" but Wesley was untouched and finished his discourse, after which he and his wife were able to make their escape when a gentle woman kindly invited them into her coach.[41] On May 9th, 1757, Wesley entered Huddersfield, remarking, "A wilder people I never saw . . . appeared ready to devour us." However, they were tolerably quiet while he preached, with only a few pieces of dirt being thrown and an interruption by the some of the town's bell ringers.[42]

Strange Happenings

Unusual occurrences happened from time to time during Methodist preaching. Such was the case on April 21st, 1739, when Wesley spoke at the Weavers Hall in Bristol. There "a young man was suddenly seized with a violent trembling all over, and, in a few minutes, the sorrows of his heart being enlarged, sunk down to the ground." Thankfully, Wesley recorded, he found peace. On the 25th day of the same month, while Wesley was preaching, "Immediately one, and another, and another sunk to the earth; they dropped on every side as if thunderstruck." Two months later, on Friday, 13th June, Wesley noted in his journal,

> I went to a society in Wapping, weary in body and faint in spirit. . . . While I was earnestly inviting sinners to enter the holiest by this new and living way, many of those who heard

---

39. Wesley, *Journal*, 14 September, 1766.
40. Wesley, *Journal*, 13 April, 1776.
41. Wesley, *Journal*, 24 April, 1765.
42. Wesley, *Journal*, 9 May, 1757.

began to call upon God with strong cries and tears. Some sunk down, and there remained no strength in them; others trembled and quaked; some were torn with a kind of convulsive motion in every part of their bodies, and so violently, that often four or five persons could not hold one of them. I have seen many hysterical and many epileptic fits; but none of them were like these, in many respects. I immediately prayed that God would not suffer those who were weak to be offended.[43]

The same thing happened when Wesley preached at Epworth. "While I was speaking," he recorded, "Several dropped down as dead and among the rest such a cry was heard of sinners groaning for the righteousness of faith as almost drowned my voice."[44] Initially, during the early days of his open-air preaching, Whitefield seemed not to experience any such manifestations. Indeed, he had doubts over the matter. But on Sunday, July 8th, 1739, he encountered a disturbance as he drew to the close of his sermon, at which, by chance, Wesley happened to be present. Wesley noted in his journal that "no sooner had he begun than four persons sunk down close to him, almost at the same moment. One of them lay without either sense or motion. A second trembled exceedingly. The third had strong convulsions all over his body, but made non noise, unless groans. The fourth, equally convulsed, called upon God, with strong cries and tears."[45] Wesley reflected, "From this time, I trust, we shall all suffer God to carry on His own work in the way that pleaseth Him."[46] After this time many who attended Whitefield's preaching were heard to cry out and seen to fall on their knees in repentance.[47] Many who heard his sermons in Scotland were seen "to be crying out" and "a very great but decent weeping and mourning was observable."[48]

Inevitably modern psychology looks for explanations of hysteria or altered states of consciousness for these extravagances in behavior. Wesley initially viewed them as the work of Satan but later came to recognize the aftereffects of them were for the most part entirely good, leaving those who experienced them with peace of mind and a sense of well-being. It

---

43. Wesley, *Journal*, 15 June, 1739.
44. Wesley, *Journal*, 12 July, 1742.
45. Wesley, *Journal*, 15 June, 1739.
46. Wesley, *Journal*, 7 July, 1739.
47. Macfarlan, *Revivals of the Eighteenth Century*, 73–74.
48. Rankin, *MS Journal*, in Tyerman, *Life of the Rev George Whitefield*, 2:393.

was noticeable that as the years passed the number and intensity of such occurrences diminished.[49]

Both Whitefield and the Wesleys were remarkable preachers through whom the eighteenth-century revival came to England. Whitefield, who spent nearly half of his ministry in the American colonies, is estimated to have preached 18,000 formal sermons and given thousands more in house, homes, prisons, ships, and places of learning. Wesley, who lived twenty years longer than Whitefield, is reported to have preached 40,000 times and traveled over a quarter of a million miles.[50]

Fervent Participatory Worship

The revival proclaimed by the early Methodists was an assurance of sins forgiven through the death of Christ and a new birth in him through the Holy Spirit. It resulted in an outpouring of love into the hearts of those who believed. Such a transforming experience could, as Whitefield and the Wesleys knew well, only be sustained by fervent and joyous spiritual worship. Above all this meant singing both individually and publicly with others. In this Charles Wesley had a major and profound impact. He was possibly one of the greatest English poets of all time. The words literally seemed to flow from his pen. In addition to his many preachments, he was the author of several thousand hymns,[51] many of which have stood the test of time. John Tyson, in his biography of Charles Wesley, spoke of his hymns as "weapons forged for Wesleyan evangelism."[52] His hymns both express orthodox creedal theology and the doctrines and experience of the evangelical revival. This is seen for example in "Love divine, all loves excelling":

> Love divine, all loves excelling,
> Joy of heaven to earth come down.
> Fix in us thy humble dwelling,
> All Thy faithful mercies crown:
> Jesus Thou art all compassion,
> Pure unbounded love Thou art;
> Visit us with Thy salvation
> Enter every trembling heart.

49. Davies, *Methodism*, 71.
50. Moorman, *History of the Church in England*, 298 and 301.
51. Tyson, *Assist Me to Proclaim*, ix.
52. Tyson, *Assist Me to Proclaim*, ix.

John Wesley described the Methodist hymnbook as "a little body of practical divinity,"[53] meaning that people were learning the teachings of Jesus by singing them. Many of Charles's hymns had repetitive choruses which made them more memorable.

Another aspect of fervent early Methodist worship was their love feasts, which Wesley had first encountered among the Moravian Christians. Essentially, they were the agape meals which the Christians of the early church shared between the bread and wine of Communion. The central part consisted in the sharing of a simple meal of small portions of bread or cake and drinking from a "loving cup."[54] There was often vibrant singing and extempore prayers which, together with testimony and words of exhortation, created strong bonds of fellowship and unity. Entry to love feasts was usually by ticket.

There can be no doubting that the vibrant nature of early Methodist worship sustained the revival at a high level. Wesleyan Methodism continued to grow rapidly to the end of the century and beyond.

Reaching Parts of the Church of England

Several Church of England parochial clergy were impacted by the Methodists and carried the revival into their parishes. Some even became associate leaders and helpers. Among their number was William Grimshaw, the vicar of Haworth in Yorkshire. His church only had 525 seats, but often a thousand and more crowded into the building on a Sunday.[55] He became a recognized Methodist leader who itinerated across the Yorkshire moors. About 6,000 hearers assembled in the churchyard to listen to Whitefield in 1749, and over a thousand took communion. In 1753, Whitefield once again proved a crowd-puller, with Grimshaw writing, "we have lately had Mr Whitefield in these parts. . . . In my church he assisted me in administering the Lord's Supper to as many communicants who sipped away 35 bottles of wine to within a gill."[56] Vincent Perronet, vicar of Shoreham in Kent, became a respected adviser and defender of Methodism. John Berridge became vicar of Everton in Bedfordshire in

---

53. Wesley, *Collection of Hymns*, Preface (para. 6).
54. See Baker, *Methodism and the Love Feast*, 15.
55. Baker, *William Grimshaw*, 239.
56. Whitefield, "Letter to Lady Huntingdon," 17 June 1758, in Whitefield, *Works*, 3:236.

1752 and experienced a revival which spread over the neighboring countryside, with scenes that were the equal of Whitefield's earlier preaching to the miners of Kingswood. Perhaps most prominent was John Fletcher, whose meeting with Wesley persuaded him to become a Methodist. He was ordained and later became vicar of Madeley in Shropshire. For a while he became the overseer and "President of Trevecca College" where the Countess of Huntingdon's Calvinistic Methodists trained for the ministry.[57] Charles Wesley, who was a little more closely attached to the Established Church, seems to have made a particular attempt to extend Methodism among the clergy.

Lay Helpers

Both the Wesleys and Whitefield employed laypeople at all levels in their societies. Wesley trained some as full-time preachers. These he called "helpers." Such men and women were chosen on account of their personal knowledge and experience of salvation. They were given a probationary period of one year, with prescribed reading, after which, if successful, they were appointed to a particular location. In 1753, Wesley published *Twelve Rules of a Helper*, which set a demanding standard for those commissioned. Its rules included "never be unemployed for a moment; never be triflingly employed. Converse sparingly with young women in private. . . . Do not affect the gentleman. . . . A preacher of the Gospel is the servant of all. Be ashamed of nothing but sin."[58] Quite possibly as a result of his mother who preached when his father was absent from Epworth rectory, Wesley took the radical step of choosing a number of female helpers, writing on one occasion, "God owns the ministry of women in the conversion of sinners and who am I that I should withstand God?"[59] Prominent among them was Mary Bosanquet (1739–1815) who was authorized as a traveling preacher in 1787. Some of Wesley's helpers became quite well known, among them the Montgomery shoemaker, Thomas Olivers (1725–99). His hymn "The God of Abraham Praise" revealed a deep understanding of Scripture. John Nelson (1707–74), a Yorkshire stonemason, traveled with Wesley for a time and was then entrusted with Methodist work in Leeds, Manchester, Sheffield, and York,

---

57. Jones et al., *Elect Methodists*, 116.
58. Davies, *Methodism*, 81.
59. Wearmouth, *Methodism and the Common People*, 227.

which were then relatively small places. Wesley had many helpers, both men and women, who sustained the revival by their intentional proclamation of the New Birth and the witness of the Holy Spirit in the life of the believer. Their preaching, in the words of Dr. Johnson of dictionary fame, was "in a plain and familiar manner, which is the only way to do good to the common people."[60]

Major Social Concern

As was noted in the first chapter, one of the most significant and biblical characteristics of a genuine revival is a positive impact on the society and culture in which it occurs. In this regard the eighteenth-century Methodist Revival is particularly noteworthy. From the very outset in the days of the Holy Club, members had made the poor their particular concern. Whitefield, who had grown up in difficult circumstances, always had a heart and concern for the poor, which led to his founding and building an orphanage. In later years he concentrated on preaching alone while John Wesley in particular made social action a primary concern. He frequently styled himself as "God's steward of the poor." In 1757, he wrote, "I love the poor, in many of them I find pure, genuine grace."[61]

Wesley had a deep compassion for the needy. Just one year before his death we find him wading knee-deep through the snow on Bristol streets collecting money for those who were too poor to afford medicine or medical help. He himself set up a medical dispensary in connection with his Foundery headquarters and wrote a book entitled *Primitive Physic* which offered all kinds of remedies and practical help and advice to counteract various ailments and sicknesses. By 1750, a number of Wesleyan societies were also offering medical care and making use of Wesley's remedies. Other Methodist societies lent small sums of money to their members or helped those who were unemployed find work. Methodist benefit societies later became a marked feature of the wider evangelical world.

In addition to all of this, Wesley was a constant writer and publisher. He used his pen to raise the issues of the conditions in the new towns; unemployment; the land question; taxation; the national debt; East India Company stock; the distribution of wealth, luxury, dress, and money; intemperance; smuggling; highway robbery; and the status of women.

60. Semmel, *Methodist Revolution*, 20.
61. Telford, *Letters of John Wesley*, 3:229.

In 1773, he wrote *Thoughts on the Present Scarcity of Provisions* in which he asked the leading question, "Why is food so dead? Methodists were among the first to begin the systematic visitation of prisoners and above all slavery."[62] He published his *Thoughts on Slavery* in 1774, and in a letter written to William Wilberforce in 1791 he described the trade as "the execrable sum of all villainies."[63] In 1807, Wilberforce eventually brought the trade to an end following a lengthy fight in Parliament. Wesley and his fellow Methodist made a great contribution to education. He founded a school for miners at Kingswood in 1748 (not to be confused with Whitefield's Kingswood school), and he was a strong advocate of Sunday schools and a great supporter of Robert Raikes's campaigns to establish them.

Learning from the Methodist Revival

There were lessons to be learned from some aspects of the revival. Prominent among them were the disagreements over the issue of election, predestination, free grace, and salvation for all. There is no doubt that the public nature of these controversies was not a happy spectacle and hindered the progress of the revival. It would have been altogether better if Whitefield and the Wesleys had resisted the temptation to engage in a pamphlet war. The Wesleys, for their part, were adamant that an unchangeable and irresistible decree that a certain number were inevitably damned made the gospel preaching without purpose. They were also concerned that those who believed their salvation was decidedly certain regardless of their behavior might be tempted into immoral behavior. Such did in fact happen on a few occasions. Whitefield accused the Wesleys of teaching a doctrine of holiness which amounted to a belief in "sinless perfection." It should be said, however, that this was a term which John and Charles both rejected. John was, however, to agree to speak in terms of a perfection in love.

Neither John Wesley nor Whitefield enjoyed warm and happy relationships with their wives. There were several women who through no fault of their own caused Wesley spiritual and emotional turmoil, among them Sophy Hopkey in Georgia, and then Grace Murray, whom he would have married had not his brother Charles intervened. His

---

62. For details see Rack, *Reasonable Enthusiast*, 262. Concern for prisoners became a particular concern of Methodist lay preachers.

63. Wesley, *Letters*, 8:6–7, in Skevington Wood, *Inextinguishable Blaze*, 241.

eventual marriage to Mary Vazeille, a wealthy widow, took place in February 1751.[64] It was something of a disaster. There were hopes that she might accompany Wesley on his travels, but it soon emerged that she was not suited to an itinerant lifestyle. She resented her husband's long absences and told her friends he no longer loved her. Eventually they separated although they were never divorced. Whitefield had a not dissimilar experience. He had wanted to marry Elizabeth Delamotte for whom he had strong feelings, but his proposal of marriage revealed his total inability to express his love for her. He could only offer the hope of managing his orphanage. Eventually he married Elizabeth James, a widow from Abergavenny, in November 1741. She was a dedicated Christian woman, but the marriage seems not to have been warm and intimate with Whitefield sometimes being separated from her for many months at a time.[65] Wesley's two brothers, Samuel and Charles, were both happily married but both he and Whitefield did not follow their examples.

Positives

The Methodist revival was demonstrably born of *inspired preaching*, most notably on the part of Whitefield and the Wesleys but by no means confined to them. They both inspired and taught hundreds of laymen and laywomen the vital importance of straightforward teaching. Methodist preaching was applied theology. It was, in John Wesley's words, "the plain truth for the plain man."[66] Both Whitefield and John Wesley were dramatists who spoke without notes and both had powerful voices which could be heard by 20,000 people and more.[67] Methodist preaching caused many preachers who weren't part of the revival to abandon the practice of reading their sermons.

The message which both Whitefield and the Wesleys proclaimed was God's love for all demonstrated by his coming in the person of Jesus. Whitefield's appeals to the crowds, it should be said, appeared not a jot different from those of the Wesleys, although in practice he believed only the elect could respond. The heart of their Methodist message was the biblical doctrine of justification, or being made right with God though faith in

---

64. See Hattersley, *John Wesley*, 241–45.
65. See Scotland, *George Whitefield*, 138–40, and 314–16.
66. Wesley, *Sermons on Several Occasions*, preface, para. 3.
67. Rack, *Reasonable Enthusiast*, 346.

the atoning death of Jesus. It was not obtained by human effort but simply received as a gift from God. The essential ingredient of this doctrine of justification was that it could be experienced as the Holy Spirit filled new believers with divine love. This message of free pardon for all from a God who loved all had a particular appeal to the poor and marginalized.

Last Word

The Methodist revival may well have saved England from a "bloody revolution" such as that which occurred in the American colonies and France, as the French historian Elie Halévy (1870–1937) asserted.[68] Regardless of how we regard Halévy's thesis, the fact is the revival humanized the culture of the British Isles. It changed the face of the nation. Right from their days in the Oxford Holy Club, the Methodist leaders were social carers. They fully recognized that the proclamation of Jesus' words needed to be validated by Jesus' works of practical care and service. It is estimated that in 1791, the year of Wesley's death, there were as many as 300,000 members in Wesley's Methodist societies.[69] To this should be added the well-known fact that there were more than that number who joined in Methodist worship but shrank from becoming full members. Added to this, there were large numbers of Elect Methodists in England and more especially in Wales. Other churches, most notably the Church of England and the Baptist churches, also experienced very significant growth due to the impact of the Methodists. The Methodist revival was one of the most significant in history. It was, as both Wesley and Whitefield strongly articulated, truly a sovereign work of God. It magnified and lifted up the name of Jesus and it was marked by a renewal of the church in worship and song. The Methodists effectively discipled those who came to faith so that the revival had an enduring impact both on the lives of the new Christian believers and on the morality and culture of the nation.

---

68. Halévy, *History of the English People*, 1:372.
69. Rack, *Reasonable Enthusiast*, 438.

5

The Revival in the Southern Colonies of America

In 1796, James McGready (1763–1817), a Presbyterian minister, moved from North Carolina to Southern Kentucky where he had been placed in charge of three congregations. Here, just four years later, he became the human instrument which signaled the beginning of the greatest and most influential revival in the history of America. Known as "the Second Great Awakening" it was initially confined to Logan County. But then, in the summer of 1800, McGready began to take the revival to a number of places in Tennessee and Kentucky. By 1803, the revival spread into the Carolinas and western Pennsylvania. Reed and Matheson wrote in 1835, "The Second Great Awakening has to be one of the most remarkable and extensive revivals ever known."[1] Ian Murray declared that "the Second Great Awakening has to be one of the most significant turning points in church history."[2] And Mark Noll gave it as his view that "The Second Great Awakening was the most influential revival of Christianity in the history of the United States."[3]

---

1. Reed and Matheson, *Narrative of the Visit to American Churches*, 2:2.
2. Murray, *Revival and Revivalism*, 117.
3. Noll, *History of Christianity*, 166.

The Social Context

The context in which the awakening was set was one in which a great many of the inhabitants of the newly formed country of America were in low spirits. The War of Independence, 1775–83, had left the nation with both optimism and disappointment. The Anglican Church, whose clergy had sided with the defeated British, was particularly discouraged as were the majority of Methodists who had stood firm with the "Old Country." Many Americans were still being impacted by the spirit of the French Revolution. Thomas Paine's *Age of Reason* was still fueling people's doubts about the miraculous aspects of the Christian faith. Many of the elite and intellectuals were being drawn into deism, which asserted that God did not interfere with events on Earth.

The newly formed Southern states of Kentucky (1792) and Tennessee (1797) shared all these concerns but had the added difficulties of being on the nation's western frontier with Indian territory. Life and society were often understandably rough and harsh, particularly in the mountainous Appalachian regions. There was always a risk to living in isolated territory and from a sudden conflict with hostile indigenous peoples. In 1790, a Kentucky judge had reported that in the previous seven years "fifteen hundred souls had been killed or taken prisoner" by the Indians.[4] Denominational leaders also expressed the fear that many of the recent settlers were falling into heathenism and godless ways.

Notwithstanding this discouraging and raw environment there had been faithful and consistent preaching in Kentucky, Tennessee, and neighboring Virginia. From 1798–1800, observers began to sense an upturn in spiritual life and a growing concern among Christians, including those in Kentucky, to pray.[5] Peter Cartwright, who later became a Methodist minister, was brought up in Logan County in Kentucky. While still a youth he remembered "a revival of religion broke out" in 1799, and "scores joined our society." A church was built and became part of the Cumberland circuit.[6] By 1800, there was a general feeling of expectancy that the time was right for a revival to come. And so it was that James McGready was able to seize the moment.

McGready was an orthodox Calvinist who believed in the importance of both piety and education. He was ordained in 1790 and served

---

4. Murray, *Revival and Revivalism*, 145.
5. Murray, *Revival and Revivalism*, 129.
6. Cartwright, *Backwoods Preacher*, 4–5.

congregations in North Carolina before moving south to Kentucky. In consequence of his revival experiences McGready became convinced that the gospel was there for everyone and not simply for the elect, as Presbyterians and other followers of Calvin's views maintained. He was appointed in 1796 to serve three congregations at Red River, Muddy River, and Gasper River.

Initially, McGready found in these communities a "universal deadness and stupidity."[7] However, by the following year there were calls for prayer and he began to speak to his people about the need for revival and urged them to set aside a day each month for prayer and fasting.[8] At the same time some in the Gasper River community had begun to ask, "Is Christianity a felt thing? If I were converted would I feel and know it?" In 1798, McGready began to sense some moving of God's Spirit in all three congregations such that by the summer "there was a general awakening which deepened throughout the next twelve months." Finally, in June 1799, a four-day sacramental meeting was held at the Red River during which "many of the most bold and daring sinners of the country were brought to cover their faces and weep bitterly."[9] McGready was assisted by two Presbyterian ministers (William Hodges and John Rankin) and two McGee brothers (William, a Presbyterian minister, and John, a Methodist minister). During preaching by McGready, Hodges, and Rankin, many of those present were reduced to tears. Then, on the final day John McGee could no longer keep silent and, standing up, exhorted the people "to let the Lord God Omnipotent rule in their hearts." He recalled "the power of God was upon me . . . and losing sight of fear of man, I went through the house shouting and exhorting with all possible ecstasy and energy."[10] "Soon the floor was 'covered by the slain'" and "their screams for mercy pierced the heavens." McGready reported that the most notorious "profane swearers and Sabbath breakers were pricked to the heart and cried out 'What shall we do to be saved?'"[11]

More was to follow when a month later camp meetings were held at Gasper River. These were occasions usually held in the warmer months when large, and sometimes huge, numbers came to an appointed place

---

7. Murray, *Revival and Revivalism*, 150.
8. Conkin, *Cane Ridge America's Pentecost*.
9. Details taken from Murray, *Revival and Revivalism*, 150.
10. Hudson, *Religion in America*, 138.
11. Johnson, *Frontier Camp Meeting*, 34–35.

with full camping equipment. They lasted anywhere from two or three days up to a week, with people sharing friendship, stories, and their Christian faith. Preaching, prayer times, and socializing continued throughout the day. Many of those attending were overcome with deep emotion and fell to the ground. McGready wrote, as follows in his *Narrative of the Revival in Logan Count*:

> On Saturday evening after the congregation had been dismissed... the greater part of the ministers and several hundreds of the people remained at the meeting house all night. Through every part of the multitude there could be found some awakened souls, struggling in the pangs of the new birth, ready to faint or die for Christ, almost on the brink of desperation. Others again ... beginning to tell the sweet wonders which they saw in Christ. Minsters and experienced Christians were everywhere engaged praying, exhorting, conversing and trying to lead enquiring souls to the Lord Jesus. In this exercise the night was spent till near the break of day.[12]

Towards the close of the sermon on the Sunday McGready reported that "the cries of the distressed" rose almost above the voice of the preacher, and "no person seemed to wish to go home—hunger and sleep seemed to affect nobody—eternal things were the first concern." He continued.

> Here awakening and converting work was to be found in every part of the multitude.... Sober professors, who had been communicants for many years, now lying prostrate on the ground crying out: "I have been a professor; I have been a communicant; O! I have been deceived, I have no religion.... I feel the pains of hell in my body! O! I would have despised any person a few days ago who would have acted as I am doing now!—But O! I cannot help it!"... Little children, young men and women, and old grey headed people, persons of every description, white and black, were to be found in the most extreme distress.[13]

But greater things even than Gasper River were on the horizon. During Friday, 6th of August, 1801, huge numbers began arriving at Cane Ridge for the summer sacramental meeting. But long before that day it had been made clear that this was going to be no ordinary meeting. One traveler wrote to a friend in Baltimore that he was on his way "to the greatest meeting of its kind ever known." He observed that "religion has got to such a

---

12. McGready, "Narrative of the Revival," 192, 193, 194.
13. McGready, "Narrative of the Revival," 192, 193, 194.

height here, that the people attend from a great distance; on this occasion I doubt not but that there will be 10,000 people and 500 wagons."[14]

Cane Ridge was planned as a sacramental gathering for Presbyterians, with tables set up for people to sit down to eat and drink the bread and wine. But such was the anticipation that many Methodists and others came simply to share in the camaraderie, listen to the preaching, and take part in the gatherings for prayer, exhortation, and teaching. A young Peter Cartwright, who later became a Methodist pastor and was active in the revival, recorded in his autobiography:

**Camp Meetings, ca. 1829. Hugh Bridport, Lithographer.
Source unknown. Public domain.**

> Ministers from almost all the denominations flocked in from far and near. The meeting was kept up by night and day. Thousands heard of the mighty work, and came on foot, horseback, in carriages, and wagons. It was supposed that there were in attendance at times during the meeting from twelve to twenty-five thousand people. Hundreds fell prostrate under the mighty power of God as slain in battle. Stands were erected in the woods from which preachers of different churches proclaimed repentance toward

---

14. Patterson, "Letter to a Friend in Baltimore," 7 August, 1801 in *Methodist Magazine* 25 (1802) 23, in Conkin, *Cane Ridge America's Pentecost*, 83.

God and faith in our Lord Jesus Christ, and it was supposed, by eye and ear witnesses, that between one and two thousand souls were happily and powerfully converted to God during the meeting. It was not unusual for one, two, three, and four to seven preachers to be addressing the listening thousands at the same time from the different stands erected for the purpose."[15]

Inevitably, those who went to Cane Ridge had differing opinions regarding what they saw and participated in. The Rev. John Lyle kept a full account of his experiences in his diary. He exhorted those who were seeking Christ and preached on at least one occasion. Yet he was not totally taken with all that happened. On the Saturday, the 7th of August, 1801, he found McNemar's sermon on "I am not ashamed of the Gospel of Christ" to be "a discourse unintelligible to myself and others with whom I conversed about it."[16] Some of the Methodist ministers he came across he described as "hot-headed men" whose doctrine "will separate the church of Christ and quench the revival."[17] However, on the morning of Sunday, the 8th of August, he went into the meeting house where he found Houston exhorting. After this gentleman had done, Lyle spoke on "The influence of the Love to God and man on the Christian character as exemplified by our Saviour in his life." It is clear from his diary entries that he enjoyed wandering round the camp area, stopping to listen to various preachers such as Mr. Marshal and Mr. Burke. He then went to the Communion and sat at the first table which was served by Mr. Blythe.[18] Lyle noted that "there were eleven hundred communicants according to the calculation of one of the elders."[19] After the sacrament was ended, Lyle noted that "Mr Blythe took me aside, we were talking about disorder and the danger of enthusiasm." Later in the evening Lyle returned to one of the evening meetings where "many were falling and rejoicing &c, & c." He then "turned into praying and exhorting among them, as did other ministers and continued I suppose near to one o'clock."[20] The following day, after breakfast, he heard Mr. Tull preaching in the meeting house and then exhorted and prayed. Later he went again to the meeting house and began with the help of others "to carry out the people and continued to carry out and pray and

---

15. Cartwright, *Backwoods Preacher*, 8.
16. Lyle, *Diary*, 8 August, 1801, in Cleveland, *Great Revival in the West*, 183.
17. Lyle, *Diary*, 8 August, 1801, in Cleveland, *Great Revival in the West*, 184.
18. Lyle, *Diary*, 8 August, 1801, in Cleveland, *Great Revival in the West*, 184.
19. Lyle, *Diary*, 8 August, 1801, in Cleveland, *Great Revival in the West*, 185.
20. Lyle, *Diary*, 8 August, 1801, in Cleveland, *Great Revival in the West*, 185.

exhort till the middle of the day or about one o'clock." These were people who had been convicted and then fell to the ground during the meetings. Most, Lyle observed, later rose up and "testified to the truths of the gospel that they had powerfully been convicted of." He detailed one man who "had been ridiculing the work of Christ" but then fell and "lay speechless for an hour or two." He eventually got up and declared "he wanted to pray and seek Christ."[21] Lyle also went to the meeting house where "he found a number of boys and girls singing and shaking hands." They were, he noted, "very loving and joyful, almost dizzy with joy."[22] After leaving Cane Ridge on Wednesday the 11th, Lyle stated that "a thousand had fallen before I came away."[23]

A certain Colonel Patterson who went to Cane Ridge recorded his impression in a letter he penned to a friend in Baltimore. His piece captures the atmosphere of the occasion very well.

> A large congregation assembled in the woods, ministers preaching day and night; the camp illuminated with candles, on trees, at waggons, and at the tent; persons falling down, and carried out of the crowd, by those next to them, and taken to some convenient place, where prayer is made for them; some Psalm or Hymn suitable for the occasion, sung. If they speak, what they say is attended to, being very solemn and affecting. But if they do not recover soon, praying and singing are kept up, alternately and sometimes a minister exhorts over them—generally a large group of people collect, and stand around, paying attention to prayer and joining in singing. Now suppose 20 of these groups around; a minister engaged in preaching to a large congregation, in the middle, some mourning, some rejoicing, and great solemnity on ever countenance, and you will form some imperfect idea of the extraordinary work.[24]

Barton Stone (1772–1844) was an ordained Presbyterian minister who was later one of the founding leaders of a new denomination known as the Disciples of Christ. On the 2nd of July, 1801, he married Elizabeth Campbell, and together they made their way to Cane Ridge. In his autobiography he wrote, "The roads were literally crowded with wagons,

---

21. Lyle, *Diary*, 9 August, 1801, in Cleveland, *Great Revival in the West*, 186.
22. Lyle, *Diary*, 9 August, 1801, in Cleveland, *Great Revival in the West*, 188–89.
23. Lyle, *Diary*, 9 August, 1801, in Cleveland, *Great Revival in the West*, 188.
24. Patterson, "Letter to a Friend in Baltimore," in Conkin, *Cane Ridge America's Pentecost*, 93.

carriages, horsemen and footmen, moving to the solemn camp." The sight of it was "affecting" and "it was judged by military men on the ground, that there were between twenty and thirty thousand collected."[25] He was impressed by the fact that four or five preachers were often to be seen all preaching at the same time in different parts of the camp ground and yet there was no confusion between them. Besides the Presbyterians there were a number of Methodist and Baptist minsters aiding in the work.[26] He gave this moving account of what he saw:

> Many things transpired there, which were so much like miracles, that if they were not, they had the same effects as miracles on infidels and unbelievers; for many of them by these were convinced that Jesus was the Christ and bowed in submission to him. This meeting continued six or seven days and nights, and would have continued longer, but provisions for such a multitude failed in the neighbourhood.[27]

The Revival Spreads

Cane Ridge not only drew Presbyterians from Tennessee and Kentucky who came to share in their annual sacramental meeting, but men, women, and children also traveled great distances. A great many who came were Methodists, Baptists, and members of other denominations. Barton Stone wrote in his autobiography of their coming from Ohio and other distant parts. Significantly he went on to relate that "those who returned home diffused the same spirit in their neighbourhoods, and the same works followed."[28] Peter Cartwright wrote in his autobiography that "from 1801 for years a blessed revival of religion spread through the entire inhabited parts of West Kentucky, Tennessee, the Carolinas, and many other parts, especially through the Cumberland country."[29]

In the immediate areas of Kentucky there was rapid growth in the Baptist churches following Cane Ridge. The Baptist Association of Kentucky increased its membership from 4,766 in 1800 to 13,569 in 1802.[30]

25. Stone, *Biography*, 37–38.
26. Stone, *Biography*, 38.
27. Stone, *Biography*, 38.
28. Stone, *Biography*, 38.
29. Cartwright, *Backwoods Preacher*, 15.
30. Murray, *Revival and Revivalism*, 155.

By 1812, there were close to 200,000 Baptists in the United States, half of them in Virginia.[31] The Methodist minister Peter Cartwright reported that the Western Conference of Tennessee, Kentucky, and Ohio Methodist Churches grew by 3,000 between 1801 and 1802.[32] Peter Cartwright was appointed to the Scioto Methodist Circuit in Ohio in 1805 and carried the revival with him.[33] Other itinerant preachers took the revival to distant parts. One of the greatest among their number was the Methodist Superintendent Francis Asbury (1745–1816). Born in Birmingham, he came to America at Wesley's behest. Convinced of Wesley's maxim "Go to those who need you most" he developed a strict routine which was "to read about one hundred pages a day; to preach in the open air every other day; and to lecture in a prayer meeting every day." Before he died, he had traveled an estimated 300,000 miles on horseback and crossed the Appalachian Mountains more than sixty times.[34] When he first arrived in America in 1771, there were four Methodist ministers caring for about 300 people. When he died in 1816, there were 2,000 ministers and 200,000 Methodists.[35]

This Second Great Awakening embraced large sections of the frontier states and their marginalized communities, together with the inhabitants of the growing towns and cities. Significantly it began to impact all parts of America. Leading ministers began, like Francis Asbury, to write letters to people in all parts of the country. Asbury recorded in his journal that he had sent reports to Methodists in Albany, New York; Lebanon, Vermont; and districts in New Hampshire.[36]

The revival also impacted education and academic institutions. Among them was Yale College, where Timothy Dwight (1752–1817) had become president in 1795. Being the grandson of Jonathan Edwards of Northampton, revival was in his blood. On his arrival he found the students almost totally devoid of any sense of the Christian faith. There were fewer than twenty in the entire college who would publicly admit to being a Christian. Dwight therefore commenced a series of sermons in the chapel on basic Christianity, engaged in good pastoral care, and

---

31. Noll, *History of Christianity*, 178.
32. Murray, *Revival and Revivalism*, 156.
33. See Cartwright, *Backwoods Preacher*, chap. 8.
34. Noll, *History of Christianity*, 173.
35. Noll, *History of Christianity*, 173.
36. Asbury, *Journals and Letters*, 3:210.

was diligent in his lecture preparation. For six years there was little to show from his endeavors, but then significantly, in 1802, prompted by the spread of the revival, 230 students, one-third of the student body, were converted. More than thirty of their number became preachers after their graduation. Prayer and praise seemed to be the delight of most students. Bennet Tyler, one of the students converted in 1802, recorded, "A great change had taken place." There was "an awful solemnity." It was commonly remarked that "Yale College had become a little temple" and many "were deeply anxious about their souls."[37]

Dwight's use of logic and philosophy in his lectures and chapel talks helped to endear the academic world to the validity of Christian doctrine and experience. As Murray observed, Yale served as an exemplar to a whole cluster of higher education colleges. In the longer term the revival prompted and inspired the founding of seminaries to prepare men to preach. Among the earliest of such institutions were Andover in Massachusetts in 1808, and Princeton Theological Seminary in 1812.

Some historians suggest that the impact of the Second Great Awakening was beginning to plateau by 1810. Others have pointed out that its impact continued to 1820, or perhaps even a little longer. Murray reminds us of five prominent leaders in the faraway northeast of the country whose lives were impacted by what had taken place in the Southern states. First, there was Edward Griffin, whose first pastorate was at Newark, New Jersey from 1801–9, where revival broke out "almost immediately."[38] Second, his longtime friend, Gardiner Spring, pastored Brick Church in New York City from 1810–73. He wrote in his *Personal Reminiscences*, "I have ever felt a deep interest in revivals of pure undefiled religion. The Church of God from the beginning has been enlarged, beautified and perpetuated by them."[39] Third, Asahel Nettleton was a Congregationalist who ministered at New Haven and traveled extensively "witnessing numerous revivals."[40] His preaching was described as "deeply experimental and powerful beyond measure."[41] Fourth was Lyman Beecher, who served at East Hampton in Long Island from 1799–1810, and then moved to Litchfield, Connecticut, where he became a prominent Christian leader.

37. Sprague, *Lectures on Revivals*, 17–18, in Murray, *Revival and Revivalism*, 140–41.
38. Murray, *Revival and Revivalism*, 201.
39. Spring, cited in Murray, *Revival and Revivalism*, 197.
40. Murray, *Revival and Revivalism*, 196, 198.
41. Murray, *Revival and Revivalism*, 199.

And the fifth, Edward Payson, was ordained in 1807 and he ministered at Portland from 1807–27. Numerous revivals took place wherever he preached. On the 19th of September, 1816, he wrote to a friend, "My meeting-house overflows, and some of the church are obliged to stay at home, on account of the impossibility of obtaining seats."[42]

Features of the Revival

Preaching and Exhorting

In the awakenings at Tennessee, Kentucky, and the adjoining states of Virginia and Ohio, there was still the acknowledgment that the revival was the result of the gracious movement of God's Spirit. There was, however, a greater effort on the part of ministers and preachers to urge people to seize the moment and commit their lives to Christ immediately. Earlier preachers such as Jonathan Edwards and George Whitefield had felt it was simply enough to present the message of God's love and trust people to make their own personal response. Preachers such as McNemar, McGready, Barton Stone, and the new revivalists engaged in "exhortation," imploring and pleading with those who were concerned about their souls to make their commitment now while there was still time. Those under conviction were urged to come to a penitent bench at the front of the camp meeting place or to step inside a circle of people and make their profession of faith public. This change in approach was a move away from the teachings of John Calvin to a conviction that everyone who heard the message could weigh it up and make their own decision.

The central and core activity at all the meetings which were held was preaching followed by exhorting. The preaching was forceful, emotional, and in your face. In consequence there is a tendency on the part of some contemporary Christians to be repelled by the rigorous and fervent proclamations of the likes of McNemar, Cartwright, and McGee. However, it needs to be remembered that the great majority of those who came to hear their spoken endeavors were not cultured sophisticates who could encounter the Lord in doctrinal sermons, silent prayer, and mystical contemplation. They were tough and rugged frontierspeople who lived in harsh and dangerous environments. They needed a raw Christian experience that could unlock their feelings and bring them joy and catharsis.

---

42. Murray, *Revival and Revivalism*, 204.

The preachers who fanned the flames of the revival preached to persuade their hearers to fully commit their lives in surrender to Christ and to experience his transforming presence. Sometimes they sought to achieve this end by vivid warnings about the nature of hell. James McGready's sermon based on the text, "The Fool has said in his heart, there is no God," was doubtless typical of hundreds of revival preachments. Ending, McGready sternly warned "the fool died accursed of God when his soul was separated from his body and the black flaming vultures of hell began to encircle him on every side. Then all the horrid crimes of his past life stared him in the face in all their glowing colours." McGready was still not quite done! "When the friends of hell dragged him into the eternal gulf, he roared and screamed like a devil."[43] His friend William Bennet said of him, "he would so array hell before the wicked that they would tremble and quake, imagining a lake of fire and brimstone yawning to overwhelm them and the hand of the Almighty thrusting them down the horrible abyss."[44] The purpose behind such rigorous speaking was to bring the hearers to make an immediate commitment of their lives to Christ. This was achieved by urging everyone who felt the need to settle the issue to respond to "the invitation to the altar" which was a designated place at the front of the meeting. Sometimes it would be an area with benches for them to sit, and on other occasions they would be invited to kneel. Those who came forward were often referred to as "mourners." They were grieving not over the loss of loved ones, but over their sins.

It became a constant practice of revival preachers to call for "mourners" at the end of every sermon. Sometimes the preacher, having finished speaking, would leave his stand and go down among the people, "exhorting" them to repentance and full surrender and to come to the altar to seek the Lord and the power of the Holy Spirit. Speaking at a camp meeting in 1806, Peter Cartwright recalled that "the altar was crowded to overflowing with mourners" when some "young ladies asked permission to set down inside it." "I told them," he said, "that if they would pray for religion, they might take a seat."[45] When people arrived at the altar other ministers gathered round them praying, singing, and urging that now is the day of salvation. Exhorting was not confined to the ministers, lay

43. McGready, *Posthumous Works*, 1:228–29 in Cleveland, *Great Revival in the West*, 45–46.

44. Davenport, *Primitive Traits in Religious Revivals*, 67 in Cleveland, *Great Revival in the West*, 47.

45. Murray, *Revival and Revivalism*, 186.

preachers, and laypeople frequently joined in. At Cane Ridge it was estimated that as many as 300 men and women were engaged in exhorting at the same time. Exhorting on this occasion was also done by many of those who had earlier fallen to the ground but had since risen up. "It was noted that on rising children, slaves, shy people, illiterates all exhorted with great effect."[46]

Open-Air Meetings

Many of the revival gatherings under the earlier preaching of George Whitefield and the Wesleys took place in fields, commons, streets, and market squares. Several types of open-air meetings became a marked feature of the Second Great Awakening.

The most frequent revival gatherings were the camp meetings which appear to have originated among the Methodists.[47] Peter Cartwright certainly believed so. People were invited to come to a chosen outdoor venue, usually where there was woodland which could provide sufficient shelter from the sun. They came with full camping equipment and provisions sufficient to last from four days up to a week. At some of the more permanent campsites a shed capable of holding about 5,000 people was constructed. During each day a number of ministers would preach and teach and there would be one large meeting in the evening. Much time was also spent in socializing and relaxation. The needs of children were also to be catered for, which made the occasions a family affair. Camp meeting grew rapidly in popularity and became the main vehicle by which the revival spread. The Methodist Bishop Francis Asbury reflected in 1809 that camp meetings "make our harvest time. . . . I hear and see great effects produced by them."[48]

Very similar to camp meetings were the sacramental gatherings which were commonly held by Presbyterians about once every quarter.[49] The central focus of these meetings was the sharing of the Lord's Supper. Long tables were set out in the meeting house or in a large tent. The communion was arranged in a series of sessions with the people seated

---

46. Conkin, *Cane Ridge America's Pentecost*, 94–95.

47. Murray, *Revival and Revivalism*, 151, suggests they emerged from Presbyterian sacramental meetings. See also Cleveland, *Great Revival in the West*, 53.

48. Asbury, *Journals and Letters*, 3:141, in Murray, *Revival and Revivalism*, 183.

49. In some places in Scotland they were held annually.

round several tables. Each was hosted by a minister who served the bread and wine. It often happened that there was a powerful and overwhelming sense of God's presence as people received the bread and wine. It was not uncommon for Baptists and Methodists to join these occasions in the years before the revival. Sacramental meetings provided opportunities of socializing and sharing experiences for those who lived in isolated settlements on the margins of society.

Another feature of the revival in the southwest was the Protracted Meeting. These gatherings were more informal in nature since only the venue and starting day was announced but the ending was left open until people sensed that an appropriate time had been reached. Catherine Cleveland suggested that they first began out of a reluctance on the part of those who were most seriously "impressed" to leave the scene of worship.[50] It often happened that sacramental and camp meetings turned into protracted meetings with preaching, worship, and religious exercises.

Physical and Emotional Phenomena

The fervency and vigor of revival preaching, the intensity of the singing, and the sheer excitement of huge expectant crowds inevitably resulted in unusual emotional responses. The most obvious of these were falling, the jerks, barking, and dancing. These were not all new. Falling, for example, had featured in the earlier revival at Northampton under Jonathan Edwards.

The most common response in the revival meetings in the Southern colonies was falling. For the Methodists this was nothing unusual since many of Wesley's hearers were stuck down to the ground, some lying motionless, others crying out for mercy or weeping. Peter Cartwright recorded in his autobiography, "I have seen more than a hundred sinners fall like dead men under one powerful sermon, and I have seen and heard more than five hundred Christians all shouting the high praises of God at once; and I will venture to assert that many thousands were awakened and converted at these meetings."[51]

The phenomenon known as the jerks was first reported in Eastern Tennessee[52] but became widespread. McNemar, who was there, described

50. Cleveland, *Great Revival in the West*, 51.
51. Cartwright, *Backwoods Preacher*, 15.
52. Cleveland, *Great Revival in the West*, 98.

them as follows, "The exercise commonly began in the head which would fly backward, and from side to side with a quick jolt which the person would naturally labour to suppress but in vain."[53] In fact, it was soon found that the more people tried to stop their twitching the more they increased. Women's headdresses, bonnets, combs, and people's hats and caps of all kinds flew into the air. During the revival at East Cumberland Peter Cartwright recorded that "saints or sinners would be taken under a warm song or sermon and seized with a convulsive jerking all over, which they could not by any possibility avoid, and the more they resisted the more they jerked. If they would not strive against it and pray in good earnest, the jerking would usually abate."[54] Cartwright also stated, "I have seen more than five hundred persons jerking at one time in my large congregations."[55] Barton Stone, in his autobiography, noted that "all classes, saints and sinners," were taken with the jerks. "They could not account for it," he continued, "but some have told me that those were the happiest seasons of their lives."[56] Most of those who were taken with the jerks would begin to dance. After a brief period, many testified to having either been converted or to feeling a deep consciousness of Jesus' presence in their lives.

What was frequently termed the dancing exercise often began with the jerks, although it was observed to be confined to believers. Those who danced "had the smile of heaven" on their faces, and when they ceased they offered prayer and praise to God.[57]

Other less-frequent phenomena were witnessed in the revival. The barking exercise was in reality a grunt which resulted from the rapid movement of the head from side to side during the jerks. It seems to have been first recorded in East Tennessee.[58] The laughing exercise was common but appears to have been "confined solely to the religious." It was described by Barton Stone as "rapturously solemn and excited solemnity in saints and sinners."[59] Stone also recorded "the singing exercise which seemed to come from the breast rather than the lips." Such music, he

---

53. Cartwright, *Backwoods Preacher*, 17.
54. Cartwright, *Backwoods Preacher*, 17.
55. Cartwright, *Backwoods Preacher*, 17.
56. Stone, *Biography*, 40.
57. Stone, *Biography*, 40.
58. Stone, *Biography*, 41.
59. Stone, *Biography*, 41.

continued, "silenced everything, and attracted the attention of all. It was most heavenly."[60]

How do we assess these phenomena? Clearly not everyone was happy. A few Presbyterians expressed their disapproval of camp meetings in their 1805 General Assembly. Cleveland took the view that on the whole, bodily exercises "tended to bring religion into disrepute."[61] She maintained that the rhetoric of the preachers alone was sufficient to stimulate the exercises of the kind witnessed in the revival. She also felt that "hypnotic suggestion" induced many to take part. In response several things can be said. The most prominent preachers were not enthusiasts or fanatics. They had undergone some training and basic education. Some were well known as careful preachers. They consistently found that after people got up from the ground or their jerks ceased, they were happy, in their right mind, and with a strong sense of Jesus' presence in their lives. Furthermore, it was apparent from the steady growth in church membership that the majority must have continued in the faith. Light hypnosis may not necessarily be dysfunctional. The experience of revival preaching and worship undoubtedly brought a cathartic and emotional release. There is a sense in which all religious experience is human experience. People differ in the ways in which they handle and respond to an overwhelming spiritual empowerment. Clearly there were excesses in the revival meetings which the prominent leaders themselves recounted. Barton Stone gave a balanced and positive summary of the phenomena.

> Thus I have given a brief account of the wonderful things that appeared in the great excitement in the beginning of this century. That there were many eccentricities, and much excitement, was acknowledged by its warmest advocates; indeed it would have been a wonder, if such things had not appeared, in the circumstances of that time. Yet the good effects were seen and acknowledged in every neighbourhood.[62]

In the end any assessment of these physical and emotional phenomena must be based on the long-term impact of the revival on the lives, society, and culture of the Southern states and beyond.

---

60. Stone, *Biography*, 42.
61. Cleveland, *Great Revival in the West*, 114.
62. Stone, *Biography*, 42.

Inspiration from the Revival in the Southern States

Church Growth

Glancing at the membership figures for major American denominations it is immediately clear that there was a huge and continuing upturn in the years immediately following the revival. In the years from 1800–1810 the membership of the Presbyterian Church grew from 70,000 to 100,000. The denomination's General Assembly of 1803 remarked, "There is scarcely a Presbytery under the care of the Assembly from which some pleasing intelligence has not been announced."[63] Baptist membership rose more starkly in the same period from 95,000 in 1800 to 160,000 in 1810.[64] Significantly half of this number were in the Southern States of Virginia, North and South Carolina, Georgia, and Kentucky.[65] The membership of the Methodist Episcopal Church totalled 104,000 in 1803[66] and by 1809 had reached 163,038.[67]

Good Leaders

The men at the forefront of the revival were for the most part men of integrity and some formal learning. James McGready was affirmed by the Transylvania Presbytery to be "one of the most honest men" who possessed and practiced "the most exemplary piety."[68] McGready became well known for the careful two-day preparation time that went into his written sermons and for his effective preaching.[69] Barton Stone was clearly a thoughtful preacher, while Peter Cartwright had passed through a Methodist training and had a long ministry following the revival.

---

63. Murray, *Revival and Revivalism*, 123–24.
64. Murray, *Revival and Revivalism*, 124.
65. Noll, *History of Christianity*, 178.
66. Briggs, *Bishop Asbury*, 341.
67. Murray, *Revival and Revivalism*, 125.
68. *Testimony of Ninian Edwards before a Committee Appointed by the Transylvania Presbytery*, 12 February, 1807, in Cleveland, *Great Revival in the West*, 103.
69. Conkin, *Cane Ridge America's Pentecost*, 53.

Social Improvement

The revival soon began to generate a widespread change in American social life. George A. Baxter, president of Washington College, Virginia, visited Kentucky in 1801 and reported:

> I found Kentucky... the most moral place I had ever been. A profane expression was hardly ever heard. A religious awe seemed to pervade the country. Upon the whole, I think the revival in Kentucky the most extraordinary that has ever visited the church of Christ.... This revival has... awed vice into silence, and brought numbers beyond calculation under serious impressions.[70]

The revival created a much-needed emphasis on temperance. The Methodists of the South had long been following Wesley's injunction to avoid spiritous liquor and to practice temperance. In 1826, *The American Education Society for the Promotion of Temperance* was founded. While Lyman Beecher (1775-1863) was at Litchfield, Connecticut (1810-26), he became increasingly concerned about the need for temperance and joined *The General Association of Connecticut for the Purpose of Temperance*. Beecher was also a strong opponent of dueling and preached a sermon on the subject after Aaron Burr, a former Congressman and Vice President to Jefferson, killed Alexander Hamilton in a duel. In 1809, a society against dueling was founded.

Opposition to Slavery

Campaigns against slavery became considerably stronger in the wake of the revival in the Southern States. Peter Cartwright wrote that "slavery is certainly a domestic, political and a moral evil." On a preaching tour in Tennessee, he encountered two families, one of which were Baptists and the other Methodists. The two families between them had "over one hundred and twenty slaves." Despite both being very humane in their treatment Cartwright felt it "my duty to bear my testimony against the moral and wrong of slavery."[71] Francis Asbury wrote in his journal on the 3rd of February, 1801, "If the Gospel will tolerate slavery, what will it

---

70. *Methodist Magazine* (London) 27 (103), 93 in Bacon, *History of American Christianity*, 237, in Hudson, *Religion in America*, 139.

71. Cartwright, *Backwoods Preacher*, 79.

not authorise?"⁷² Barton Stone was also decidedly opposed to slavery. He urged Christians to give up their slaves to the Colonization Society which would transport them back to freedom in Africa. He wrote:

> The question is no longer now as thirty years ago—is slavery right or wrong? It is settled in the nation that it is wrong, both politically and morally. The light of truth and intelligence has removed our doubts. No man can justify it, whether he be a politician, moralist or Christian.⁷³

Slavery finally came to an official end in the Northern States when New Jersey ruled for abolition in 1803. Regrettably, the situation was much slower in the South despite the outspoken preaching of Francis Asbury and other revival leaders. The Southern States did suspend their involvement in the Atlantic slave trade, which was finally prohibited by Congress in 1807,⁷⁴ but it was not until the ending of the Civil War that slave-owning came to an end.

Education and Missionary Endeavor

Two other particularly important and positive results which flowed from the revival were a drive to promote educational initiatives and the formation of mission societies. Regarding the former, the focus was on higher education, particularly of clergy and church leaders. The Great Awakening, as the revival is often termed, prompted the beginning of what became known as the Seminary Movement. The first such institution was Andover Theological Seminary in 1808, followed by Princeton in 1812. Yale Divinity School followed in 1822 after the revival had plateaued. Winthrop Hudson listed twelve other institutions of higher education which were founded after 1801 and before 1830.⁷⁵ Significantly he added, "Of five hundred and sixteen colleges and universities that were founded before the civil war, only a few had no religious affiliation."⁷⁶

The revival had brought exceptionally large numbers of people to a personal faith and commitment to Christ, and this led to a growing and widespread concern for local and home mission societies. A number

72. Asbury, *Journals and Letters*, 3 February, 1801, 3:9.
73. Stone, *Biography*, 288.
74. Wolfe, *Expansion of Evangelicalism*, 191.
75. Hudson, *Religion in America*, 155.
76. Hudson, *Religion in America*, 155-56.

of these were founded in the years immediately following the revival. Baptists founded *The Massachusetts Domestic Missionary Society* in 1802 and similar societies in Pennsylvania in 1803, Maine in 1804, and New York in 1806. The Presbyterians founded several mission societies in New York, and their General Assembly of 1802 established a Standing Committee of Missions.[77] It was not until 1819 that the Methodists formed their first missionary society, but as Hudson pointed out "they had little need of this type of organisation since every conference was in effect a missionary society and every itinerant a missionary."[78] *The American Bible Society* was founded in 1816, *The American Sunday School Union* in 1824, and the *American Tract Society* in 1825.[79]

The revival in the Southern Colonies had a huge impact on the recently formed American nation. As B. R. Lacy stressed, "The Great Revival of the early 1800s saved the new nation from French infidelity, crass materialism, rapacious greed, godlessness, and the outbreaking of violence on the frontiers."[80] There were huge numbers who came to faith in Christ and a widespread renewal and sustained growth in church membership. The revival extended to all parts of the country. It brought huge and positive changes to family, societal, and community life. There was a significant growth in education at all levels, and most notably in the foundation of seminaries, colleges, and universities. In the wake of the revival there was an immediate growth in temperance and the formation of many charitable, philanthropic, and missional societies. In short, this was a sovereign move of God which established America as a Christian nation.

---

77. Hudson, *Religion in America*, 147.
78. Hudson, *Religion in America*, 147.
79. Noll, *History of Christianity*, 168.
80. Lacy, *Revivals in the Midst of the Years*, 87.

6

The Primitive Methodist Revival, 1811–51

ON THE 30TH OF May, 1811, two Wesleyan Methodist revival local preachers and their followers held a meeting at which they agreed to join together and form a new group to be known as the Primitive Methodists. Hugh Bourne was a carpenter who hailed from the village of Bemersley on the outskirts of Stoke-on-Trent. William Clowes was a potter who worked at his uncle's Wedgewood Pottery. Both men had a deep longing and desire to see their families, friends, and communities come to Christ. Both men had been strongly attracted to the writings and ministry of the American frontier revival preacher Lorenzo Dow and the success of his camp meeting ministry. By this time Wesleyan Methodism had begun to take a deep root among the prospering middle classes. They no longer shared John Wesley's compassion and care for the poor and marginalized. This, together with the church's growing suspicion about revivals and anything that might be labeled emotional, led to the Wesleyan Annual General Conference expelling both Bourne and Clowes from membership.

Neither Bourne nor Clowes were the sort of men to be unduly worried about being turned out of their church. Not only did it spur them on to pursue their revival methods, they even succeeded in getting Lorenzo Dow to come to their newly established Primitive Methodist Church. It was so named because they wanted to get back to the early primitive Methodism of John Wesley, with the emphasis on the poor, vibrant worship, revival preaching, and exhorting sinners to give their lives to Christ.

Hugh Bourne and William Clowes

Hugh Bourne's (1772–1852) father, Joseph, was a small farmer and timber dealer who lived life in the raw and was often drunk. He was a staunch member of the established Church of England and a derider of Methodism and anything else that might be described as vital or personal religion. Inevitably, young Hugh grew up somewhat shy and diffident. Fortunately, his mother was a God-fearing, gentle woman who spent quality time with him and taught him to read and write while she worked at her spinning wheel. Her gentle kindness and affirmation created a real desire in her son for learning and eventually he even mastered the rudiments of both Greek and Hebrew. During the day Hugh Bourne worked hard as a carpenter, but his love of reading eventually led in 1799 to the event which changed his life. He recalled how one day when he was in his father's house he surrendered his life to Christ. He wrote in his journal, "I sat reading Mr Fletcher's *Letters on the Spiritual Manifestation of the Son of God*, and realised the blessing named in John 14:21 and He manifested Himself to me, and I was born again in an instant! Yea passed from death to life. The naughty was taken out of my heart and good put in . . . the Bible looked new; creation looked new; and I felt a love for all mankind."[1]

Following his conversion Hugh Bourne soon set about sharing his newfound faith in Jesus. He recorded in his journal, "My desire was that friends and enemies and all the world if possible might be saved."[2] In a short time he succeeded in converting his cousin, Daniel Shubotham, a collier whose life was widely known for drunkenness and wrongdoing. The two of them started evangelizing the hamlets and villages on the slopes of Mow Cop, a large heath-covered upland not far from Stoke-on-Trent. As a result

Hugh Bourne. Source: Kendall, *Origin and History*, Vol. 2, London, Dalton, 1906. 2 Portraits.

---

1. Kendall, *Origin and History*, 1:12.
2. Kendall, *Origin and History*, 1:12.

of their endeavors a revival broke out among the miners in the small town of Harriseahead.

It was a revival that was similar to the one which was happening at the same time in the Southern colonies of America and which soon began to attract hostility from the Wesleyan Methodist authorities in London. Harriseahead was "only slenderely attached to the official Methodism of the area"[3] and was much closer in style to the early days of John Wesley's preaching. Bourne and Shubotham and those who joined them were noted for their "conversational preaching." This, as might be expected from those who lacked any theological training, was not in chapel style; it was informal, down-to-earth, straightforward talking about Christ and salvation. As Kendall put it, "On the pit-heaps, in the delf, by the way side, the new converts talked religion. They did it in the way of direct personal appeal."[4]

Hugh Bourne, like all those used of God in revival, was a very remarkable man of prayer. From the outset of the revival he described himself as being "fitted to be a public praying labourer."[5] He established prayer meetings across the area but they were of no ordinary type. "Liveliness was the key!" Bourne wrote. "The people got to be, in a great measure, 'Israelitish' by which he meant 'noisyish.'"[6] He found and quoted the precedent for this in Ezra 3:12–13: "And all the people shouted with a great shout . . . and the noise was heard far off." This was certainly true of the prayer meetings which Bourne held at Jane Hall's cottage. Kendall recounted how the door of a home happened to be open and Elizabeth Baddeley, a miner's wife who was given to profane language, distinctly heard the sound of prayer and praise coming from Harriseahead, a mile and a half away. She came under conviction of sin and found forgiveness and new life in Christ. These cottage prayer meetings were particularly popular "because they were held in rural areas where people were isolated and devoid of other forms of entertainment."[7] They appealed to women who were often excluded from pub-based diversions.

William Clowes's (1780–1851) mother, Ann, was a Wedgewood related to the famous Josiah Wedgewood. At an early age William was apprenticed to his uncle Joseph Wedgewood at the Church Works Pottery. He soon became so efficient at his work that he could easily make

3. Kendall, *Origin and History*, 1:31.
4. Kendall, *Origin and History*, 1:31.
5. Kendall, *Origin and History*, 1:31.
6. Kendall, *Origin and History*, 1:32.
7. Werner, *Primitive Methodist Connexion*, 180.

twenty-one dozen plates in a day. His social life and behavior left much to be desired. He became a "prize dancer" and "gambling and fighting ranked among the sins of my youth."[8] Added to these ills he was frequently drunk and given to profanity. During wake week at Leek in North Staffordshire Clowes recalled how he and others held a mock prayer meeting in the parlor of a public house. The nature of this impiety was too much even for those who were drinking who fled into the street with mugs in hand. Towards the end of 1804, Clowes got into a brawl in the Dog and Duck Tavern and was very nearly caught by officers from the press-gang.

However, shortly after this, Clowes returned to his home area where he soon came under conviction concerning his sins. He wrote in his journal, "Sometimes in sleep at night I have been agitated with terrible dreams, and staring up, I have been afraid of looking out of my bed, supposing the room to be full of devils and damned spirits."[9] Clowes's anguish and distress became known by a friend who took him to Bourne's new chapel at Harriseahead. At the time Clowes had just been reading chapter 11 of the First Letter to the Corinthians with its warning against eating the bread and drinking the wine unworthily. When the bread and water of the Love Feast were passed around Clowes mistook it for the Lord's Supper and feared he was committing the unpardonable sin. The following day, the 20th of January, 1805, he attended one of the many "noisyish cottage prayer meetings" and it was there that he committed his life to Christ. He later wrote, "I believed he had saved me and it was so." H. B. Kendall wrote of his conversion in the following lines:

> Conversion in his case was like some great upheaval of nature which changes the very contours of the landscape. His growth in Christian experience and knowledge was rapid. He discharged his debts, fasted and prayed, drew up rules for holy living, opened his house for prayer meetings, took part in efforts for repressing Sabbath breaking, became an active member of a Tract Mission, and as such walked many miles and did real evangelistic work in the houses of the people. He also became the leader of two classes, and in the course of time his initials appeared on the plan as an exhorter.[10]

From the day of his conversion, Clowes became active in the work of evangelism. Every sabbath became a day of preaching and prayer. He had

8. Clowes, *Journals*, in Kendall, *Origin and History*, 1:54.
9. Clowes, *Journals*, in Kendall, *Origin and History*, 1:54.
10. Kendall, *Origin and History*, 1:54–55.

"extraordinary manifestations of the Holy Spirit," which he called "the spirit of burning."[11]

At the time of Clowes's conversion, the revival around Harriseahead had spread into several neighboring villages, hamlets, and farmsteads but was still loosely attached to Wesleyan Methodism. However, Bourne had begun to take an interest in the reports in the *Methodist Magazine* of the frontier revivals in America and the great blessings that were resulting from their camp meetings. They were well advertised ahead of time and large numbers of people came with camping equipment and food for several days to these specially chosen sites. They were mostly situated in quiet rural areas ,and the general format was a mixture of fervent worship, prayer, and revivalist preaching. A major feature was the exhortation to sinners to come to a penitent form or enclosure pen at the front of the place of worship and give their lives in surrender to Christ. Bourne was particularly impressed by Lorenzo Dow (1774–1834) who was one of the leading exponents of American camp meetings. It happened that he had been in England from 1805 and Bourne was able to invite him to Harriseahead shortly before he left for America. Dow, who had published a small pamphlet on the importance of camp meetings, urged upon his hearers their great value both in stirring the sinner and in reviving those whose faith needed rekindling. During his two-year travels, which included trips to Ireland, he had great success in Macclesfield where, on July 20th, 1806, he spoke in the street to "about five thousand' and "wrestled with mourners at night,"[12] and at Congleton where he found "more than a hundred had been taken into society since my other visit."[13] Dow came to Harriseahead in April 1807 and spoke of the great usefulness of camp meetings, observing "that occasionally something of a Pentecostal power attended them; and that for a considerable time in America, as much good had been done, and as many souls brought to God, at the camp meetings as at all the meetings put together."[14] Dow was a major influence on Bourne. He had broken with the Wesleyan Methodists and failed to comply with the instructions of his American superiors. His powerful advocacy of camp meetings proved to be a central core in Primitive Methodist evangelistic strategy. Bourne wrote "that Dow's

---

11. Ritson, *Romance of Primitive Methodism*, 48.
12. Dow, *Journal of the Dealings*, 827.
13. Dow, *Journal of the Dealings*, 865.
14. Kendall, *Origin and History*, 1:59.

constant advocacy of camp meetings and his several tracts on the subject "filled the country with camp meeting conversations."[15]

After Dow had left the area it was decided to organize such a gathering and the venue chosen was Mow Cop. This celebrated and controversial meeting took place on May 31st, 1807. John Walford recorded that people flocked to the ground from every quarter. So many hundreds unexpectedly covered the ground that a second preaching station was set up. As numbers further increased a third preaching stand was set up. Many preachers joined the meeting from Knutsford, Wheelock, Burslem, Macclesfield, and other places. Walford wrote that later in the day "the congregation increased so rapidly that a fourth preaching place was called for" and that "the atmosphere was most awful and interesting."[16] Hugh Bourne wrote of "thousands hearing with an attention as solemn as death" and the preachers who included William Clowes, James Nixon, Peter Bradburn, and Captain Edward Anderson "fired with an uncommon zeal" and "an extraordinary unction."[17] At about seven o'clock "a work began amongst the children . . . and the power of God seemed to have a great effect on the people present." The meeting "such as our eyes never beheld" and "for which many will praise God in time and eternity" finally closed about half past eight at night.[18]

Kendall, *Origin and History*, Vol. 1 (London, Roberts Bryant, 1906), 64.

15. Bourne, *History of the Primitive Methodist Church*, 414.
16. Ritson, *Romance of Primitive Methodism*, 64, and Walford, *Memoirs*, 12.
17. Ritson, *Romance of Primitive Methodism*, 64.
18. Walford, *Memoirs*, 121–24.

The time at which the Mow Cop camp meeting was held was one in which England was at war with France and there was still talk of revolution in the air. The authorities were understandably concerned about unlawful gatherings and were anxious to uphold *The Conventicle and Five Mile Acts* which prohibited unlicensed preachers. Mow Cop was just the kind of event the Wesleyan Conference was trying to avoid in order to portray themselves as upholders of government policy and the status quo. To make matters worse, some reports of the American camp meetings had made mention of instances of emotionalism with people falling, barking, jerking, and shaking. When Bourne therefore decided to hold a further camp meeting on Mow Hill which began on the 18th of July, 1807, he took the precaution of hiring the ground and securing a license. The occasion lasted till the following Tuesday evening with preaching, exhorting, and forty professing conversion.[19] Clowes "was greatly struck by the solemnity and power" which attended the preaching of James Nixon.[20]

The Wesleyan Annual Conference at Liverpool in 1807 pronounced against camp meetings, stating that "even supposing such meetings to be allowable in America, they are highly improper and likely to be of great mischief."[21] However, Bourne was not one to be easily discouraged and soon organized a further camp meeting at Norton-on-the Moors on the 23rd of August, 1807, an event for which he was expelled from membership for breaking connexional rules.

Bourne now found himself responsible for preaching and caring for thirteen places of worship. Undeterred by what had happened, he continued visiting and evangelizing the area, and his followers became known as the camp meeting Methodists. By 1809, things had progressed to the point where Bourne was able to engage James Crawfoot as an itinerant evangelist. He paid him ten shillings a week and gave him instructions to labor alternately in East Cheshire and West Staffordshire. Crawfoot had been a Wesleyan local preacher on the Northwich Circuit but had lost his position through having taken the pulpit for a group of independent Methodists at Warrington. He established a meeting in his own house on the last Saturday of each month for the promotion of holiness, which both Bourne and Clowes attended. "These occasions," Bourne reported, "increased their knowledge of the deep things of God" and they

---

19. Ritson, *Romance of Primitive Methodism*, 68.
20. Kendall, *Origin and History*, 1:75.
21. Kendall, *Origin and History*, 1:77.

"mastered the ability to remain in a state of "continual rest" in God and of "being clothed with majesty and power."[22]

In June 1810, William Clowes, who had also been successfully evangelizing in the areas around Tunstall, was removed from the Wesleyan Methodist local preachers' plan, and his membership was not renewed for the reason that he too had attended camp meetings contrary to the Methodist discipline. Many of those whom Clowes had brought to faith in Christ remained loyal and insisted on standing by him. They and others who subsequently associated with his activities were also removed from the Wesleyan class lists. Among them was James Steele, the Tunstall Sunday school superintendent. Many of his members and scholars followed him. Clowes's followers became known as "Clowesites." Clowes gave the following account of the way he ran his class meeting in the hopes that it would be a model for his followers.

> The class rapidly increased, until the house became so full, that there was hardly room to kneel. In leading my classes I used to get from six to ten to pray a minute or two each, and thus get the whole up into faith; then I found it a very easy matter to lead thirty or forty members in an hour and a quarter for I found that leading did not consist so much in talking to the members, as in getting into faith, and bringing down the cloud of God's glory, that the people might be truly blessed in their souls as well as instructed in divine things.[23]

During the months following Clowes's expulsion he developed a close and long-lasting friendship with Hugh Bourne, and he and some of his followers attended Bourne's Friday night revival services. Bourne described Clowes as "such an example of living faith as I scarcely ever met with."[24] Eventually on the 30th of May, 1811, the two groups held a joint meeting and agreed to come together and form the Primitive Methodist Church.

The Tunstall Non-Mission Law

In the early days of their new organization, the cofounders, Bourne and Clowes, made a deliberate decision not try and expand too rapidly but rather to confine themselves to their present areas around Tunstall and

---

22. *Primitive Methodist Quarterly Review* 46 (1902) 587.
23. Ritson, *Romance of Primitive Methodism*, 48.
24. Ritson, *Romance of Primitive Methodism*, 48.

Mow Cop. They felt that it was God's call that they should consolidate the revival by building up their core following rather than engaging in wider evangelistic activities which might weaken their home base. This strategy of consolidating rather than immediate evangelism became known as the "Tunstall Non-Mission Law."[25] It was stated as follows, "Let us move cautiously; not weaken ourselves by covering too much ground, but confine ourselves within our present limits, and give our strength to building up our societies."[26] In 1814, Bourne put forward a series of rules which all the members were invited to consider, change, or add to. They resulted in a church that was probably more democratic than any other in England at that time. During this period camp meetings became a growing feature and were held to be a chosen instrument of divine blessing.

The Spread of the Revival

With the passing of time, the nonexpansion policy was gradually ignored and Primitive Methodist local preachers began to extend the revival by moving out along the river Trent.[27] In many ways this was an obvious strategy since roads were poor and rail travel had not yet been developed. By 1817, several of Bourne's fellow laborers had traveled as far as Nottingham and Newark and established bases in both places. A camp meeting was held at Nottingham Forest on Whit Sunday 1816, attended by 12,000 and which "inaugurated a movement which swept across the Midlands."[28] Among other nearby places impacted were Woodhouse Eaves and Loughborough. At the former town "such multitudes attended that the village wells were drunk dry and the food supply ran out."[29] At the latter place there was "a spiritual harvest of three hundred souls." At Hinkley a camp meeting was held in the evening by lantern light and "a spell-bound multitude's cries for mercy were heard on every hand."[30] John Benton reached Round Hill near Leicester and "preached with such effect on 'the great day of Wrath is to come' that many fled from the spot, while others fell

---

25. The term "Tunstall non-mission law" was the name given to the strategy by those who were against it.
26. Kendall, *Origin and History*, 1:189.
27. Kendall, *Origin and History*, 1:29.
28. Ritson, *Romance of Primitive Methodism*, 71.
29. Ritson, *Romance of Primitive Methodism*, 71.
30. Ritson, *Romance of Primitive Methodism*, 71.

upon each other in heaps."³¹ He first entered Leicester on the 1st of March, 1818, accompanied by "a goodly number of persons from Thurmaston, Syston and the adjacent villages." They entered the town singing by way of the Melton Mowbray turnpike. The news of their coming had "spread like wildfire" and people poured into Belgrave Gate. Benton's sermon to "the vast crowd" was on the text, "Let me die the death of the righteous, and let my last end be like his." It was "stentorian, clear as a clarion and carrying far."³² From this time forward it felt as though the Lord had opened a door which none could shut and from that time Leicester was joined to who the Loughborough Primitive Methodist Circuit.

Benton (1775–1856) typified the early Primitive Methodist evangelists and preachers. He was later described by H. B. Kendall as "an unbending individual who would not be under anyone and who took his preachers' plan from no one."³³ On one occasion when he was sent a copy of the circuit plan showing the places where he was appointed to preach, he returned it with the following lines scribbled on it.

> A plan from God I have to mind,
> A better plan I cannot find.
> If you can, pray let me know.
> And round the circuit I will go.³⁴

Benton, described by Hugh Bourne as "a man let loose,"³⁵ was virtually illiterate to the point where a fellow local preacher who heard him preaching on Cannock Common said in scorn, "You are bringing a scandal to the cause of Christ, you have no learning and you do not understand grammar."³⁶ A short while after this jibe Benton was delivering a Good Friday message based on the text, "It is finished." As he proceeded with his discourse, rough colliers started to fall under conviction on every side, eyewitnesses reporting that "some groaned, others shrieked and some fell from their seats and the whole assembly was thrown into consternation; he therefore closed the Bible and went from his stand to pray for mourners; and when passing down among the people he saw his friend, the local preacher, standing and looking on with amazement. Said Benton

31. Ritson, *Romance of Primitive Methodism*, 72.
32. Kendall, *Origin and History*, 1:303.
33. Kendall, *Origin and History*, 1:113.
34. Ritson, *Romance of Primitive Methodism*, 111.
35. Ritson, *Romance of Primitive Methodism*, 111.
36. Kendall, *Origin and History*, 1:97.

to him, "This is grammar!"[37] Bourne, who had recently met with Benton, talked with him at length and encouraged him in his ministry. He then attended the Ramsor camp meeting on the 26th of May, 1811, after which he recorded, "At this meeting I received such a baptism of the Holy Spirit as I never experienced before; and I felt from this day it was my duty to be give up to the work of the ministry."[38]

William Clowes also visited Leicester later in the same year and recorded in his journal:

> The multitude on this occasion were exceedingly well-behaved; a deep solemnity reigned over the meeting, and all was still and quiet as if we had been in chapel. We terminated the proceedings about twelve o'clock, and at half past one we held a prayer meeting in Orchard Street. The gathering together again was very numerous. Vast numbers stood on the outside, many were powerfully affected, and cried for pardoning mercy, and their cries were not in vain. It was supposed that about twenty souls found the Lord and rejoiced; the prayer meeting continued till six o'clock in the evening.[39]

Some lay preachers traveled as far as Oldham in the northwest where, in 1822, some 14,000 people were present and "a season of extraordinary Pentecostal power was experienced."[40] From Newark, missionaries pushed their way north, following the course of the Trent to Gainsborough, where they were able to start a work in 1819. From these two points they were then able to fan out across the northern part of Lincolnshire and then move northwards into Yorkshire and up into the coalfields of Durham. Johnny Oxtoby reached Filey in Yorkshire in 1824, where he declared well before his arrival "the Lord has a great work to do."[41] So it was proved with Joseph Ritson later writing, "A revival began, which completely revolutionised the moral condition of the place, and laid the foundations of a powerful church, which abides to this day."[42] Some Primitive Methodist preachers went on to Norwich and Fakenham, which became independent centers by 1825. Others continued southwards from Nottingham, possibly through Spalding, and on to Kings

37. Kendall, *Origin and History*, 1:96–97.
38. Kendall, *Origin and History*, 1:98.
39. Clowes, *Journals*, 130–40.
40. Ritson, *Romance of Primitive Methodism*, 72
41. Kendall, *Origin and History*, 2:104.
42. Ritson, *Romance of Primitive Methodism*, 115.

Lynn, which became an established center in 1821. A number of evangelists headed southwards from Nottingham to Loughborough, which by 1822 became the center of a circuit which had forty-two preaching places on it, including Leicester and Coventry. It is noticeably clear from Kendall's account that in the 1820s Primitive Methodist missionaries were making effective inroads among the Luddites of the Midlands, the fishing communities of Filey and Flamborough, along the North Yorkshire coast, with the miners of the midlands and Northumberland and Durham, as well as the rick-burning farm laborers of Lincolnshire and East Anglia.[43] The revival at Filey was remarkable by any standards. A Mr. Dent who was present later wrote:

> There were many cases of prostrations in connection with that great work. I have seen more than fifteen at one meeting, some of whom were sober-minded Christians as humble as they were earnest. And what was observable, there was nothing in the voice or manner of the preacher to account for such effects; no vociferation, no highly impassioned address He [J. Oxtoby] stood as steadily, and talked as calmly, as I ever witnessed anyone do. . . . He did not take falling down as a certain proof of obtaining entire sanctification; but ascribed much to physical cause—to nervous weakness. . . . It was wonderful how some persons so affected were preserved from physical harm. I remember seeing men fall suddenly backwards on stone flags without being hurt, and on one occasion, in a dwelling house, a man fell against a fire-place, the fire burning at the time, without being injured.[44]

The revival in Filey saw the morals of the village rapidly improved. "Religion wrought for sobriety, thrift, softening of manners, social peace, and domestic concord."[45] The fishermen abandoned Sunday fishing to keep the sabbath. They found they caught more fish in six days than they had previously done in seven. Kendall remarked that Filey became a model fishing town.[46] Wherever Bourne and Clowes and their many lay preachers and helpers found a good response to their preaching and made converts, their town or village was put on the circuit plan as a preaching station. The circuits were a copy of the Wesleyan Methodists, with a group of preaching stations in a local area placed under one leader

43. Kendall, *Origin and History*, 1:212–18; 2:100–102.
44. Kendall, *Origin and History*, 2:147.
45. Kendall, *Origin and History*, 2:105.
46. Kendall, *Origin and History*, 2:105.

who was responsible for appointing preachers and supervising pastoral care. The very first Primitive circuit was based around Tunstall, from which it took its name. Neither Bourne nor Clowes had probably ever contemplated setting up an organization similar to that of the Wesleyan Methodist connexion from which they had both been expelled, but they soon came to recognize it was a pastoral necessity. Both men were godly, strong, and able leaders, but Clowes was a particularly gifted preacher. Joseph Ritson wrote of him as follows:

> Like a flame of fire, he swept over Staffordshire, through Derbyshire, Nottinghamshire, Lancashire, Leicestershire, Yorkshire, until he reached the sea at Hull, the scene of his early exploits in sin and folly. But here was to be the scene of far greater exploits in the service of Jesus Christ. In less than four months four hundred persons had been gathered into Christian fellowship, and in less than a year Hull was a circuit. It then became a centre of the most astounding evangelistic achievements, embracing Yorkshire, Durham, Northumberland, Cumberland, Westmorland; and extending as far as Lincoln, Norfolk, and yet more distant places. Within seven years, twenty-one independent circuits had been made, with a membership of 8,455, which with the membership of Hull itself, made a total of 11,996.[47]

There were a host of others who played vital roles in the Primitive Methodist Revival. Among them were Robert Key and John Stamp. Robert Key (1805–76) was an early pioneer in every sense of the word. Little is known of his early years save that he was born in the village of Upton-All-Saints on the Norfolk-Suffolk border and as an adult worked as a coal-heaver on the docksides at Great Yarmouth, where he kept company with a gang of poachers, gamblers, and cock-fighters. He was converted to Christ in 1826, and became a traveling preacher two years later. In Victorian times he became known as "the apostle of mid-Norfolk" because he proved to be a major influence in the villages round East Dereham. He is recorded as trudging the roads and lanes of this isolated area often begging for hospitality. The years of 1825–42 were a remarkable period of expansion and advance in East Anglia. In 1825, the six Norfolk circuits had a membership of only 1,546, with thirteen ministers. By 1842, thanks to Key's untiring labors, this had risen to a figure of 9,072 with fifty-nine ministers.

---

47. Ritson, *Romance of Primitive Methodism*, 103.

The Primitive Methodist Revival, 1811-51

John Stamp is worthy of a passing mention since he typifies so many of the Primitive Methodist preachers who literally gave their all to carry the gospel forward. He was a Primitive Methodist traveling preacher stationed at Louth in Lincolnshire from 1836–39. In that time, he wrote, "I have walked more than 10,000 miles, have preached upwards of 1,500 sermons and have visited near 6,000 families."[48] A prominent pioneering preacher in the South was John Ride, who was converted in 1813. He was placed at Brinkworth (1828–31), Shefford (1832–36), Reading (1837–43), and London (1844–47). His ministry was remarkable by any standards. From Reading, under his direction, the work spread to Aylesbury in Buckinghamshire, which became a circuit in 1840, and from there to Luton in Bedfordshire, which was made a circuit in 1843. In the same year branches were established in Oxford and Witney, Thame and Camden. Further outposts were established in Andover, Romsey, Lymington, and the New Forest. The Reading, High Wycombe, and Windsor branches were made circuits in 1848.[49]

By the middle of the nineteenth century Primitive Methodism was firmly established in four major areas: the South Midlands; the North West Midlands; East Anglia, including Lincolnshire; and the northeast, embracing the coastal areas of Yorkshire and Durham. In 1811, the Primitive Methodists numbered only 200 members, but at their Conference in 1820 there were 7,842 members.[50] Primitive Methodism continued to expand rapidly, reaching a membership of 84,660 by 1843.[51] Then when the government held a religious census on the last Sunday in March 1851, it showed that 266,555 attended Primitive Methodist places of worship.[52] This steady and solid growth in numbers clearly indicated that most converts had continued steadfastly in their faith. Furthermore, it demonstrated the genuineness of the revival. Primitive Methodism continued to expand until the First World War, but the revival began to plateau in the second half of the nineteenth century as the church entered what was described as "a period of slackening energies, introversionism and denominationalism."[53] There were now larger and grander buildings and

---

48. Obelkevich, *Religion and Rural Society*, 246.

49. Kendall, *Origin and History*, 2:314.

50. Armstrong, *Church of England and the Methodists*, 210.

51. Bourne, H., Letter to John Browason, 13 May, 1843, in Englesea Museum, Englesea, UK M MS ENBPM 1990.033.

52. Thompson, *Nonconformity in the Nineteenth Century*, 153.

53. Obelkevich, *Religion and Rural Society*, 220–21.

calmer worship in some of the larger chapels, together with greater theological training for its circuit ministers. Significantly, William Clowes died in 1851, and Hugh Bourne in 1852.

Features of the Revival

Female Preaching

Following in the footsteps of John Wesley, Hugh Bourne, who authored a book in 1808 entitled *Remarks on the Ministry of Women*, was clear that women had an important role to play in both preaching and leading. Julia Werner pointed out that in 1818 one in five Primitive Methodist preachers was a woman.[54] Dorothy Graham identified ninety female itinerants, and suggested that there may have been more.[55] Sarah Kirkland (1794–1880) was one of the first women preachers, and although she was never formally appointed to a specific "station," she was held in high esteem, not least because she had been recruited by Bourne himself and played a significant role in establishing Primitive Methodism in a number of important places in the North Midlands.[56] R. W. Ambler observed that female preachers such as Ann Carr and Sarah Healand "linked early Primitive Methodism to the domestic lives of the rural workers of South Lincolnshire by helping to assert the role of women in providing a refuge against the stresses of social change through a religious experience in the home."[57] Among the women who were notable preachers, Ritson highlighted Sarah Kirkland, who pioneered work in Cheshire, Nottingham, Derby, and Yorkshire, and was a frequent speaker at camp meetings. After her preaching at Bulwell sixty persons joined the society. Later in the year she preached there again at a camp meeting to "an immense multitude."[58] In 1816, she missioned the colliery village of Ilkeston, which resulted in "a marvellous reformation."[59] The high point of female Primitive Methodist preaching was probably the early 1840s since after 1842 no more women were appointed as itinerants, the last one being Elizabeth Bultitude who

---

54. Werner, *Primitive Methodist Connexion*, 142.
55. Wilson, *Constrained by Zeal*, 206.
56. Milburn, *Primitive Methodism*, 15.
57. Ambler, *Ranters, Revivalists and Reformers*, 47.
58. Ritson, *Romance of Primitive Methodism*, 137.
59. Ritson, *Romance of Primitive Methodism*, 134–39.

travelled as a full-time preacher for thirty-one years and retired in 1862. Joseph Ritson rightly emphasized that "devoted women played a large part in the work of preaching in the early days."[60]

Conversation Preaching

There can be no doubt that the importance that Primitive Methodists attached to conversation preaching was a major factor in attracting new people into their open-air meetings and chapel congregations. The people who attended their gatherings were those whose formal education was minimal. They were not able to appreciate or stomach a carefully thought-out pulpit homily. Rather they needed someone who could bring them face to face with the Jesus who could give them hope and strength in the harsh demands of their work in agriculture as well as the mines and factories. Primitive Methodist local preachers were known, like John Wesley, as those who preached "the plain truth to the plain man."[61] Conversation preaching was a personalized way of relating the Christian faith to the issues of everyday living at a time when Wesleyan Methodists were favoring more formalized pulpit preaching.

The Power of the Holy Spirit

Primitive Methodists lived in a world in which Satan, heaven, hell, angels, demons, and witches were ever-present realities. Their religion was a fervent and powerful experience of the presence of Jesus. Their meetings and chapel worship were powerful outpourings of the Holy Spirit often accompanied by religious exercises such as falling and shouting. There was often an emphasis on bringing the high power of God down on the assembled company through fervent singing, praise, and shouting. On one occasion Bourne related how he was struck down by the power of the Spirit as he came home past the praying place in Mr Heath's field. "I felt," he wrote, "as if I was held by an irresistible power, and I sank down into nothing before it, and everything I did was contrary to God. I felt it die away. I gave myself up to God. Immediately came 'the spirit of burning,'

---

60. Ritson, *Romance of Primitive Methodism*, 138.
61. Wesley, *Sermons on Several Occasions*, Preface (para. 3).

and I was made 'a habitation through the Spirit.' I wondered at myself; I could scarcely believe what the Spirit witnessed."[62]

The experience of God's presence on these occasions was more than enough to overcome hidden fears, the fetishes of rural superstition, and haunted domains. Additionally, Bourne had discovered in 1809 that he had the gift of being able to impart the power of God's spirit through the laying on of hands.[63] This in turn gave him the confidence to exorcise a demonic spirit from a woman in Harriseahead.[64] As a young man William Clowes had grappled with the Kidsgrove bogget and later in life he had been disturbed by his encounters with a woman at Ramsor of whom Bourne wrote: "I believe she will prove to be a witch. These are the head labourers under Satan, like as the fathers are the head labourers under Jesus Christ. . . . For witches throughout the world all meet and have connection with the power of the devil."[65]

Primitive Methodists, with their strong belief in the reality of demons and the world of unseen spirits, lacked any sort of systematic theology. This, however, had its plus side since it meant their message was sharply focused on the heart of the Christian gospel and the power of Jesus to bring salvation, forgiveness, and newness of life. Their preaching was a straightforward dualism between heaven for the righteous and hell for the others. They had a strong faith in the power of Jesus over the presence of evil and the demonic. Exorcisms and binding the forces of darkness were not infrequent. Flora Thompson, in *Lark Rise to Candleford*, so well captured the feeling of what Primitive Methodist meetings must have been like. She wrote that it was "a poor people's religion, simple and crude; but its adherents brought it more fervour than was shown by the church congregations and appeared to obtain more comfort and support from it than the church could give."[66]

Camp Meetings

There is no doubt that the Primitive Methodist strong commitment to camp meetings was the very heart and significant contributor to their

---

62. Ward, *Religion and Society*, 78.
63. Werner, *Primitive Methodist Connexion*, 70.
64. Werner, *Primitive Methodist Connexion*, 70.
65. Ward, "Religion of the People," 242.
66. Thompson, *Lark Rise to Candleford*, 125.

successful evangelism. They were of course the major reason for their separation from the Wesleyan parent body. Whilst it was the case that William Clowes never took to camp meetings with quite the same enthusiasm as Hugh Bourne did,[67] they nevertheless were an important feature in the Hull and Yorkshire area over which Clowes presided. Julia Werner observed that the American camp meetings were "both spiritual as well as social events."[68] In rural England, where Primitive Methodism took strong root, camp meetings were able to fulfill a similar function, bringing together those who otherwise would have lived isolated lives. Camp meetings were also the ideal vehicle to foster religious experience that brought excitement, catharsis, and wholeness to a segment of society who suffered long hours of work, harsh conditions, and had little in the way of joy or happiness.

Impact on Society

Education

One of the marked features of the Primitive Methodist Revival was its impact on society and culture at almost every level. Their theology may have been limited, but it was always practical and pastoral. It brought huge impact on the education of children through day schools and, more importantly, Sunday schools. In 1838, there were 58,188 scholars in Primitive Methodist Sunday schools with 9,801 teachers. By 1849 numbers had increased to 94,876 scholars with 18,169 teachers.[69] The *Primitive Methodist Magazine* emphasized, "We owe much to Sunday schools. In their moral influence they have worked wonders for England. . . . They have been the means of placing numbers in distinguished social positions."[70]

An important aspect of Primitive Methodist educational activities was the founding of the Book Room in 1821 at Bemersley in Staffordshire, with Hugh's brother, James, as its President, and the publication of the denominational magazine with Hugh Bourne serving as editor until 1842. The Book Room printed a huge volume of spelling books, tracts, cheap literature, and Sunday school material. Many early trade

---

67. Kendall, *Origin and History*, 1:87.
68. Werner, *Primitive Methodist Connexion*, 46.
69. Cubberley, *History of Education*, 617.
70. *Primitive Methodist Magazine* (1849), 342.

union leaders testified that their only education was because of their Primitive Methodist Sunday school.

Temperance

Total abstinence was a cause with a political aspect[71] to it and one in which the Primitive Methodists took an active role. Somewhat surprisingly the church did not finally establish its own temperance league until 1882, when members were encouraged to pledge, "I do hereby agree, by God's help to abstain from all intoxicating drinks as beverages and will endeavour to promote the interests of this society."[72] The reason for this late action was, as William Cutts had reminded Conference members in his Presidential Address of the same year, that from its very beginning Primitive Methodism "has been on the side of total abstinence" and that "Mr Hugh Bourne was a total abstainer from all intoxicating drink before any total abstinence societies were formed in the country."[73]

The public start of total abstinence began on the 1st of September, 1832, when "the seven men of Preston" made total abstinence pledges at the close of a temperance meeting.[74] Of the seven men, John King (1795–1885), Joseph Richardson, and Richard Turner (1790–1846) were Primitive Methodists. It was the last-named individual who was wont to say: "I am the happiest man alive for who can be happier than a teetotal Primitive Methodist!"[75] Significantly, several early missionaries who were sent out from Preston were also Primitive Methodists. James Teare (1804–68) was a Manx shoemaker who always spoke at temperance meetings with an open Bible in his hands, and Thomas Whittaker (1813–99) was often driven by images of hell which had remained with him since his Sunday school days. A widely known Primitive Methodist temperance worker was George Charlton, of whom Kendall wrote, "Among temperance advocates he stood in the foremost rank. He was a most effective temperance speaker. Dealing with facts which could not be gainsaid . . . he made a powerful impression and carried his audience

---

71. See Kent, *Holding the Fort*, 88, where the author points out that teetotalism had an appeal in that it enabled its followers to reject the social values and behavior they were supposed to regard as their superiors.

72. Cutts, "Presidential Address," 109.

73. Scotland, *Methodism and the Revolt of the Field*, 163.

74. Kendall, *Origin and History*, 2:129.

75. Kendall, *Origin and History*, 2:129.

with him."[76] Richard Horne (1813–80) hailed from Stoke-on-Trent. He took the pledge, along with his father, on 7th March 1836. In 1845, he gave up his employment and worked full-time for the British Temperance League until 1876. Horne's diary records that in 1868 he delivered 234 temperance lectures, besides preaching most Sundays. He also noted that he had travelled 7,166 miles and that 62,140 attended his meetings, with 530 people signing the pledge.[77] Thomas Burt noted that the Primitive Methodists played a leading role in setting up and organizing temperance meetings in the mining communities in the 1830s.[78] Kendall observed the many leading minsters of the connexion became pledged abstainers and zealous advocates of the cause.

Chartism

Primitive Methodists were active in the Chartist Movement, the name deriving from the Charter for Parliamentary Reform which the Working Men's Association prepared and presented to Parliament in 1839, 1842, and 1848. It proposed votes for everyone, secret ballot to protect electors from intimidation, abolition of property qualifications for MPs, payment for MPs so that people with modest incomes could give up their livelihood to attend to the needs of government, equal-sized constituencies, and Annual Parliamentary elections. Despite huge public rallies, support from several newspapers, and the establishment of local branches, the Chartist Agenda was not met with immediate success. However, with the passing of the years all the first five points of the Charter were accepted and enshrined in Parliamentary acts. Revivalist Primitive Methodism played a noticeable role in Chartism. It supplied a number of leaders at both National and local levels. For example, Thomas Cooper (1805–77) was the leader of Leicester Chartism and Thomas Skevington (1801–50), a Primitive Methodist travelling preacher, was the leading figure in Loughborough Chartism. Joseph Capper, a Primitive Methodist local preacher and prominent Chartist speaker in Staffordshire, was imprisoned in 1842. The real influence of Primitive Methodism was seen in the way the Chartists borrowed their organizational model. There were local Chartist meetings similar to the Methodist Class meetings and there were

---

76. Kendall, *Origin and History*, 2:193.
77. *Primitive Methodist Magazine*, Vol 5 (New Series) 247–49.
78. Burt, "Methodism and the Northern Miners," 303.

Chartist preachers, districts and circuits. *The Sheffield Iris* of the 3rd of September, 1839, warned that upwards of a hundred Chartist class meetings had been formed in every part of the town. Meetings were often held in Primitive Methodist chapels and began with a Christian hymn and prayers. Most telling of all were the Chartist camp meetings which were a direct borrowing from Primitive Methodism. Between 1839 and 1850, there are mentions of almost 400 Chartist camp meetings in *The Northern Star* newspaper. The most significant year was 1842, with ninety Chartist camp meetings being recorded.[79] Others were observed in Manchester, Tower Hamlets, Brighton, Bristol, Worcester, Durham, and Nottingham.

Trade Unions

Primitive Methodism gave many significant leaders to the mineworkers' unions most notably in Durham, Yorkshire, and the Midlands.[80] Tommy Hepburn (1795–1864), a Primitive Methodist local preacher, was the leader of the first combination founded in Durham in 1832. Hepburn emerged as a shrewd and able negotiator and led a successful strike against the pit owners. He refused to discuss any terms with the Marquis of Londonderry unless he first knelt down with him to ask for the Lord's guidance.[81] In an article written in 1882, Thomas Burt MP stated that in the 1830s many of the miners' leaders were Primitive Methodist local preachers. They had learned from their church the two most important lessons—the method of organizing men and the way to speak in public.[82] Burt added, "In 1831 among the leaders and most frequent speakers at Union meetings were Thomas Hepburn, Ralph Atchison, and Charles Parkinson. And again, in 1844, there were Mark Dent, Robert Archer, John Tulip, and Thomas Pratt. "All these were Primitive Methodist preachers."[83] The Primitive Methodists came to make a far greater and significant contribution to the origin and development of trade unions in the second half of the nineteenth century, but by this time the Primitive Methodist Revival had largely plateaued.

79. Wearmouth, *Methodism and the Working-Class Movements*, 129–63.
80. *Primitive Methodist Quarterly Review* (1883). See also Griffin, "Methodism and Trade Unionism."
81. *Durham Chronicle*, 14 May, 1831.
82. Burt, "Methodism and the Northern Miners," 303.
83. Burt, "Methodism and the Northern Miners," 303.

In the second half of the nineteenth century, by which time the revival was beginning to decline, Primitive Methodism contributed in several major ways to the growth of trade unionism, most notably by providing a basic training in public speaking and in business skills in a way that other denominations did not. In addition to the provision of Sunday schools, it gave men opportunities to stand in front of their fellows as exhorters, local preachers, and class leaders. Such offices as chapel and society steward provided a chance to laboring men and women to learn simple business and administrative skills. In addition, Methodist conversion instilled in many ordinary men and women a sense of self-worth and dignity and gave them a desire to better their place in society. The result of all this was that many of the more articulate laborers were Methodists.

An Inspirational Legacy

The Primitive Methodist Revival was remarkable for several reasons. It was a revival which was brought about through the vision, prayers, worship, courage, and determination of ordinary working men and women. Joseph Ritson emphasized that "the founders of the Connexion were local preachers for years before they were set apart wholly to the work of the ministry. . . . It was from the ranks of this class that the ministry was drawn."[84] Primitive Methodists effectively facilitated the revival because they communicated their faith in the language and culture of the society in which they found themselves. It was a revival which was both thoroughly Christ-centered and fully related to the needs of the people to whom it came. It was home-based and transformed family life and relationships. Like all revivals it was a work of the Spirit of God, with people being transformed spiritually, emotionally, mentally, and physically. Drunkards were turned into law-abiding, godly men and women who campaigned for temperance and total abstinence. Men, women, and children who were illiterate were taught to read and write. Converts were then able to study the Scriptures for themselves, which in turn gave them a new set of biblical Christian values on which to shape their lives, including justice, compassion, and equality, especially of women. The revival was sustained and extended by vibrant worship, watchnights, and love feasts. It was in the small, intimate, weekly class meetings where people sang, prayed, and shared their lives and Christian experience that converts learned to value

---

84. Ritson, *Romance of Primitive Methodism*, 177.

themselves and were then prompted to reach out to others. The Primitive Methodist Revival, with its emphasis on the forgiveness and the power of the Holy Spirit, conveyed self-confidence and the courage to stand up for themselves and for just living and working conditions and pay.

The Primitive Methodist Revival was sharply focused on one particular people group. From the very beginning their evangelistic efforts were focused on the working classes. Everything they did, in what James Obelkevich described as their "heroic age of missionary expansion" and "their age of revivalism and consolidation," was focused on the working poor.[85] They built chapels that were plain and much in the style and appearance of large versions of laborers' cottages where the poor didn't feel uncomfortable or out of place. Their preaching was conversational in style and their content always straightforward and easily understandable. Their religion offered a fervent and immediate experience of the risen Christ and the intensity of their singing and praying offered a catharsis which was able to touch the lives of those who lived and worked in the raw environment of the fields and the damp and heat of the mines and factories of the Industrial Revolution.

Many working poor were drawn to Christ in large numbers by the Primitive Methodists on account of their involvement in political issues and, most notably, their founding and active support of trade unions. The laboring classes were aware that Primitive Methodists were people who cared for their human rights and championed better working conditions based on biblical justice. They felt a strong degree of solidarity with their local preachers who were their leaders, stewards, and Sunday school teachers. This was their church, which they felt they owned. Their preachers did not engage in occasional acts of charity, like their Church of England counterparts, out of a sense of duty or because they were paid to. Rather they fought for conditions that would make charitable donations of broth and blankets unnecessary. Furthermore, many of their number did not give credence to a fixed social hierarchy which believed that some were born to privilege and money while others had been decreed to labor for a mere pittance and be content, as Prayer Book Catechism put it, "with that state wherein God had been pleased to call them."[86] The Primitive Methodist Revival was a revival of democratic religion with democratic principles; it was, above all, a radical, vibrant, Christian lifestyle.

85. Obelkevich, *Religion and Rural Society*, 220.
86. Anonymous, *Book of Common Prayer*, 344.

7

Revival in Upper New York State, 1824-32

In 1818, a young man began his legal training at Benjamin Wright's law firm in the town of Adams in New York State. Sometime after his arrival he started to attend Sunday worship at the Presbyterian Church. There he soon found himself challenged by the sermons of its minister, George Gale. Eventually he was brought face to face with the issue of "whether I would accept Christ as presented in the Gospel, or pursue a worldly course of life."[1] On Sunday, October 7th, 1821, he finally made up his mind to "settle the question of his soul's salvation at once" and "make his peace with God."[2] But it was not until the following Wednesday that he finally accepted "the offer of Gospel salvation."[3] So instead of going to his office that morning he went out after breakfast into a grove of woods north of the village and cried out, "Lord, I take thee at thy word. Now thou knowest that I do search for thee with all my heart."[4]

On returning to his office at lunch time he found it impossible to do any work. Instead, he picked up his bass viol as he often did and played and sang some music. After a brief period he recalled that suddenly "it

---

1. Finney, *Memoirs*, 14.
2. Finney, *Memoirs*, 16.
3. Finney, *Memoirs*, 18.
4. Finney, *Memoirs*, 20.

seemed as if I met the Lord Jesus Christ face to face." He described his experience as follows.

> But as I returned and was about to take a seat by the fire, I received a mighty baptism of the Holy Ghost. Without expecting it, without ever having the thought in my mind that there was any such thing for me, without any recollection that I had ever heard the thing mentioned by any person in the world, at a moment entirely unexpected by me, the Holy Spirit descended upon me in a manner that seemed to go through me, body and soul. I could feel the impression, like a wave of electricity, going through and through me. Indeed it seemed to come in waves of liquid love,—for I could not express it in any other way. And yet it did not seem like water, but rather as the breath of God. I can recollect distinctly that it seemed to me, as these waves passed over me, that they literally moved my hair like a passing breeze. No words can express the wonderful love that was shed abroad in my heart. These waves came over me, and over me one after another, until I recollect I cried out, "I shall die if these waves continue to pass over me." I said to the Lord, "Lord I cannot bear any more." Yet I had no fear of death.[5]

The man who received this overwhelming experience of God was Charles Finney. He was destined to become the leader and instrument of a continuous stream of powerful local revivals which extended for more than a decade in the towns and cities of Upper New York State.

Charles Finney

Charles was born on the 29th of August, 1792 to Sylvester and Rebecca Finney, neither of whom were Christians. When he was about two years of age, his parents, who were farmers, moved west from Warren, Connecticut to Hanover, Oneida County in New York State, which Finney later recalled was "to a great extent a wilderness."[6] After his early education he attended Hamilton Oneida Institute in order to prepare himself for his law studies, and this in turn brought him to the town of Adams.

After his overwhelming conversion, Finney's whole life was soon radically changed. He later wrote, "I was quite willing to preach the

---

5. Finney, *Memoirs*, 23–24.
6. Finney, *Memoirs*, 4.

gospel."⁷ He began at once to share his newfound faith whenever the opportunity arose. Many of the inhabitants of Adams who had believed him to be a hapless individual were profoundly challenged by his changed life. Soon afterwards his parents and his youngest brother, George, were converted. Finney wrote of those early days, "I used to spend a great deal of time in prayer; sometimes, I thought, literally praying 'without ceasing.' I also found it very profitable, and felt very much inclined, to hold frequent days of private fasting."⁸

**Portrait of Charles Finney by Samuel Waldo (1783–1867)
Courtesy of Oberlin College Archives.**

7. Finney, *Memoirs*, 28.
8. Finney, *Memoirs*, 39.

Shortly after this, Finney began theological studies tutored by his pastor, George Gale. He soon found that he did not share Gale's views that not everyone could be saved. He did however gain from him a knowledge of Hebrew and Greek. He was examined by the St Lawrence Presbytery at Adams, who unanimously voted to license him to preach the gospel on December 30th, 1823.[9] After he had given his first sermon, Gale said to him, "Mr Finney I shall be very much ashamed to have it known, wherever you go, that you have studied theology with me."[10] He subsequently spoke very harshly of Finney's views. Notwithstanding his mentor's opinions of him, Finney was ordained by the Presbytery of St Lawrence at Evans Mills on the 1st of July, 1824.[11] In October that same year he married Lydia Andrews of Whitestown, Oneida County.

Campaigns in the Northeastern States, 1824-32

Since he had had little training for the ministry, Finney did not expect to be invited to labor in large towns and cities or to be invited to speak to cultivated congregations. "I intended to go," he wrote in his *Memoirs*, "into the new settlements and preach in the schoolhouses, and barns and groves, as best I could."[12] Accordingly, he set out in 1824 on what proved to be almost a decade of continuing revival in Upper New York State, an area on the margins of society subject to economic strains and political upheavals. It was known also as the "burned-over district" on account of its previous history of religious excitement. At the outset of his ministry Finney had very limited financial support. He did, however, receive funding from *The Female Missionary Society of the Western District of the State of New York*. On the 17th of March, 1824, they formally agreed to pay him a salary of $600 a year to labor as a missionary "in the Northern parts of the County of Jefferson and other destitute places in the vicinity as his discretion shall dictate."[13] Finney began in his home area of Jefferson County, but gradually, as the news of his successes became increasingly well known, the number of invitations multiplied hugely. In

9. Finney, *Memoirs*, 54.
10. Finney, *Memoirs*, 54.
11. Finney, *Memoirs*, 77.
12. Finney, *Memoirs*, 77.
13. Letter of appointment, *Finney Papers*, Oberlin College Library, cited in McLoughlin, *Modern Revivalism*, 26.

fact, by 1830 he was receiving requests from major towns and cities. The following glimpses at some of Finney's campaigns witness to the remarkable power and moving of the Holy Spirit.

Evans Mills, Antwerp, and Le Raysville (April–October 1824)

He began in his own home area of Jefferson County, New York State, preaching in the villages of Evans Mills, Antwerp, and Le Raysville. Of Evans Mills Finney wrote, "the people thronged en masse to hear me preach."[14] Close to the town there was a small settlement of Germans with their own church but with no pastor. The result of Finney's preaching was "the conversion of the whole church" and "nearly all the community of Germans."[15] Finney wrote in his *Autobiography* that "during the six months that I laboured in that region, I rode from town to town and from settlement to settlement and preached the Gospel as I had opportunity."[16] He was encouraged because when he left his law office in Adams he recalled "my health had run down a good deal but before six months were completed my health was entirely restored." He continued, "I preached out of doors, I preached in barns, I preached in school-houses, and a glorious revival spread all over that new region of country."[17]

When Finney first arrived at Antwerp he heard "a vast amount of profanity" and wrote, "I thought I had never heard so much in any place that I had ever visited. In every business place all were cursing and swearing, and I felt I had arrived upon the borders of hell."[18] However, the impact of his preaching at Antwerp soon heralded a wonderful and unexpected change. "The Lord let me loose upon them in a wonderful manner," he later recalled. The results were remarkable by any standard as his recollections make abundantly plain. He preached on the text "Up get ye out of this place for the Lord will destroy this city." He had not spoken "for more than a quarter of an hour" when "the congregation began to fall from their seats; and fell in every direction and cried for mercy" and "within less than ten minutes the whole congregation was either on their knees

---

14. Finney, *Memoirs*, 64.
15. Finney, *Memoirs*, 76–77.
16. Finney, *Autobiography*, 64.
17. Finney, *Autobiography*, 64.
18. Finney, *Autobiography*, 80.

or prostrate."[19] Finney's preaching at Le Raysville brought a comparable response. Finney noted in his *Autobiography*, "After labouring there a few weeks, the great mass of the inhabitants were converted; and among the rest Judge C__, a man, in point of influence, standing head and shoulders above the people."[20] Finney recorded that at the close of one of his sermons "I called on any who would give their hearts to God, to come and take a front seat... a large number arose in different parts and came forward; and a goodly number appeared to give their hearts to God on the spot."[21]

Gouverneur (April–September 1825)

From April to the end of September 1825, Finney labored at Gouverneur in St Lawrence County. It had earlier been revealed to him "in a most unexpected manner that God was going to pour out his Spirit at Gouverneur, and that I must go there and preach." In obedience he did so and "with remarkable effect." On the first night a group of skeptics and universalists were convicted and converted. Gouverneur was a large farming town settled by well-to-do inhabitants. "The great majority of them," Finney wrote, "I am confident were in that revival converted to Christ."[22]

Rome (January 1826)

After seeing powerful moves of the Spirit of the Lord in St Lawrence County, Finney moved on to Rome in Onieda County at the start of the new year. There he preached almost every day for three weeks. During his time in the town there was much emphasis on prayer, and at some of the gatherings the church was more than half-full with praying people. Indeed, Finney recalled, "the town was full of prayer." "Go where you would," he wrote, "you heard the voice of prayer."[23] It was at Rome that Finney began the practice at the evening services of asking those who had committed their lives to Christ to come forward publicly. Most did so, and on average there were twenty-five a day. In all, Finney was able

---

19. Finney, *Memoirs*, 101–2.
20. Finney, *Autobiography*, 81.
21. Finney, *Autobiography*, 95–96.
22. Finney, *Memoirs*, 130.
23. Finney, *Memoirs*, 168.

to report that there were nearly 500 conversions. This number included nearly all the local lawyers, merchants, and physicians.[24]

Looking back on his time in Rome in 1825, he recalled, "Convictions were so deep and universal that we would sometimes go into a house and find some in a kneeling posture and some prostrate on the floor. Some bathing the temples of their friends with camphor, and rubbing them to keep them from fainting and, as they feared, from dying."[25] After one of his meetings so many people responded to Finney's challenge to repent and commit their lives to Christ that it was decided to have an inquiry meeting the following morning in the courthouse. At the appointed hour so many came that "we spent a good part of the day in giving instruction, and the work went on with wonderful power. So many came forward on the following evening that the Inquiry Meeting had to be held next morning in the church."[26] The state of things in the neighborhood of Rome during the revival was such "that no one could come into the town without feeling awe-stricken with the impression that God was there."[27] The sheriff of Utica had to visit Rome on business and found that as he crossed the old canal about a mile from the town "a strange impression came over him, an awe so deep that he could not shake it off. He felt as if God pervaded the whole atmosphere." He stopped at Mr F__'s hotel, and observed that the hotelier "looked just as he himself felt, as if he were afraid to speak."[28]

After great encouragement at Rome, Finney moved on to Utica where a yet more powerful revival began. There he stayed in the home of the minister Samuel Aitkin[29] and preached for several months from the pulpit of the First Presbyterian Church. Finney recalled, "The word took immediate effect, and the place became filled with the manifested influence of the Holy Spirit."[30] Men entering the town on business "felt as if God pervaded the whole atmosphere" and "some were converted without even attending the meetings."[31] The revival reached a cotton mill owned

---

24. Finney, *Memoirs*, 164.
25. Finney, *Memoirs*, 103, 198, and 203. See also Finney, *Autobiography*, 136.
26. Finney, *Autobiography*, 137.
27. Finney, *Autobiography*, 141.
28. Finney, *Autobiography*, 142.
29. See Murray, *Revival and Revivalism*, 230.
30. Finney, *Memoirs*, 172.
31. Sherwood Eddy, *Spiritual Awakening*, 9.

by a Mr Wolcott at Oriskany Creek. Finney was invited to look round the buildings and while he was doing so "many men came under conviction and burst into tears." Woolcot, an unconverted man of good morals and high standing in the local community, ordered his superintendent, "Stop the mill, and let the people attend to religion; for it is more important that our souls be saved than this factory run."[32]

Auburn (June–late August 1826)

In the summer of 1826, Finney moved on to Auburn at the request of Dr Dirck Cornelius Lancing, the pastor of the First Presbyterian Church. Owing to spurious reports of Finney's recent ministry, a group of clergy from churches in the neighborhood banded together in an effort to prevent his coming to hold further meetings.[33] Finney wrote, "I shook from head to foot, like a man in an ague fit,"[34] but the Lord showed him that he must press ahead. He therefore took to serious private prayer and was rewarded "with such a sense of God's presence that he felt as if he were Moses on Mount Sinai."[35] The revival spirit filled Auburn just as it had the cities and villages of Oneida and Jefferson Counties before that.[36] Fifty-four were admitted to membership at First Church as a result of the revival, a smaller number than in some previous years. This may have been a reflection of the opposition Finney encountered at Auburn. Nevertheless, "there were a great many interesting conversions around Auburn and vicinity and also in all the neighbouring towns throughout that part of the state, as the work spread in every direction."[37] Finney later wrote that he stayed at Auburn for six sabbaths and that the pastor, Mr. Clary, "found that in the six weeks five-hundred souls had been converted."[38]

---

32. Finney, *Memoirs*, 183.
33. Finney, *Memoirs*, 195.
34. Finney, *Memoirs*, 195.
35. Hambrick-Stowe, *Charles G. Finney*, 56.
36. Hambrick-Stowe, *Charles G. Finney*, 57.
37. Hambrick-Stowe, *Charles G. Finney*, 56–61.
38. Finney, *Autobiography*, 257.

Troy (October 1826—April 1827)

Early in 1826, Finney accepted the invitation of the Revd Nathan Smith Beman (1785–1871) to "labour with them for revival."[39] The *Troy Review* noted that inquiry meetings were held at the close of all Finney's main evening meetings and that by the time he left a hundred had joined the Presbyterian church.[40] The revival also swept through the Troy Female Seminary. The pioneer women's rights leader, Elizabeth Cady Stanton, who was a sixteen-year-old pupil at the time, later recalled "that it went through the seminary 'like an epidemic.'"[41] Nonetheless, the revival, as Hambrick Stowe noted, was marked by a very earnest spirit of prayer and "Troy produced a multitude of heartfelt conversions, and many leaders were awakened."[42]

Philadelphia

After experiencing such encouragement at Troy, Finney went on to Philadelphia in January 1828, at the insistence of James Patterson (1779–1837), who was the minister of the First Presbyterian Church of Northern Liberties. There a "powerful revival' very quickly took hold of the congregation with several hundred representatives from most of the city's different denominations attending Finney's anxious meetings.[43] As the reports of his labors spread, he was invited to preach in all the city's Presbyterian churches except Arch Street Church.[44] After several months, it was decided to hold the meetings in one place, and Race Street German Reformed Church was chosen. It was the city's largest church with a capacity for 3,000 worshipers. Finney preached there from mid-August until the end of January 1829. People from all parts of the city flocked to hear him and "some hundreds" were converted.[45] Then, in spring 1829, many lumber men who floated timber into the city started to attend the meetings. When they returned back home to the forest regions along the

---

39. *Troy Review* in Finney, *Memoirs*, 210. See also note 38.
40. Finney, *Memoirs*, 210. See also note 37.
41. Finney, *Memoirs*, 210.
42. Hambrick-Stowe, *Charles G. Finney*, 65.
43. Finney, *Memoirs*, 248.
44. Finney, *Memoirs*, 248.
45. Finney, *Memoirs*, 255.

Delaware River they prayed for an outpouring of the Holy Spirit. Their efforts, Finney recorded, "were immediately blessed" and the revival began to spread across their region. Finney later recorded that "it spread to such an extent that in many cases persons would be convicted who had not attended any meetings, and were almost as ignorant as heathen."[46] Looking back, Finney wrote:

> I think I laboured in Philadelphia about a year and a half. In all that time there was no abatement of the revival, that I could see. The converts became numerous; but I never had any knowledge of their exact number. I never laboured anywhere where I was received more cordially; and where Christians, and especially converts appeared better than they did. There was no jar or schism; and I never heard of any disastrous influence resulting from that revival.[47]

New York City (October 17th, 1829—May 1830)

While Finney was at Whitestown in Oneida County he was invited to go to the City of New York. There Anson Green (1781–1853), a leading metal importer and wealthy manufacturer, hearing that he had not been invited to any of the city's pulpits, secured the use of a vacant church in Vandewater Street.[48] Finney remained in the city for eight months. He did not limit his labors solely to Green's church and recalled that the number of converts "was large."[49] During the revival, Lewis Tappan (1788–1873), a prominent New York merchant and a Unitarian who had opposed the work, was converted. He became a major figure in the anti-slave trade campaigns and subsequently was a strong supporter of Oberlin College, where black and white pupils were taught together.[50] This revival led on to the formation of seven free Presbyterian churches in New York City, composed largely of the new converts.

---

46. Finney, *Memoirs*, 260.
47. Finney, *Autobiography*, 203–4.
48. Finney, *Memoirs*, 285–86.
49. Finney, *Memoirs*, 287.
50. See Sherwood Eddy, *Spiritual Awakening*, 11.

Rochester (September 10th, 1831—mid-June 1832)

While at New York City, Finney received a pressing invitation to go to the Presbyterian Church at Rochester. Their pastor, Joel Parker (1799–1873), had recently left the city to take a church in New York and urged Finney to do a few months' supply preaching. Rochester in the 1820s was the fastest growing city in the United States and its religious life was in a downward spiral.[51] Finney nevertheless felt prompted to take up the offer and arrived with his wife on the 10th of September, 1831. At Rochester, Finney started to use what he termed "the anxious seat," something which he stated in his *Memoirs* he had not used before "except in rare instances." He had occasionally asked people in his congregations to "stand up" to confess their faith, but he believed that the higher classes "needed help to overcome their fear of being known as anxious inquirers." In this new practice certain seats at the front of the building were left empty and those who were willing to renounce their sins and give themselves to Christ were invited to come and sit on them as the meetings drew to a close.[52] Significantly, Finney soon observed that lawyers, physicians, and merchants, indeed "all the most intelligent class of society" were more readily influenced to give themselves to God by this means." Apart from the use of the "anxious seat"[53] the means which Finney employed in promoting this revival remained the same as those he had used in his previous campaigns.

Out of a population of about 10,000 in 1831, there were an estimated 800 converts, with some 1,200 joining the churches which made up the Rochester Presbytery.[54] Finney wrote in his *Memoirs* that "the revival was so powerful, it gathered in such great numbers of the most influential class of society."[55] Among those who professed conversion were fourteen lawyers, twenty-four merchants and physicians, one general, three colonels, one sheriff, and a bank cashier.[56] The revival brought remarkable change in the moral and subsequent history of Rochester. The city's leading prosecuting attorney, who was himself converted, reported years afterwards, "I have been examining the records of the criminal courts, and I find this striking fact, that whereas our city has increased since that revival

---

51. Finney, *Memoirs*, 299–301.
52. Finney, *Memoirs*, 307.
53. Finney, *Memoirs*, 323.
54. Finney, *Memoirs*, 318 and n88.
55. Finney, *Memoirs*, 323.
56. Finney, *Memoirs*, 327 and n118.

threefold, there is not one third as many prosecutions for crime as there had been up to that time."[57] A Mr. C. P. Bush also reported, "The courts had little to do, and the jail was nearly empty for years afterwards."[58] The town's theater remained closed from 1832 till the later 1850s.[59] Years after the revival in Rochester Dr. Beecher remarked, "That was the greatest work of God, and the greatest revival of religion, that the world has ever seen in so short a time. One hundred thousand, were reported as having connected themselves with the churches, as the result. This is unparalleled in the history of the church, and of the progress of religion."[60]

Boston (September 1831—August 1832)

At Rochester, Finney had seen the blessings that had flowed as local churches worked together. He was therefore reluctant to accept offers to preach in Boston until there was a general agreement from the clergy as a whole. Eventually a united invitation came and Finney was welcomed by Lyman Beecher (1775-1863) who had been a vigorous opponent of his revival services. Finney arrived in September 1831 and began preaching at Park Street Congregational Chapel where he soon found his sermons "were not at all palatable" and caused many professed Christians "to back away."[61] He preached in various churches and reported "a blessed work of grace" with a large number of persons converted in different parts of the city." "Indeed," he continued, "the work was more or less extensive throughout the city."[62]

Boston must have been something of a disappointment for Finney, coming as it did so soon after the powerful move of God's Spirit in the meetings at Rochester. By this time, Finney must have realized that the past ten years of continuous travel and preaching were beginning to sap his physical and spiritual energy. It therefore came as no surprise that he accepted a call to go to New York City and moved there with his wife and children in May 1832. Yet there was not the slightest sign that he had, like the Old Testament king Saul, lost his anointing. Two wealthy

---

57. Finney, *Memoirs*, 318.
58. Finney, *Memoirs*, 319 and n91.
59. Finney, *Memoirs*, 318.
60. Finney, *Autobiography*, 253.
61. Finney, *Memoirs*, 347.
62. Finney, *Memoirs*, 353.

individuals, Lewis Tappan and William Green, purchased the Chatham Garden Theater and converted it into a place of worship which could also provide office space for charitable societies. Finney began preaching on the 6th of May, 1832, and saw an immediate positive response: "The Spirit of the Lord," he reported, "was poured out upon us, and we had an extensive revival that Spring and Summer." It was such that Lewis Tappan stated that "within three months there was a moral change in that part of the city and every grog shop in the area had to close."[63] Finney was formally installed as pastor on the 28th of September.

Very shortly afterwards Finney was seized with cholera but recovered by the end of October. He then preached for twenty-four evenings in succession, with great effect. Between 400 and 500 declared themselves as "inquirers" at the end of the meetings. Chatham Street congregations were soon so large that a group was sent off to another part of the city to plant the Fourth Free Presbyterian Church. Finney found his new congregation to be a united praying and working people who were happy to walk the streets and invite people to the meetings. Both Finney and his church were strongly opposed to slaveholding, and he frequently preached on the matter. Black people were welcome at all services and Finney refused communion to slaveholders, believing this to be "a decidedly good influence on the individuals and the church a whole."[64] Finney's sermons on the subject of slavery were vivid as he spoke for example of "two millions of degraded heathen in our land" who "stretch forth their hands, all shackled and bleeding, and send forth an agonising cry to God."[65]

In 1834, Finney suffered a break in his health and took time away to recover. On his return he was concerned to discover that the *New York Evangelist*, which had been a warm supporter of his ministry, was on the verge of financial collapse because of its anti-slavery stance. In what proved a very successful means of saving it, Finney agreed to preach a series of lectures on the subject of revival with the substance of each one printed in the paper. The lectures were afterwards published in May 1835 as *Lectures on Revival*. They were translated into French and German and widely read in America and Europe.

---

63. *Christian Register*, 28 February, 1846 cited in Finney, *Memoirs*, 357n5.
64. Hambrick-Stowe, *Charles G. Finney*, 142.
65. Hambrick-Stowe, *Charles G. Finney*, 142.

Oberlin College (1835-75)

With the passing of time, Finney became increasingly alienated from the old-school Presbyterians and eventually resigned from the Presbytery in 1836. In the meantime, a new church had been built and on the 10th of April of that same year Finney was installed as minister at the purpose-built Broadway Tabernacle. As things turned out, Finney did not stay in the post very long. The majority of students in training for the ministry at Lane Presbyterian Seminary were forced to leave the institution because they were forbidden to speak out against slavery. This led Arthur Tappan to approach Finney with a proposal that if he would come out West and instruct the students he would cover all expenses. This resulted in the founding of Oberlin College in Ohio, with Finney becoming Professor of Theology after the trustees agreed "to receive coloured people on the same conditions that we did white people" and "never to interfere with the internal regulations of the school."[66] Initially it was hoped Finney would still be able to spend some months each year at the church in New York but it soon became clear that Oberlin College and its chapel for which he was responsible was an all-consuming commitment. Finney's links with the Tabernacle finally ended on April 6th, 1837.

Broadway Tabernacle. Source F. Palmer and Co. Public domain.

66. Finney, *Memoirs*, 380.

Oberlin College, which was named after Jean Frederick Oberlin, the Strasbourg pastor and philanthropist, came to be known for its support for abolitionism. It served as a safe haven for slaves who were escaping to the Northern States. Finney recalled that several slaves were "secreted here" and that their friends "aided their escape through the fields of high standing corn and through woods."[67] "Coloured students," as Finney called them in his autobiography, were welcomed and treated on equal terms.[68] They boarded in the same halls, ate at the same tables, and shared the same classrooms.

Finney's move to Oberlin marked the ending of a decade of intense revival in the towns and cities of New York State. Finney now found himself occupied with the college chapel, lecturing, research, publishing, and with the pastoral care of the students. In 1851, he was unanimously elected as President of the College. He soon found it was no longer possible even to return to the church which had been built for him in New York. He was, however, in this later phase of his life, to return to some of the places which in times past had been the scenes of powerful revivals. These included Rochester in 1842[69] and Rome in 1854 and 1855.[70]

Features of the Revival

The Importance of Prayer

It soon became clear to Finney that prayer was a vital ingredient in any revival. He emphasized the need for what he termed "prevailing prayer" and devoted a whole chapter to it in his *Lectures on Revival*. He outlined eleven characteristics of "prevailing prayer" which included "having a definite object, submission to God's will, perseverance and faith."[71] He also spoke and wrote of "travailing prayer,"[72] the agony of the soul that we see in Jesus. We have already noted the powerful effect of prayer gatherings at Rome in Oneida County, where Finney preached every day for three weeks in 1826. The same was also true at De Kalb, a village

---

67. Finney, *Memoirs*, 413.
68. Finney, *Memoirs*, 411–12.
69. Finney, *Autobiography*, 298–305.
70. Finney, *Autobiography*, 356–62.
71. Finney, *Revivals of Religion*, Lecture 4.
72. Finney, *Revivals of Religion*, Lecture 4, 65–66.

sixteen miles north of Gouverneur, which Finney visited in 1825. He recalled, "Not only were prayer meetings multiplied and fully attended, not only was there great solemnity in those meetings, but there was a mighty spirit of secret prayer." Christians, he recorded, prayed a great deal, many of them spending many hours in private. It was also the case that two or more would take the promise: "If two of you shall agree on earth as touching anything that they ask, it shall be done for them of My Father which is in heaven." "Answers," Finney stated, "were so multiplied that no one could escape the conviction that God was daily and hourly answering."[73] The same emphasis on prayer was seen at Auburn,[74] and at Finney's campaigns in the town of Troy during the autumn of 1826 and the spring of 1827, which were "marked by a very earnest spirit of prayer" and produced "a multitude of heartfelt conversions."[75] Finney was always quick to remind others that prayer was "an essential link"[76] before a revival could take place. In a letter sent to *The Revivalist*, Finney wrote that "Prayer, closet prayer, social, public, earnest, agonising, prevailing prayer, praying everywhere, lifting up holy hands without wrath or doubting, has been the great fundamental fact in the use of means."[77]

Finney's Straightforward Preaching

Finney was an imposing figure in the pulpit, standing six feet two inches tall, slim, and good-looking. According to one report, "his piercing eyes stared out from their deep sockets with frightening intensity, and when he spoke . . . guilt-ridden auditors quailed and fainted under his gaze."[78] Finney's preaching often stirred the emotions of his hearers. When he gestured, people in his congregations sometimes ducked as if he were throwing things at them. When he described the fall of sinners he often pointed to the ceiling and as he let his finger slowly drop people at the back of the building would sometimes stand to watch the final entry into hell. He sought to bring those who were not Christians to a point where they would be convicted over their sinfulness and in consequence turn

---

73. Finney, *Autobiography*, 118.
74. Hambrick-Stowe, *Charles G. Finney*, 57.
75. Hambrick-Stowe, *Charles G. Finney*, 65.
76. Finney, *Revivals of Religion*, 49.
77. *The Revivalist* (1859), 32.
78. McLoughlin, *Modern Revivalism*, 17.

to Christ for forgiveness. He believed that conversion was a work of man and that it happened in a specific moment in time.[79] Finney regarded human beings as naturally sluggish and believed that rational thinking was heavily influenced by the physical senses. He therefore believed it quite right and proper to stir the senses in order to regain the attention of people whose minds were starting to drift from the message. Finney encouraged ministers of the gospel "to address the feelings enough to secure attention, and then deal with the conscience, and probe to the quick. Appeals to the feelings alone will never convert sinners."[80] But he added, "If attention flags at any time, appeal to the feelings again, and rouse it up; but do your work with conscience."[81]

Finney firmly believed that preaching should be conversational. "Preaching to be understood," he wrote in his *Lectures on Revival*, "should be colloquial in style. A minister must preach as he would talk, if he wishes to be fully understood."[82] Looking back to his early days as a preacher Finney recalled that on one occasion at Evans Mills some of his fellow clergy complained that "I let down the dignity of the pulpit and was a disgrace to the ministerial profession, that I talked like a lawyer at the bar." However, Finney's reply was, "Show me the fruits of your ministry, and if they so far exceed mine as to give evidence that you have found a more excellent way, I will adopt your views."[83]

Pressing for Decisions

From the very outset of his ministry the aim of all Finney's revival preaching was to press his hearers to make a personal commitment to Christ and receive forgiveness for their sins. Although Finney was clear that every conversion was brought about by the Holy Spirit, he was strongly of the view every single person has the will and ability to make their own decision

---

79. Finney, *Lectures on Systematic Theology*, 290. "What is implied in regeneration. 1. The nature of the change shows that it must be instantaneous. It is a change of choice or intention. This must be instantaneous. The preparatory work of conviction and enlightening the mind may have been gradual and progressive. But when regeneration occurs, it must be instantaneous." See also 217: "There are many passages which represent the conversion of sinners as the work of men."

80. Finney, *Lectures on Systematic Theology*, 241.

81. Finney, *Lectures on Systematic Theology*, 241.

82. Finney, *Revivals of Religion*, 233.

83. Comment by Harding, *Revivals of Religion*, 163n1.

for Christ.[84] His first assignment where revival immediately broke out was six months of preaching at Evans Mills and Antwerp. He recorded, "I was obliged to take much pains in giving instruction to inquirers. . . . I tried to show them that all delay was only an evasion of present duty; that all praying for a new heart was only trying to throw the responsibility of their conversion upon God; and that all efforts to do duty, while they did not give their hearts to God, were hypocritical and delusive."[85]

As the revivals continued, Finney tried and developed new ways to bring his hearers to the point of commitment.[86] At Rome in January 1826, for example, Finney began the practice at the evening meetings of asking those who had professed conversion to Christ during that day to come forward and report themselves. This produced remarkable results with a total of nearly 500 reported conversions in the space of the month. There is no doubt that there must have been psychological pressure on the new converts to identify themselves in this way, but it was a method that proved to be singularly effective. At Troy, Finney introduced what he called "the inquiry meeting." This was a more private gathering that took place immediately after the main revival preaching came to a close. The thinking behind it was that people might feel more at ease to talk and make a personal decision away from the general public glare. It worked with great effect at Troy in the autumn of 1826 and the spring of 1827. In January 1828, Finney went to Philadelphia where his revival services took a "powerful hold." On this occasion he held what he termed "anxious meetings."[87] These were similar in style to the "inquiry meeting" but were designed to focus specifically on those who were "anxious" about their standing before God. After leaving Philadelphia, Finney spent the winter of 1829-30 at Reading, a city about forty miles to the west. On the third Sunday evening of his time there he invited any "who wanted to know how to be saved" to come to an inquiry meeting the following evening. Despite it being a snowy day, the lecture room, which was nearly as large as the body of the church above, was full. On looking around, the minister, Dr. Greer, observed "that most of the impenitent persons in his congregation were present; and among them, those who were regarded

---

84. In a sermon entitled "The Doctrine of Election," Finney denied that people were saved solely for the reason that they were of the elect while others were predestined to be eternally lost in hell (*Sermons on Important Subjects*, 209-22).

85. Finney, *Autobiography*, 62.

86. Finney, *Autobiography*, 210.

87. Finney, *Autobiography*, 248.

as the most respectable and influential." After speaking at length Finney asked all who wanted to surrender to Christ to kneel with him. There followed "an awful solemnity and stillness punctuated with sobs, sighs and weeping." Finney later recorded, "The great majority of Dr Greer's congregation were converted in the revival."[88] So effective were these "after meetings" that in the summer of 1831 he made a further development when he received an invitation to undertake supply preaching at the Third Presbyterian Church in Rochester. The "anxious seat" was to prove another very effective feature of Finney's revival meetings, as people from all sections of society, from the highest to the lowest, stood up publicly to acknowledge their willingness to follow Christ. Having done so they were invited to come forward and sit on one of the anxious seats. Rochester marked the maturing of Finney's revival techniques, and by the time the revival ended, Finney had an established reputation as an evangelist in demand in both east and west.

Publicity and Music.

Finney made wide use of publicity. In the 1820s, he had relied on the *Western Recorder* for reliable news reports of his labors. Later, when he moved east, he turned to *The New York Evangelist* for support. These two papers, together with *The Oberlin Evangelist*, he used as the means of correcting misrepresentations of his teaching and theology and of promoting revival in more distant places. His published books, particularly *Lectures on Revival*, enjoyed huge sales in both America and overseas, and created an appetite for deeper Christian experience. The *Lectures* were first published on May 15th, 1835, and 12,000 copies sold immediately in America.

Finney was also acutely aware of the importance and value of music. In particular, he looked for music with good melodies which would be easy to sing and stir the emotions. When he came to New York in 1832, he teamed up with Thomas Hastings of Utica as his music and choir director. In addition to being an excellent conductor, Hastings was writing new hymns which were beginning to catch on with the wider public who were drawn into Finney's campaigns.

---

88. Finney, *Autobiography*, 219, 224.

Independent Meeting Places

One valuable strategy that Finney learned during the revival was the use of independent premises in which to hold his meetings. Finney wrote, "I found it to be true wherever I tried it, that the best way to promote revivals of religion was to hold independent meetings; that is, meetings in large halls, where they can be obtained, to which all denominations may come."[89] Finney believed that in the United States that "the true way to labour for souls is to avoid having connection with any one particular denomination; but to preach the true Gospel, and make a stand in halls, or even in streets when the weather is favourable, where no denominational feelings and peculiarities can straiten the influences of the Spirit of God."[90]

Social Change

Although the heart of Finney's revival preaching was always to bring the sinner to repentance, his understanding of revival was also integrally tied to issues of social justice. He was firmly of the view that to overlook social justice was to cause God to withhold his blessings. His preaching brought change and improvement in all aspects of living. In some places theaters were closed. Such was the case at Rochester where both the theater and the circus were purchased by a group of wealthy Christians and then shut down because they were felt to promote dissolute and ungodly behavior.[91] Finney was a strong advocate of temperance, and many of his converts became staunch campaigners and supporters of temperance societies. In 1826, in the wake of the revival, his friend, Lyman Beecher, founded *The American Society for the Promotion of Temperance*.[92] It was his firm belief, shared by Finney, that the consumption of alcohol fueled violent crime, poverty, and domestic violence. The revival in Rochester led to the founding of several temperance societies. Finney was a strong supporter of education, with black and white men and women treated equally in every way. Following the revival in Rochester, Finney recorded, "The moral aspect of things was greatly changed. It was a young city, full of thrift,

---

89. Hambrick-Stowe, *Charles G. Finney*, 262.
90. Hambrick-Stowe, *Charles G. Finney*, 262.
91. Hambrick-Stowe, *Charles G. Finney*, 110.
92. Hambrick-Stowe, *Charles G. Finney*, 111.

enterprise, and sin. The inhabitants were intelligent and enterprising; but as the revival swept though, and converted the most influential, the change was wonderful." Many years later it was reported that "whereas our city has increased three-fold since the revival, there are not one third as many prosecutions as there had been up to that time. This is the wonderful influence that that revival had upon the community."[93]

Finney was, as we have seen, a major opponent of slavery in all its forms. At New York he was one of the founding members of *The New York Anti-Slavery Society* in 1833. Both he and his congregation were strongly opposed to slaveholding, and he frequently spoke against it. Finney, as has been noted, welcomed black men and women to the Lord's Table and refused to serve communion to slaveholders at his New York chapel, believing this to be "a decidedly good influence on individuals and the church as a whole."[94] His sermons on the subject of slavery were vivid as he spoke, for example, of "the two millions of degraded heathen in our land" who "stretch forth an agonising cry to God."[95] Another more personal aspect of Finney's social concern was seen in May 1850, when he invited the congregation at one of his services to confess and restore any money or material objects they had dishonestly taken. He reported that "almost every form of crime was thus searched out and confessed."[96] Finney recalled that he had had similar instances following one of his addresses at Rochester, New York.[97]

The Status of Women

From the beginning of his ministry Finney had given full place to women. As early as 1827, the Oneida Presbytery had criticized his decision to allow females to pray in the presence of men and to pray for individuals by name.[98] There were other ways in which Finney enhanced the role of women in his revival campaigns. Hambrick-Stowe noted that evangelical women played a key role in promoting the revival in Philadelphia by

93. Finney, *Autobiography*, 250.
94. Hambrick-Stowe, *Charles G. Finney*, 142.
95. Hambrick-Stowe, *Charles G. Finney*, 142.
96. Finney, *Autobiography*, 343.
97. Finney, *Autobiography*, 389.
98. George Gale, "Letter to Finney," 14 March, 1827, cited in McLoughlin, *Modern Revivalism*, 30.

organizing bands of visitors and praying with women for the conversion of their husbands.[99] Significantly, Finney had found when in his New York pastorate that "our ladies were not afraid to go and gather all classes from the neighbourhood round about into our meetings."[100] During his later revival meetings Finney's wife took on an increasing role preaching at large gatherings for women. The many letters she received from women friends and others involved in the revival reveal her to be a valued organizer, counselor, and prayer coordinator.[101]

An Inspirational Revival

In his role in this decade-long revival in Upper New York State Finney revealed a capacity to extend and develop some of the practices of past revivals while embracing some new ones. His campaigns were always centered on prayer, public preaching, visitation, and inquirers' meetings. Finney was strongly of the view that while men and women have free choice to commit their lives to Christ, it was vital to work in cooperation with the Holy Spirit. As he saw it, all revivals are works of God which demand a human response. One of the reasons Finney was so effective was his steadfast determination to persuade men and women to follow Christ. "I have said before," he emphasized. "that the means that I had all along used thus far in promoting revivals, were much prayer secret and social, public preaching, personal conversation, and visitation from house to house for that purpose: and when inquirers became multiplied I appointed meetings for them and invited those that were inquiring to meet where I gave them instructions suited to their necessities."[102] Religion, Finney stressed, is "a work of man." Once a person has become converted their life now "consists in obeying God."[103] This is every believer's duty.

The revival in Upper New York State was a very powerful and sustained move of God which brought many thousands to faith in Christ and spawned a huge growth in church membership across the entire nation. Its message was spread widely through Finney's writing and printed sermons, as well as journals such as *The New York Evangelist* and

99. Hambrick-Stowe, *Charles G. Finney*, 80–81.
100. Finney, *Memoirs*, 359.
101. Hambrick-Stowe, *Charles G. Finney*, 83–84.
102. Finney, *Memoirs*, 158.
103. Finney, *Revivals of Religion*, 1.

The Oberlin Evangelist. The revival transformed society by proclaiming a gospel which included justice for women and freedom for slaves. It promoted temperance and uplifted family life and relationships. It led to widespread educational endeavors at all levels, which resulted in the training of converts, many of whom became preachers who threw in their lot with the revival.

8

The Welsh Revival of 1904

THE WELSH REVIVAL BEGAN in the early months of 1904 and was characterized by waves of powerful preaching, prayer, and worship gatherings across the country, but with a particular focus in the South. One of the first places to be impacted was the church at New Quay pastored by the Reverend Joseph Jenkins (1829–1859). For some time he had been concerned about the apathy he felt in his own life and had been seeking a deeper experience of God. Then, in September 1904, Seth Joshua (1859–1925), a denominational evangelist of the Calvinistic Methodist Church, arrived and found "a remarkable "revival spirit" in evidence. He later stated that he had "never seen the power of the Holy Spirit so powerfully manifested among the people as at this place just now."[1] Joshua further noted:

> 19th Revival is breaking out here in greater power . . . the young receive the greatest measure of blessing. They break out into prayer, praise testimony and exhortation.
>
> 20th I cannot leave the building until 12 and even 1 o'clock in the morning—I closed the service several times and yet it would break out again quite beyond control of human power.
>
> 21st Yes, several souls . . . they are not drunkards or open sinners, but are members of the true church not grafted into the true Vine . . . the joy is intense.

1. Orr, *Flaming Tongue*, 3.

23rd I am of the opinion that forty conversions took place this week.²

Among those who were profoundly touched at Joshua's meetings was a young man named Evan Roberts. Although not the only human instrument God used to bring about the Welsh Revival, Evan Roberts was to become the central figure in what took place.

Evan Roberts (1878–1951)

Evan John Roberts was born to Henry and Hannah Roberts on July 8th, 1878. His parents were devoted Christians and Bible reading, family prayers, and Sunday school were a regular part of his early years. His father broke a leg in the mine, causing Evan to begin working there before his twelfth birthday. His first assignment was as a doorboy, opening and closing the metal doors for tunnel traffic. When he was nineteen, there was an explosion in the pit and he was fortunate to escape. Roberts had no interest in sports or amusements but he was an avid reader who devoured novels, poetry, and theological books such as A. A. Hodge's *The Outlines of Theology*. Roberts never married. In rest periods in the mine he would read the Bible and pray. He was well regarded by his fellow miners and became a trade unionist.

Early on he became a communicant member of Moriah Church in Loughor, which was part of the Welsh Calvinistic Methodist denomination. Later, as his Christian faith matured, he became superintendent of the Sunday school at Pisgah, Moriah's mission church. In 1900, when he had returned to Loughor, he formed a prayer circle at Pisgah which aimed to encourage members to participate in public worship as prompted by the Holy Spirit. He developed a growing, consuming interest in revival and on one occasion wrote to a friend, "For ten or eleven years I have prayed for a revival. I could sit up all night to read or talk about revivals.... It was the Spirit that moved me to think about a revival."³

After having been in the mines for twelve years, Evan Roberts took up an apprenticeship as a blacksmith with his uncle on September 15th, 1902. Soon after, however, he became convinced he should enter the church's ministry. He sat the denominational examinations in preparation to enter the Newcastle Emlyn Academy. Shortly before he began

2. Orr, *Flaming Tongue*, 4.
3. Orr, *Flaming Tongue*, 4.

his studies he had a remarkable mystical experience which lasted for a number of nights during which he was awakened at 1:00 a.m. and had periods of intense communion with God. Then, shortly after the start of his studies at the Academy, Roberts attended a meeting conducted by Seth Joshua on the 15th of September, 1904. Joshua had been concerned that there was a growing emphasis on the necessity of intellectual qualifications for the ministry and had started to pray that the Lord would choose a young man from the mines or field to raise up his work. He was unaware that the answer to his prayer was actually present in his meeting at Blaenanerch. It was a powerful occasion at the close of which Joshua prayed, "Bend us, O Lord." Through his prayer the Holy Spirit struck a deep chord in the young man Evan Roberts, and he cried out, "Bend me! Bend me! Bend me! Bend us!"[4]

Evan Roberts knew in this moment that he had reached a crisis point in his Christian life and he felt compelled to pray in public. He "felt a living power pervading my bosom"[5] and was overwhelmed by the verse, "God commendeth His Love toward us."[6] This was a defining moment, "the most sublime day of his life," and Roberts knew without a doubt that an extraordinary work was beginning."[7] He returned to Newcastle Emlyn to pray for his first team which was to consist of Sidney Evans, himself, and some young women from New Quay. He put his ministerial training on hold and withdrew his life savings of 200 pounds for their support. Principal Phillips of Emlyn Academy later wrote that "Evan Roberts was like a particle of radium in our midst. Its fire was consuming and felt abroad as something which took away sleep, cleared the channel of tears and sped golden wheels of prayer throughout the area."[8]

Sidney Evans, who later married Roberts's sister, was told by Evan Roberts that "I have a vision of all Wales being lifted up to heaven. We are going to see the mightiest revival that Wales has ever known."[9] Roberts returned home on the 31st of October, 1904, needing to convince his parents, his sisters, and his brother Dan of his mission to Wales. They were perhaps understandably uneasy about his confidence and certainty.

---

4. Jones, *Voices from the Welsh Revival*, 19–20; Orr, *Flaming Tongue*, 5.
5. Orr, *Flaming Tongue*, 5.
6. Orr, *Flaming Tongue*, 5.
7. Orr, *Flaming Tongue*, 5.
8. Orr, *Flaming Tongue*, 6.
9. Orr, *Flaming Tongue*, 6.

However, Roberts went to see the ministers of Moriah Church, its daughter church in Goreseinon, and its mission chapel in Pisgah. They granted him permission to use the premises to hold his meetings. And so began his quest to win 100,000 men and women for Christ in Wales.

Roberts's Meetings

Roberts's role in the revival has been variously interpreted. Some regard him as a catalyst or instrument of the revival, while others at the opposite end of the spectrum see him as an individual who often did little more than be present at the meetings. Roberts began his ministry with just seventeen people attending an after-meeting. He asked each of them to testify to their faith. All of them eventually did so, including Roberts's three sisters. Other meetings soon followed in Pisgah, Gorseinon, and elsewhere. Roberts was evidently confident that revival was indeed coming, for on Friday November 4th, 1904, he penned a letter to the editor of a Sunday newspaper asking for an estimate for printing notepaper. He wrote, "We are on the eve of a great and grand revival, the greatest the world has ever seen. Do not think that the writer is a mad man."[10] On the Saturday night following, Roberts addressed a crowded church on "Be filled with the Holy Spirit." The meeting lasted five hours. On the Monday night the prayer meeting went on for three hours past midnight: "so great was the number of people present that windows were broken for air."[11] *The Western Mail* of 10th of November reported the following.

> A remarkable religious revival is now taking place in Loughor. For some days a young man named Evan Roberts, a native of Loughor, has been besieged by dense crowds of people unable to obtain admission. Such excitement has prevailed that the road on which the chapel is situated has been lined with people from end to end. Roberts who speaks in Welsh, opens his discourse by saying that he does not know what he is going to say but that when he is in communion with the Holy Spirit, the Holy Spirit will speak, and he will be the medium of His Wisdom. The preacher soon after launches into a fervent and at times impassioned oration. His statements have the most stirring effects upon his listeners. Many who have disbelieved Christianity for years are returning to the fold of their younger days.

---

10. Orr, *Flaming Tongue*, 7.
11. Orr, *Flaming Tongue*, 7.

> One night, so great was the enthusiasm invoked by the young revivalist that, after his sermon which lasted two hours, the vast congregation remained praying and singing until two-thirty in the morning. Shopkeepers are closing early in order to get a place in the chapel, and tin and steel workers throng the place in working clothes. There were also reports of other shops being cleared of provisions by people who had travelled long distances to the meetings.[12]

Evan Roberts issued a fourfold call to his congregations: to confess Christ publicly and openly; to give full obedience to the Holy Spirit in order to be filled with the Spirit; to confess known sins; and to put away doubtful things.[13] Roberts also taught the fast-growing congregations to say the prayer he had taught the young people, "Send thy spirit now for Jesus' sake."[14]

From late December 1904 to May 1905, the period which spans the revival, a minimum of six meetings were held each day in many large industrial villages and even more in big towns, not counting overflow meetings and all-night meetings. Roberts and his associates could not have been present at more than 10 percent of these instances.[15]

On many occasions Roberts made use of young women assistants. At Neath, Roberts came with Annie Davies and Mary Davies.[16] At Maesteg, on another occasion, a meeting was held in Bethania Chapel. Once again Evan Roberts was accompanied by Miss Annie Davies and Miss Mary Davies. Annie Davies "delivered a brief address, urging all to accept salvation . . . delivered with simplicity."[17] The congregation were so aroused that a scene which beggars description followed. Scores were speaking, shouting, gesticulating, praying, testifying, and then all the voices were merged in a triumphant rendering of "Crown the Lord My Saviour."[18] Annie May Rees was a gifted speaker before the revival, and she accompanied Roberts on a number of occasions.[19]

---

12. *Western Mail*, 10 November, 1904.
13. Jones, *Voices from the Welsh Revival*, 33.
14. Jones, *Voices from the Welsh Revival*, 33.
15. Jones, *Voices from the Welsh Revival*, 65.
16. Jones, *Voices from the Welsh Revival*, 43.
17. Jones, *Voices from the Welsh Revival*, 46.
18. Jones, *Voices from the Welsh Revival*, 46.
19. Jones, *Voices from the Welsh Revival*, 53.

Copyright unknown. Revival Library. Org. High Street,
Bishops Waltham, Hants, SO32 1AA.

It often happened that the crowds were too densely packed to allow Roberts and his helpers to come down from the platform and move freely among the distressed sinners. When this happened he experimented for a while using a network of Christian counselors that had been used by Seth Joshua and in earlier times by the American evangelist R. A. Torrey.[20]

---

20. Jones, *Voices from the Welsh Revival*, 49.

Features of the Revival

Teams of Young People

Roberts was totally committed to the doctrine of the priesthood of all believers and always sought to share the work with others. In the early days of the revival he sent out teams of young people, including his brother Dan Roberts and Sidney Evans, who was about twenty at the time. Other helpers were even younger. Annie Davies was eighteen, Mary Roberts sixteen, and Annie May Rees and Florrie Evans both fifteen. Rees was a gifted singer and speaker who was trained by Roberts to serve as his substitute when he was ill or unable to be present.[21] Roberts was strongly committed to women's ministry and was happy for them to lead meetings without himself being present.

Music and Singing

Roberts realized the importance of music and singing at the meetings. Singing became an important and predominant aspect in the revival gatherings. It was seen as a key way to enter into God's presence. Rather than entrusting this to one individual musician, Roberts worked with a team of singers, including Priscilla Watkins, Lavinia Looker, and Annie May Rees. In some quarters the revival was termed "the singing revival."[22] Annie Davies, who was a professionally trained singer, became well-known for leading worship and singing the hymn "Here Is Love Vast as the Ocean." She was often referred to as "the nightingale of the revival."[23] The singing had a particular impact on the uncommitted who attended the meetings. The Welsh have always been known for their love of song so that it was to be expected that singing would be a major feature of the revival. Whilst it was true that singing sometimes had a hypnotic effect on the worshipers this was never intended. In the vast majority of occasions it provided people with a safe environment in which to release emotional hurts and pain.

At Dowlais, Roberts spent three days that climaxed in a meeting at Hebron Baptist Chapel, where "every traditional and much-loved revival

---

21. See Lowe, *Carriers of Fire*, 54–55.
22. Jones, *Voices from the Welsh Revival*, 54.
23. Lowe, *Carriers of Fire*, 59.

hymn was sung over and over."²⁴ D. M. Phillips called "Here Is Love Vast as the Ocean" the "Great Hymn of the Revival" because it was sung so many times at so many meetings.²⁵ At some of the gatherings when Roberts was not present the character of the worship was different. At Bethania Chapel in Morriston, for example, the hymns were sung with "a slow impressiveness."²⁶

It was not uncommon for the singing to begin well before the meetings started. A typical instance was that on Wednesday, December 14th, 1904, at Merthyr in the Taff Vale. Accompanied by his host, Mr. Edwin Morgan and by Miss Annie Davies, Roberts walked through the dark muddy streets and a surging, singing crowd followed him all the way.²⁷

Preaching

From November 1904 Roberts visited numerous chapels in the Welsh valleys preaching on the transforming power of the cross and the joy of the Holy Spirit.²⁸ Although he had no formal training he was much sought after as a preacher. He was always reluctant to schedule engagements ahead of time, his practice being rather to wait for the Spirit's prompting. Roberts rarely preached in a formal style, preferring to speak as he felt directed by the Spirit. Many of his talks were brief and not based on one particular text. He frequently spoke on the themes of Jesus' love and kingship.

Roberts thought of his mission as being first and foremost to the churches. His conviction was that once the churches were on fire for God nonbelievers would be converted. Roberts appears to have been more concerned with reviving the church and the baptism of the Spirit than converting non-Christians.

Phenomena

Religious phenomena of various kinds were observed at the meetings. An article in *The Lancet* of November 26th, 1904²⁹ described in some-

24. Jones, *Voices from the Welsh Revival*, 44.
25. Jones, *Voices from the Welsh Revival*, 43.
26. Jones, *Voices from the Welsh Revival*, 71.
27. Jones, *Voices from the Welsh Revival*, 47.
28. Adams, *Diary of Revival*, 121.
29. Hughes-Roberts, "Sketches from the History of Psychiatry," 296–98

what hostile tones "the scenes of disorder . . . meetings prolonged well into the night . . . of women taken in a state of collapse; of strong men sobbing and bearing testimony in quivering broken accents, but incidentally not neglecting their usual occupations."[30] At Pisgah "big showers came, with people crying for forgiveness, making up old quarrels, paying their debts."[31] *The Western Mail* reported that "at one meeting Roberts fell prostrate and remained on his face on the floor for some time seeming to be in agony, while on another occasion he was observed to be weeping like a child."[32]

Informality

Many of the meetings were unplanned and proceeded without any preconceived structure or organization. As in other revivals there were people who seemed unconcerned about the time as they were caught up in praise and worship. People seemed to be unaware of tiredness or hunger. Joseph Jenkins, one of the revivalists, tried more formal teaching at Tregaron, but the people soon broke into the freedom of an open meeting.

On many occasions Evan Roberts was present at the meetings but took very little part in the proceedings. He was sometimes reported as having sat for three hours without saying anything. Dr. F. B. Meyer reported that Roberts "will not go in front of the Divine Spirit but is willing to stand aside and remain in the background unless he is perfectly sure that the Spirit of God is moving him. It is a profound lesson."[33] One Englishman journeyed to South Wales looking forward to hearing Evan Roberts preach. He was taken aback when he was told that Roberts "does not tell people where to expect him. He tells them that they need the Lord Jesus Christ, and that they will find him in the nearest church."[34] At Bryn-teg Chapel, for instance, "no one had announced the meeting yet the crowds had packed the place."[35] At Gorseinon, a Mr. Webb recalled,

---

30. Hughes-Roberts, "Sketches from the History of Psychiatry," 296.
31. Jones, *Voices from the Welsh Revival*, 33.
32. Hughes-Roberts, "Sketches from the History of Psychiatry," 296.
33. Jones, *Voices from the Welsh Revival*, 29.
34. Orr, *Flaming Tongue*, 13.
35. Jones, *Voices from the Welsh Revival*, 29.

The Welsh Revival of 1904

"How remarkable that we would be at a meeting all through the night, then return home about 5 a.m. so as to be at work by 6.00 a m."[36]

Participation

The meetings were characterized by "praying, testifying, praising, singing and exhorting." The emphasis was primarily on experience, particularly the blessing of the Holy Spirit, though this did not mean Scripture was ignored. This was largely due to the fact that Roberts did not see himself as having a teaching role. He was reported to speak "like a brother" and would often walk up and down the aisles during his addresses, asking people if they were ready to stand up and confess Christ. On Sunday evening of November 6th at Moriah after taking charge of the meeting, "Roberts went from seat to seat and asking everyone personally whether they were willing to stand up and confess Jesus Christ."[37] On many occasions Roberts did not even have to preach in order to see people come to Christ; the Holy Spirit was working freely apart from him. He sometimes wept as he spoke as the Spirit enabled him to let go his emotions.

Children and Young People

In many places children and young people were greatly affected by the revival and would pray at school during their lunch breaks. "Let's play open-air meetings" became a favorite game in one school.[38] Women and young people played an important part in the character of the revival meetings.[39] Women were encouraged to follow the promptings of the Holy Spirit to sing, share their testimonies, and even on occasion to preach. In fact, the first tokens of the revival took place at a youth meeting led by Roberts on the 31st of October, 1904, at New Quay. Dr. F. B. Meyer, who visited many of the localities of the revival, observed that very little money was spent on advertising details and venues of meetings. Yet remarkably meeting houses were often overcrowded hours before the announced starting time.

---

36. Jones, *Voices from the Welsh Revival*, 34.
37. Jones, *Voices from the Welsh Revival*, 30; Lowe, *Carriers of Fire*, 41.
38. Jones, *Instrument of Revival*, 206.
39. Lowe, *Carriers of Fire*, 24–31.

The Spread of the Revival

From his home area Roberts went to the industrial valleys of South Wales where he reaped an extensive spiritual harvest. By the end of 1904, some 32,000 converts had been counted, mainly in South Wales.[40] Roberts made a significant impact when he preached to a thousand people in the great Congregational Chapel in Aberdare on the 14th of November, 1904.[41] During the revival it has been estimated that 1 in 20 of the population yielded their lives to Christ.[42] By the end of 1904, the effects of the revival were felt in Pembroke with one minister reporting he had received forty-four new members on one Sunday.[43] In Porth the chapel was filled to capacity and the movement spread up the Rhonda Valley.[44]

Evan Roberts extended his ministry into the Swansea Valley with crowds of 2,500–3,000 filling the chapel at Morriston but declined to hold meetings in the Welsh metropolis.[45] Notwithstanding there were extraordinary scenes in Cardiff's Baptist Tabernacle with 260 converts in one year. At a meeting there in January 1905, there were reported to be almost as many nationalities as on the day of Pentecost, with visitors from France, Sweden, Greece, and Italy.[46] At Bangor, in North Wales, there were reports of crowded congregations with many people praying audibly. At Anglesey, a political meeting organized in support of David Lloyd George, later to become Prime Minister, turned into a revival meeting when the audience sang a hymn.[47]

The revival reached its greatest extent in Wales in 1905. Totals of new church members were reported in the local press; 70,000 in two months, 85,000 in five, and more than 100,000 in half a year. Edwin Orr was of the view that the statistics suggested that 2,225,000, or a tenth of the population, could have been impacted.[48] *The Royal Commission on*

---

40. Evans, "Welsh Revival of 1904," 21.

41. Jones, *Voices from the Welsh Revival*, 40.

42. This figure is computed is computed on the basis of Orr's estimate of 2,225,000 being impacted by the revival (see bottom of the page). See Orr, *Flaming Tongue*, 15. One-in-twenty is considerably less than Orr appears to have suggested.

43. Orr, *Flaming Tongue*, 15.

44. Jones, *Voices from the Welsh Revival*, 228.

45. Orr, *Flaming Tongue*, 11.

46. Jones, *Voices from the Welsh Revival*, 77.

47. Jones, *Voices from the Welsh Revival*, 134.

48. Orr, *Flaming Tongue*, 15.

Religious Bodies in Wales, published in 1910, noted that the revival in 1904 and 1905 was without parallel in Wales since the revival of 1859. The revival was reported to have continued its intensity until the close of 1906.[49]

Before the end of 1905, fully one-third of the population of Wales were registered communicant members of the Anglican and Free Church denominations. Individual statistics submitted by the churches showed some remarkable influences. Among them were New Quay, where 75 percent of the population were church members. Generally speaking, membership was highest in the Welsh-speaking areas. In Cardiff, which was Anglicized, membership was at 17 percent and adherents at 35 percent of the population of 164,296.[50]

The Anglican Church in Wales was impacted by the revival to a small extent. For the twenty years prior to 1905, Anglican confirmations hovered around the 10,000 mark, but in the peak years they reached 13,000 and averaged 12,000 in the seven years following the revival. Anglicans in general, it should be said, were fairly disparaging of the revival and its long unstructured meetings along with a lack of respect for its clergy.[51]

Students at the University of Bangor were impacted. At one point all lectures were cut and 300 students gathered for prayer in a student lounge.[52] Four major Welsh Free Church denominations announced a total of 80,000 additions in the months of revival.[53] The Free Church Sunday schools increased their attendance by 10 percent during the revival years.[54] The Calvinistic Methodists and the Congregationalist leaders expressed their support for the revival as did the Wesleyan Methodists and the Quakers.[55]

Roberts was convinced "that the Spirit which was so evident in his meetings would spread not only to England, but throughout the world."[56] His conviction proved to be correct. The revival clearly had a wide impact, with visitors from around the world coming to visit the main

---

49. *Royal Commission on Religious Bodies in Wales*, 33, in Orr, *Flaming Tongue*, 15.
50. Orr, *Flaming Tongue*, 15.
51. Brown, *Religion and Society*, 64.
52. Jones, *Voices from the Welsh Revival*, 98.
53. Orr, *Flaming Tongue*, 47–49.
54. Orr, *Flaming Tongue*, 17.
55. Orr, *Flaming Tongue*, 27.
56. Evans, "Welsh Revival of 1904," 22.

centers of activity.⁵⁷ Many parts of England were impacted. A group of 300 Welshmen went to the 1905 Keswick convention. Dr. A .T. Pierson, who led a midnight prayer meeting, reported, "nothing like this had ever been seen at Keswick before."⁵⁸ In 1905, the Archbishop of Canterbury held a conference to discuss the revival and found unanimous support. In the summer of the following year a conference of English bishops met to discuss the revival. Baptist membership increased from 360,789 in 1903 to 400,348 in 1908.⁵⁹ They embraced the revival wholeheartedly, and the Baptist Union Assembly devoted a session to discuss it. There was a revival movement in the Metropolitan Tabernacle, where Thomas Spurgeon was the pastor, with meetings lasting till three in the morning and 720 professed conversions in a short period. Quakers welcomed the movement and the Salvation Army responded with a headline in *War Cry*, "Spread the Revival Spirit; Many Corps Aflame with Revival Fervour." The year 1905 was heralded as "A Memorable Year with Notable Advances."⁶⁰ Both the Primitive Methodists and the Wesleyans witnessed a significant impact on their membership with the Primitive Methodist Conference of 1905 reporting an increase of 50,021 members in 1905.⁶¹

Social Impacts of the Revival

At Ammanford, swearing in the mines gave place to praise, and the taverns were emptied of rowdy customers. In the wake of the revival a *Cardiff Citizens Union* was formed to suppress drunkenness, immorality, and gambling. It succeeded in closing down a number of brothels and shutting down sixty taverns. Swansea police noted that there had not been a single charge for drunkenness during the 1905 New Year holiday. The chief constable of Cardiff showed that the number of convictions for drunkenness in the populous county of Glamorgan declined from 11,282 in 1904 to 8,164 in 1905 and further to 5,490 in 1906.⁶² Sir Marchant Williams, a magistrate, spoke of the decline in the number of convictions in his jurisdiction:

57. Jones, *Voices from the Welsh Revival*, 144.
58. Orr, *Flaming Tongue*, 44.
59. Orr, *Flaming Tongue*, 47–48.
60. Orr, *Flaming Tongue*, 48.
61. Orr, *Flaming Tongue*, 48.
62. Orr, *Flaming Tongue*, 18.

> In the month of February 1905, the total number of cases of drunkenness and disorderly conduct, for example, dealt with at Merthyr, Abercynon, and Mountain Ash, was 164; in the corresponding month of last year the total number of such cases dealt with at these courts was 212. This means a reduction of 23 per cent or so.[63]

Instances of drunkenness in Wales were in excess of 20,000 a year before the revival but dropped 33 percent in the years immediately following.[64]

The Miners Associations moved away from their traditional practice and refused to hold meetings in licensed premises. Mary Jones, a leading figure in North Wales, expressed her surprise at the social effect that the revival had brought:

> The policemen tell me that the public houses are nearly empty, the streets are quiet and swearing is rarely heard . . . the pit ponies could no longer understand the miners' instructions because of the absence of oaths and curses. . . . At Llanfair in Anglesey all public houses except one were closed. . . . It was claimed that three months of the revival had done more to sober the county than the temperance effort of many years.[65]

Edwin Orr, using statistics from the Registrar-General, showed that there was a decline in the number of illegitimate births in every county in Wales 1904–7.[66] Another social aspect of the Welsh Revival, which was also later witnessed in the later East African Revival,[67] was the confession of sin and in some cases costly confessions of wrongdoing were acknowledged. In a number of cases long-standing debts were repaid and compensation made for injustices. In Swansea it was found that many working folk were taking their aged parents out of the workhouse to which they had been unkindly assigned.

---

63. Davies, (Awstin), *Religious Revival of 1904*, published by *The Western Daily Press*, Issue 18 (titled "Drunkards Reformed").
64. Orr, *Flaming Tongue*, 18.
65. Griffin, *Firestorms of Revival*, 227.
66. Orr, *Flaming Tongue*, 18.
67. Bewes, *Under the Thorn Tree*, 9.

A Church-Focused Revival

The Welsh Revival began in the churches. From the beginning Roberts was of the view that if the churches could only come alive with the presence of Christ the world outside was soon come to faith. Dr. G. Campbell Morgan of Westminster Chapel asked the question, "What is the character of this revival?" He gave his own answer.

> It is a church revival. I do not mean by that merely a revival among church members . . . meetings are held in the chapels, all up and down the valleys, and it began among church members; and when it touches the outside man, it makes him a church member at once. . . . It is a movement in which the true functions and forces of the church are being exercised and fulfilled.[68]

However, it was an awakening that lacked organization or central control. Campbell Morgan commented that it was "characterised by a series of perpetual interruptions and disorderliness."[69] It was marked out by long meetings of earnest and united prayer which often went past the hour of midnight. Such meetings were noted in many places in the years immediately preceding and these grew in fuller measure during the revival itself.

Roberts's Leadership

Roberts was acutely aware of the dangers of taking the center stage and public acclaim. Although he was known across the world he refused to give interviews to the newspapers whether they were British, European, or further overseas. He firmly avoided being photographed with his family. Visitors to the revival were astounded to witness crowded and powerful meetings where people sang and testified, while the leader said very little, remained silent, or sometimes did not come when people were expecting him. Roberts remained free of even a hint of scandal. He did not live off revival giving, but he did rely on gifts and support from a group of friends.

---

68. Orr, *Flaming Tongue*, 20.
69. Orr, *Flaming Tongue*, 20.

Doubts and Criticisms Expressed about Roberts

Some critics claimed that Roberts was "a clairvoyant and a clairaudient,"[70] while others held that he possessed the charismatic gift of discernment. The journalist W. T. Stead believed Roberts had a genuine gift of discernment. He reported that Roberts had discerned dishonesty on the part of one of the house-to-house visitors in the preparations for his Liverpool meetings. He even correctly revealed that the young man had forged a signature on a previous occasion. Roberts also gained a reputation for his interest in handshakes and holding people's hands during a conversation. He had written on one occasion, "There is power and a secret in a handshake... It is the Holy Spirit who has taught me how to shake hands."[71]

Roberts received some criticism for his handling of the meetings. Some psychological journals were of the view that the converts' experiences were either self-induced or resulted from Roberts's rhetoric. It is generally recognized that the fervent atmosphere of revival meetings with exuberant worship can have a releasing and cathartic impact in the lives of the congregation. On such occasions, deep hurts, unconscious guilt, emotional pain, and scars from the past can be released often with shouts and other manifestations. Some may possibly have responded to Roberts's preaching through autosuggestion, but it has been pointed out that the average tough Welsh mine workers and their families were more likely to have been hardened against religious enthusiasm.

There were of course critics of the revival. In January 1905, for example, the Rev. Peter Price, the minister of Bethania Chapel, put down the movement as "a sham revival, a mockery, a blasphemous travesty of the real thing, it being the work of its chief figure Evan Roberts." In contrast he claimed that the revival in his own church was the real one. He provoked a storm of protest. A magistrate in Merthyr Tydfil, Sir Thomas Marchant Williams, replied "that judged by results in a court Evan Roberts was a success in the way that he was not."[72]

Inevitably, living life at Roberts's pace was going to have serious consequences, and by the later months of 1905 there were reports that Roberts was suffering from ill health brought about by incessant travel, irregular hours, long meetings, and the strain of working a sixteen-hour day. Other leading individuals in the revival also suffered from stress,

---

70. Orr, *Flaming Tongue*, 21.
71. Hughes-Roberts, "Sketches from the History of Psychiatry," 296–98.
72. Matthews, *I Saw the Welsh Revival*, 110–11.

among them Sidney Evans and Samuel Jenkins, both of whom were temporarily sidelined with nervous tension. Significantly, when Evan Roberts was holding meetings in Liverpool his friends persuaded him to have a medical examination. He did so and his examiners reported: "We find him mentally and physically quite sound. He is suffering from the effects of overwork, and we consider it advisable that he should have a period of rest."[73] Roberts did take time out for a few weeks but then resumed the task with his previous vigor, writing to a friend, "The mountains are high, my hope is higher; The Mountains are strong—my faith is stronger; The Mountains will depart—my God never."[74]

In assessing Roberts we need to take note of the fact that in a number of ways he lacked discernment, wisdom, and accountability. If he had developed better self-management skills the revival might well have lasted longer and taken deeper roots. It was not until he suffered a complete breakdown that he sought advice and help. It would have been wise for Roberts to have had greater accountability and to have shared more of the ministry with his trusted friends. This could have been achieved through his local churches or his personal network.

The revival is sometimes referred to as "The Evan Roberts Revival" despite his constant assertion that it was God's revival. R. B. Jones pointed out that Roberts would say "he was more the child than the founder of the work."[75] On another occasion Roberts spoke humbly, "I am only one agent in what is going to be a multitude . . . Not I, but God working in me . . . It is his work and it is His glory."[76]

Roberts's role in the revival did decline but it did not signal its end. Others took up his mantle and continued the work of preaching and teaching. Among them were Keri Jones, Joseph Jenkins, Seth Joshua, and Nantlais Williams (1874–1959). In the extreme Southwest "extraordinary meetings" were held by Joshua with a report that at one of them "as many as twelve hundred were on their knees praying simultaneously."[77]

There were criticisms of the revival from some sociologists who treated the Welsh Revival as "an outbreak of repressed racial passions

---

73. Hughes, *Evan Roberts*, 89, in Orr, *Flaming Tongue*, 25.
74. Hughes, *Evan Roberts*, 89, in Orr, *Flaming Tongue*, 25.
75. Jones, *Rent Heavens*, 16–17.
76. Jones, *Instrument of Revival*, 94.
77. *The Advance*, 16 February, 1905 in Orr, *Flaming Tongue*, 27.

and hopes, which were later diverted into political causes."[78] There was of course at the time a struggle over Welsh identity which included the use of the Welsh language. At the same time the Anglican Church in Wales was struggling to free itself from the Church of England. There are those who have argued that people warmed to the revival because it was in their own language.

Jessie Penn-Lewis (1861–1927)

One of the more puzzling aspects of the Welsh Revival is the impact which Mrs. Penn-Lewis came to have over Evan Roberts. Born in Neath, the daughter of a Calvinistic Methodist minister, she moved to Leicester and was married to the city treasurer. She eventually became both a keynote speaker and organizer of the Keswick Convention and the Welsh Keswick which was held at Llandrindod Wells. She was determined to meet Roberts because she declared herself concerned about things in his ministry. He steadfastly ignored her invitations to Leicester until by the end of January 1906 he became mentally and spiritually rundown at the close of his Caernarvonshire Mission. When this turned out to be a nervous breakdown he went to live with Penn-Lewis and her husband in their Leicester home. For many years she held a great deal of influence over Roberts. Indeed, at times he seemed to be controlled by her. He lived the life of a near recluse until his return to Wales in 1925.

Penn-Lewis persuaded Roberts that his spiritual gifts were the cause of his depression and that the supernatural experiences of the Welsh Revival were spurious and that he had been deceived. Her well-known book *War on the Saints*, which she published in 1909, discredited the revival and much of the phenomena associated with it. Written with Roberts, and endorsed by him, it is doubtful that it contains much of his own thoughts or input. It's difficult to know exactly what Penn-Lewis's motivations were, but there can be no doubt that Roberts's support and alleged co-authorship undoubtedly increased her book sales and gained her more preaching engagements. Penn-Lewis ministered in Scandinavia, Russia, North America, as well as in Europe.

As Roberts withdrew into the confines of Penn-Lewis's residence the revival waned and eventually came to a halt. On this ground a case can be made for Roberts being a catalyst of the revival since when he withdrew

---

78. See Jones, *Voices from the Welsh Revival*, 256–57.

the revival petered out. Surprisingly, Roberts remained with the Penn-Lewises for another eight years, helping with her *Overcomer* magazine.[79] By the 1920s, Roberts began writing his own pamphlets whilst staying in Brighton. He moved back to Wales following Penn-Lewis's death in 1926, but he disappeared from public life and lived quietly in Cardiff. He died in a Cardiff hospital on 29th January, 1951, aged seventy-two, in a mentally fit condition. A memorial in his honor stands outside Loughor Chapel.

Inspiration from the Revival

The Context on the Welsh Revival

Notwithstanding J. V. Morgan's contention that "The Welsh Revival of 1904–5 was not preceded by any peculiar apathy,"[80] it has to be said that the close of the nineteenth century in Wales was a time of great social change which created mental and moral uncertainty. Industrial strife was on the increase and the population was becoming increasingly urbanized. Socialism was a growing feature, offering material betterment at a time when many churches were still upholders of the old hierarchical social status quo. Many were also angered at the privileges granted to the Church of England in Wales which was only attended by small numbers compared with the Free Churches. There is no doubt that the alarm felt by many people in the face of these developments attracted them to a revival which offered the comfort and assurance of an immediate experience. This darkening horizon is significant because by definition a revival is about bringing back to life what is dead or dying. All the great revivals have necessarily been preceded by a downward spiral in religious, social, spiritual, and economic life.

Roberts's Leadership Qualities

Roberts exemplified some good leadership qualities. He was a Welsh-speaking coalminer who had worked in the pits from the age of thirteen and knew the struggles of life in the valleys. He had a deep and vigorous spiritual life. For thirteen years he had been steeped in prayer, earnestly

---

79. Liardon, *God's Generals*, 101.
80. Cited in Kay, *Pentecostalism*, 62.

pleading for a move of God.[81] He did not believe that he was the source of the revival but rather merely an "agent" of it. He remained humble and obedient to the Holy Spirit and always consciously did his utmost to give the Spirit room to direct the emphasis of each meeting. On the other hand, he was sometimes overly dependent on what he perceived to be the Spirit's promptings. This factor, common in many revivals, meant that there were occasions when he lacked accountability and discernment from others. It was this failing which contributed to his having a breakdown and eventually accepting the help offered by Mrs. Jessie Penn-Lewis.

One of the lessons which stands out in this and a number of other revivals is the danger of leadership burnout. Roberts himself suffered from periods of acute exhaustion at the beginning of 1906. Had he paced himself and established a more satisfactory work-life balance the revival might well have continued longer and achieved an even greater impact. The same criticism could be made of other major leaders in revival times, including George Whitefield and more recently Douglas Campbell in the Hebridean revival.

Evans may be right, at least in some degree, in his assertion that Roberts was guilty of a "culpable neglect of the divinely-ordained instrument of preaching,"[82] although there is a harshness in his comment. This said, we need to accept the fact that Roberts understood his primary aim to be that of reviving the church rather than teaching the faith to church congregations or converting the masses. This may partly account for the fact that Roberts spent little time instructing and discipling new converts. Clearly, therefore, Roberts's role in the revival was not a ministry of the word but a ministry of the gifts and presence of the Holy Spirit. Eifion Evans (1931–2017) was probably correct in his assessment of the revival, writing that

> Both during and after the Revival, clear teaching on the meaning of regeneration and justification, on the true nature of Christian experience, and the Christian's walk and warfare in a sinful world, would have been salutary. Sadly, these areas were neglected. Instead there was much loose talk about the "baptism of the Spirit" and "being filled with the Spirit." . . . An obsession with instant experiences of the Spirit, at the expense of the gradual,

---

81. Joyner, *Power to Change the World*, chap. 3.
82. Evans, *Welsh Revival of 1904*, 184.

progressive ministry of the Spirit in and to the believer in sanctifying grace, proved highly detrimental to future stability.[83]

Clearly Roberts lacked sufficient theological training to provide such a biblical backbone to the revival, yet there were other leaders who shared in the work who could have done so. For reasons not altogether clear, they did not. Possibly it was due to a fear that such teaching might quench the work of the Spirit.

Nevertheless, Roberts inspires in us the importance of prayer which is clearly the one essential ingredient in every great revival. It was because Roberts learned the practice of prevailing prayer that so many of those who attended his meetings came to faith in Christ. He was also undoubtedly a man who carried the presence of Christ with him.

Theological Content

During the revival, W. T. Stead had seriously questioned Roberts about the lack of teaching, preaching, and control over those leading the meetings. Roberts had responded, "Why should I teach when the Spirit is teaching? What they need is salvation. . . . It is not knowledge they lack."[84] The reality of the situation, however, was that many of those who were impacted by the revival needed others who could help them reflect and process their experiences. They needed a Jonathan Edwards, a George Whitefield, or one of the Wesleys to help them measure and weigh their newfound experiences in the light of Scripture. In fact, Roberts was later happy to state with Penn-Lewis that "every believer must test all teachers to-day for himself by the Word of God and their attitude to the atoning Cross of Christ, and other fundamental truths of the Gospel."[85] With the passing of time, Roberts, possibly also prompted by Penn-Lewis, wrote in *War on the Saints* that there was a lack of discernment in some of the meetings which allowed demonic activity to mingle with genuine moves of the Spirit. "The aftermath of the Revival in Wales which was a true work of God," he wrote, "revealed numbers of honest souls swept off their feet by evil supernatural powers, which they were not able to discern from the true working of God."[86] J. C. Metcalfe stated in the preface to

83. Evans, "Welsh Revival of 1904," 23–24.
84. Stead and Morgan, *Welsh Revival*, 79.
85. Penn-Lewis and Roberts, *War on the Saints*, 14.
86. Penn-Lewis and Roberts, *War on the Saints*, 48.

War on the Saints, "An aftermath of the Welsh Revival at the dawn of the present century was the rise of extreme cults."[87]

A related aspect to the limited theological content was the lack of a support structure where those new to the faith could interact with others who had greater spiritual knowledge and understanding. At the very least this would have provided a rudimentary theological grounding and accountability. It was something which could have been learned from the Wesleys and Whitefield, who set up a network of class and small group meetings with trained and leaders.

Impacted Culture and Society

When all is said and done this awakening in Wales bore all the marks of a genuine revival. It made a significant impact on the life, worship, and culture of Wales and countries beyond. Although this awakening was not nurtured, matured, and extended as well as it could have been, it produced a steep decline in drunkenness and crime. Family and work relationships were greatly improved, and conditions in the mines and on the factory floors were upgraded and humanized. There can also be no doubting that the Welsh Revival was a sovereign move of God which significantly stirred not merely the spiritual life of the British Isles but that of a number of other nations across the globe. Indeed, it has been called "the first truly world-wide awakening."[88] The Bishop of St David's declared the movement "convincing evidence that it is a manifestation of the Spirit."[89] Archdeacon Owen Evans and Lord Hugh Cecil, Anglican members of the Royal Commission on Religious Bodies in Wales, stated in 1910 that the revival was "a powerful spiritual movement, which attracted deep and wide interest among Christian people outside Wales, and cannot but have left thousands of lives permanently much better for it."[90] It brought marked impetus to the evangelical cause in China,[91] Korea,[92] and India.[93]

---

87. Penn-Lewis and Roberts, *War on the Saints*, 9.

88. Hopkins, *Industrialisation and Society*, 137.

89. Orr, *Flaming Tongue*, 16.

90. *Royal Commission on Religious Bodies in Wales*, 135, cited in Orr, *Flaming Tongue*, 17.

91. Goforth, *By My Spirit*, 33.

92. McClymond, "Christian Revival and Renewal Movements," 254.

93. See Anderson, *Introduction to Pentecostalism*, 37.

It strengthened the Christian cause in Japan and brought awakenings in South Africa and South America.[94] Very importantly, it helped to ignite the Azusa Street Revival in the United States, which followed in 1906 and birthed the modern Pentecostal movement.[95]

---

94. See Joyner, *Power to Change the World*, chap. 2.
95. See for example Robeck, *Azusa Street Mission and Revival*.

9

The Azusa Street Revival

EARLY IN 1906, WILLIAM Seymour, a black preacher, was invited to stay and teach in Los Angeles. Meetings were held in April at 214 Bonnie Brae Street where he and several others received the baptism of the Holy Spirit and spoke in tongues. Reports of the speaking in tongues soon spread through the neighborhood and black and white men and women thronged the streets to hear Seymour speak.[1] The core of his message was that the only biblical evidence of the baptism of the Holy Spirit was speaking in tongues. It may not have seemed very significant to the humble group of black and white men and women who attended the meetings, but, as often happens, the things which many regard as foolish or insignificant turn out to be of paramount importance. Such indeed proved to be the case. The early days were marked by fervent prayer, speaking in tongues, earnest new hymns, and the healing of the sick. Azusa people called it "know salvation." As their journal, *The Apostolic Faith,* put it, "If God for Christ's sake has forgiven you, you know it. And if you do not know it better than anything else in this world, you are still in your sins." Frank Bartleman who was at Azusa Street from the beginning, wrote, "In the early days of Azusa you could hardly keep the saints off their knees. Whenever two saints met, they invariably went to prayer."[2]

As the succeeding pages will show, it was from these inauspicious, humble beginnings that what proved to be one of the most impactful

1. *The Apostolic Faith* 1.2 (1906).
2. Bartleman, *Azusa Street Revival,* 136, 146.

and influential revivals in the history of the Christian church was born. It birthed the modern Pentecostal, apostolic, and the later charismatic movements which followed in its wake. Those who came to Azusa Street carried the revival back to every corner of America while others fanned out across the globe. Not only did thousands of converts form new congregations, many of the historic denominational churches across the world discovered a new vitality and spiritual reality through the baptism of the Holy Spirit. Seymour and his followers, it should be noted, believed in a three-stage way of salvation: justification, sanctification, and baptism of the Holy Spirit. Strangely, perhaps, many of the groups which emerged from Azusa reduced the three stages to two, maintaining that conversion and sanctification (being made holy) occurred at the same time. William Durham, who played a strong part in the revival, believed that from the moment of their conversion a man or woman was totally acceptable to the Lord. They may not be obviously or outwardly sanctified (holy), but their old nature had been crucified and the Holy Spirit implanted in their heart. Durham was expelled by Seymour from his Apostolic Faith Church.

Why Los Angeles?

At the beginning of the twentieth century, Los Angeles was already a fast-growing and rapidly expanding city of some 228,000.[3] Many settlers were arriving from the Midwest. An estimated one-third of the population professed to have some kind of religious membership.[4] Many others belonged to newly arising sects which were not included in the official statistics. The diaries and writings of holiness seekers such as Florence Crawford and Frank Bartleman give glimpses of the burgeoning number of apostolic and holiness missions scattered through the metropolis. Bartleman visited Peniel Mission on 227 South Main Street in December 1904, and shortly afterwards reported that "souls began to weep their way to Calvary."[5] A short time later he reported that a powerful awakening had broken out in the Lake Avenue Methodist Episcopal Church in Pasadena. There was no dominant preacher, but he found "a wonderful work of the Spirit" and "the

---

3. *Los Angeles Herald*, 15 April 1906.
4. *Los Angeles Herald*, 18 April 1906.
5. Bartleman, *Azusa Street Revival*, 1, 8–9.

altar full of seeking souls."[6] Bartleman also preached a number of times at Lamanda Park where "the fire fell in a wonderful way."[7]

The Welsh Revival

Many Americans were inspired by accounts of the Welsh Revival of 1904, taken from the British press, and began to pray for "the latter-day rains"[8] of the last days to fall on the nation. Others were enthused by reading S. B. Shaw's *Great Revival in Wales*.[9] Joseph Smale, the pastor of the First Baptist Church of Los Angeles, returned from Wales in June 1905. He had conversed with Evan Roberts and was now in earnest for a similar move of God's Spirit in his own church.[10] On April the 8th, Bartleman heard F. B. Mever from London preach a sermon in which he described the great revival going on in Wales. Bartleman wrote, "My soul was stirred to its depths, having read of this revival shortly before."[11] This inspired him to write to Evan Roberts, asking him to pray for California, and he received Roberts's reply: "Congregate the people together who are willing to make a total surrender. Pray, wait and receive God's promises."[12] Someone sent Bartleman 5,000 pamphlets on "The Revival in Wales," and he distributed them among the city's churches where "they had a wonderful quickening influence."[13] In August 1905, he received a second letter from Roberts in which he expressed how pleased he was "to learn the good news of how you are beginning to experience wonderful things."[14] It was clear there was a feeling running throughout much of the city that God was about to do something extraordinary.

In the Welsh Revival no one knew if the anticipated preacher would be present, but the people came to see what God would do. The leading British Nonconformist, G. Campbell Morgan, paid a short visit to Wales "and was deeply stirred by the movement's intensity." "It is," he declared,

---

6. Bartleman, *Azusa Street Revival*, 11.
7. Bartleman, *Azusa Street Revival*, 14.
8. Bartleman, *Azusa Street Revival*, 52.
9. Blumhofer, *Assemblies of God*, 1:100.
10. Bartleman, *Azusa Street Revival*, 15.
11. Bartleman, *Azusa Street Revival*, 10.
12. Bartleman, *Azusa Street Revival*, 17.
13. Bartleman, *Azusa Street Revival*, 20.
14. Bartleman, *Azusa Street Revival*, 25.

"Pentecost continued, without a moment's doubt."[15] This spontaneity and informality in place of a pattern of regular preaching and systematic teaching impacted the ethos of the revival worship of Los Angeles.

William Seymour

William J. Seymour (1870–1920) was born to Simon and Phyllis Seymour in Centerville, Louisiana. It was an area brutalized by the slave traffic and the rampages of the Klu Klux Klan. His parents had been freed from slavery just a few years earlier but continued to work on the plantations. Seymour lacked formal education but taught himself a great deal through reading the Bible. At an early point he came to a faith in Jesus, whom he believed was the only liberator of the human race.[16] At the age of twenty-five, he did what few black men did and left his Louisiana homeland and struck out north for the thriving city of Indianapolis. After a short spell there as a waiter he settled in Cincinnati, Ohio, where he joined a holiness group known as *The Evening Lights,* which later came to be known as the *Church of God Reformation Movement.* Although they did not wear rings or makeup and did not dance or play cards, they were people of joy and happiness in their faith. Seymour was ordained by the Evening Lights and began traveling as an itinerant, providing his own support.

On the course of his travels Seymour reached Houston where he met a Mrs. Lucy Farrow who attended meetings run by the evangelist Charles F. Parham. Parham had recently opened a Bible school in Houston and at Farrow's insistence Seymour enrolled. He did not agree with everything Parham taught, but he did accept Parham's teaching on Pentecost and the Holy Spirit. Shortly after completing his studies, Seymour received a letter from a Miss Neeley Terry, urging him to come to Los Angeles to be the pastor of a congregation that had separated from a Nazarene church. A large congregation assembled to hear his first sermon which was based on Acts 2:4. In it Seymour taught that a person was not baptized in the Holy Spirit unless they had spoken in tongues, although at this stage he had not yet received the gift himself.

---

15. See Campbell Morgan, "The Lesson of Revival," in Blumhofer, *Assemblies of God,* 1:100.

16. "The Inside Story of the Outpouring of the Holy Spirit, Azusa Street," April 1906, in *The Apostolic Faith* 1 (1939) 1–3.

William Seymour. Unknown Source. Public Domain.

Returning to the church after lunch with the Lee family, Seymour found that the building had been padlocked and he excluded from any further preaching. In light of this, the Lee family felt it was their duty to offer him a place in their home at 214 North Bonnie Brae Street. Seymour accepted their offer and meetings led by him began in late February 1906. He began by leading them in a ten-day fast to seek for the baptism of the Holy Spirit. On the third day Mr. Lee asked Seymour to visit him and pray for his healing. Seymour anointed Lee with oil and prayed for him. He was immediately healed and so he laid hands on him and he spoke out loudly in tongues. That evening, when they met at Bonnie Brae, Seymour led the worship in testimony and songs. Lee and several others spoke in tongues and for three days they rejoiced in "early Pentecost restored."[17]

17. Liardon, *Great Azusa Street Revival*, 25.

News spread rapidly, crowds began to fill every room in the house, and many more gathered outside. There was loud shouting interlaced with times of quiet, with many falling under the power of the Spirit, some of whom remained motionless for three to five hours. At last, on the 12th of April, 1906, Seymour experienced his own baptism in the Holy Spirit. It was now obvious that a larger premises had to be found as soon as possible. Eventually Seymour found the disused Methodist Church at 312 Azusa Street. This was to be the location and focus of the famous revival which impacted both America and the worldwide church. Later, in the spring of 1907, Seymour and his congregation were able to purchase the building for $15,000.[18]

Azusa Street Mission, 1907. Unknown source. Public domain.

The Revival Spreads

The disused church had been used as a stable and storage warehouse while the upstairs remained as a small accommodation. Seymour and his little flock soon cleared the ground floor of the discarded building materials and other debris. Seating was provided in the form of large

---

18. See article in *The Apostolic Faith* 1.6 (1907).

planks resting on empty nail kegs. Two empty packing boxes served as a pulpit.[19] Frank Bartleman, a local lay preacher, attended the meetings and "found God working mightily." He was particularly impressed with Seymour's humility, the complete informality, and the lack of any formalized structure to the worship.[20] The worship, which sometimes lasted all day, focused on "tarrying," spontaneous singing of new hymns and songs without musical accompaniment, messages in tongues, and prayers for the healing of the sick and other needs.[21] The sermons were in English, or in tongues with interpretation.

The Los Angeles press picked up the story, announcing "a New Sect on Azusa Street."[22] The following day, however, there was a major earthquake in San Francisco which for several weeks diverted the attention of the papers elsewhere. That, however, did not stop hundreds fleeing to Azusa to repent of their sins, hear the message of the gospel, and receive the anointing of the Holy Spirit. Frank Bartleman, who had been attending the Azusa Street meetings, immediately capitalized on the situation by distributing his tract, *The Last Call*, in 25,000 lots.[23] He wrote, "The San Francisco earthquake was surely the voice of God to the people on the Pacific Coast. It was used mightily in conviction, for the gracious after revival."[24] "A very 'dead-line,'" he observed, "seemed to be drawn around Azusa Mission by the Spirit. When men came within three blocks of the place they were seized with conviction."[25] Scores of people were seen dropping prostrate in the streets before they even got to the mission. Many would rise, speaking in tongues without any assistance from those inside the building.[26] Things had moved slowly in the early weeks, with relatively small numbers attending, but gradually the tide arose. Bartleman wrote in June 1906:

> The work was getting clearer and stronger at "Azusa." God was working mightily. It seemed that everyone had to go to "Azusa." Missionaries were gathered there from Africa, India, and the

19. Anderson, *Vision of the Disinherited*, 66.
20. Blumhofer, *Assemblies of God*, 1:98.
21. Noll, *Old Religion in a New World*, 151, and see also Wacker, *Heaven Below*.
22. Blumhofer, *Assemblies of God*, 1:99.
23. Bartleman, *Azusa Street Revival*, 47.
24. Bartleman, *Azusa Street Revival*, 49.
25. Bartleman, *Azusa Street Revival*, 49.
26. Tinney, "In the Tradition of William J. Seymour," 17, in Liardon, *Great Azusa Street Revival*, 36.

islands of the sea. Preachers and workers had crossed the continent, and come from distant islands, with an irresistible drawing to Los Angeles. . . . They had come up for "Pentecost," though they little realised it. It was God's call. Holiness meetings, tents and missions began to close up for lack of attendance. Their people were at "Azusa." Brother and Sister Garr closed the Burning Bush hall, came to "Azusa," received the "baptism," and were soon on their way to India to spread the fire. Even Brother Smale had to come to "Azusa," to look up his members. He invited them back home, promised them liberty in the Spirit, and for a time God wrought mightily at the New Testament Church also.[27]

In July, Bartleman reported to the *Way of Faith*, "Pentecost has come to Los Angeles."[28] The news of it spread fast in both the secular and religious press. Every day trains unloaded large numbers of visitors who had come from all parts of the continent.[29] People from every class across the world wanted to hear Seymour speak.[30]

An upper room was opened on the top floor for those who were "tarrying for their Pentecost." The mission was open twenty-four hours a day, and the revival continued day and night. Meetings ran from ten in the morning and often ran till late in the night and sometimes until two or three in the morning. People spoke in tongues, interpreted, prophesied, cast out demons, healed innumerable diseases, played musical instruments, and harmoniously sang new songs composed spontaneously by the Spirit in what was known as "the heavenly chorus."[31] Members of Azusa carried small bottles of oil with them, visited the sick, and offered to pray for any who were unwell. There was a strong emphasis on healing and handkerchiefs were sent in to be blessed and distributed to the sick.[32] *The Apostolic Faith* reported, "Many have laid aside their glasses and had their eyesight perfectly restored. The deaf have had their healing restored" and "Canes, crutches, medicine bottles, and glasses are being thrown aside as God heals. That is the safe way. No need to keep an old crutch or medicine

---

27. Bartleman, *Azusa Street Revival*, 49–50.
28. Anderson, *Vision of the Disinherited*, 67.
29. Tinney, "In the Tradition of William J. Seymour," 17, in Liardon, *Great Azusa Street Revival*, 36.
30. Lake, *Adventures with God*, 18, in Liardon, *Great Azusa Street Revival*, 37.
31. Anderson, *Vision of the Disinherited*, 68.
32. Blumhofer, *Assemblies of God*, 1:104.

bottle of any kind after God heals you."[33] A lengthy article in the same paper, entitled "The Precious Atonement," included this following lines:

> Thank God, we have a living Christ among us to heal our diseases. He will heal every case. The prophet has said, "with his stripes we are healed" and it was fulfilled when Jesus came. . . . Now if Jesus bore our sicknesses, why should we bear them? So we get full salvation through the atonement of Jesus.[34]

Seymour was clear that through Jesus' atoning death we receive forgiveness, sanctification, and healing for our bodies. "Sickness and disease," he declared, "are destroyed through the precious atonement of Jesus."[35] Despite the fervent Pentecostal emphasis Seymour kept the cross central in his preaching and teaching. "When we leave the blood out," he wrote, "Satan has power to switch us into fanaticism, but no powers of hell are able to make their way through the blood."[36] "Through the precious atonement," he asserted, "we have freedom from all sin, though we are living in this world."[37] In these early days it was observed, "you could hardly keep the saints off their knees. Whenever two saints met, they invariably went to prayer. This fervent desire for prayer gradually diminished in intensity as the year passed.[38]

At an early point Seymour invited his mentor Charles Parham to come to Los Angeles. As things turned out, Parham was appalled and disappointed both by the worship style and the interracial character of the services. Sitting at the front he saw what he perceived as "manifestations of the flesh, spiritual control and hypnotism at the altar." Parham was clearly a racist and denounced Seymour as a "Pope" and Azusa as "a counterfeit Pentecost" where "men and women, whites and blacks, knelt together or fell across one another."[39] Bartleman corrected this accusation, pointing out that in fact the hypnotists had nothing to do with the mission. They were outsiders who "came to test the extent of their influence."[40] Parham attended and preached at no more than three Azusa Street services

33. *The Apostolic Faith* 1 (1906).
34. *The Apostolic Faith* 1 (1906).
35. *The Apostolic Faith* 1 (1906).
36. *The Apostolic Faith* 1.2 (1906).
37. *The Apostolic Faith* 1.2 (1906).
38. Bartleman, *Azusa Street Revival*, 136.
39. Parham, *Apostolic Faith* (1912) 4.
40. Bartleman, *Azusa Street Revival*, 45.

after which he was barred from the mission. He continued to hold a "long-harboured bitterness" against the mission's success. Most, however, shared Bartleman's view that Azusa was "holy ground" and they stayed with Seymour, many of them receiving the baptism in the Holy Spirit.[41]

A number of those who attended the Azusa meetings recorded their impressions. A. S. Worrell, the Bible translator, recorded that "Great emphasis was placed on the blood of Christ for cleansing" and "a high standard was held up for a clean life." He went on to state that "Divine love was wonderfully manifest in the meetings.... We seemed to live in a sea of pure love. The Lord fought our battles for us in those days.... We lived in his wonderful immediate presence. And nothing contrary to His pure spirit was allowed there."[42] It was observed that there was never any competition, jealousy or rivalry between Azusa and other churches in either the immediate area or in other parts of the city. John G. Lake, who later came to have a powerful healing ministry, visited the Azusa Street meetings. In his book, *Adventures with God,* he later wrote of Seymour:

> He has the funniest vocabulary. But I want to tell you, there were doctors, lawyers, and professors, listening to the marvellous things coming from his lips. It was not what he said in words, it was what he said from his spirit to my heart that showed me he had more of God in his life than any man I had met up to that time. It was God in him that attracted people.[43]

The December 1906 issue of *The Apostolic Faith* reported that "the fire was still falling" and that "hundreds of souls have received salvation and healing." The article went on to report that "the revival has spread through towns about Los Angeles and through the state and all over the United States in different places, and across the Ocean."[44] The February and March 1907 issues of *The Apostolic Faith* reported that the work at Azusa Street Mission was "growing more powerful than ever" and offered praise to God that "meetings continue every day with seekers at every service" and with the three daily meetings almost running into each other. It concluded with a statement that "the spirit of unity, love and power is manifest."[45] Later in May, the Mission set aside three days of fasting and

---

41. Blumhofer, *Assemblies of God*, 1:109.
42. Bartleman, *Azusa Street Revival*, 50.
43. Liardon, *Great Azusa Street Revival*, 38–39.
44. *The Apostolic Faith* 1.4 (1906).
45. *The Apostolic Faith* 1.6 (1907).

prayer for more power in the meetings and were greatly encouraged as a result "with souls slain all about the altar the second night." The Azusa team "felt an increase of power every night."[46]

As in the case of other revivals there were occasions when the level of intensity ebbed and flowed. When Seymour was away for a brief period early in 1911 his place was filled by William H. Durham from Chicago and the saints who had moved elsewhere flocked back in large numbers and the old church building was filled again with the high praises of God. They called it "the second shower of the latter rain." On one Sunday evening, 500 had to be turned away. Bartleman recorded that 1911 was a particularly wonderful year when "much of the old-time power and glory of the Azusa Mission returned to us."[47]

The Revival Transported

News of revival was spread by the secular press, the most notable being the *Los Angeles Times*, which was decidedly hostile to the Azusa meetings. The issue of the 18th of April carried an article entitled "Weird Babel of Tongues." It announced,

> The newest religious sect has started in Los Angeles. Breathing strange utterances and mouthing a creed which it would seem no sane mortal could understand, the newest religious sect has started in Los Angeles. Meetings are held in a tumble-down shack on Azusa Street, near San Pedro Street, and devotees of the weird doctrine practice the most fanatical rites, preach the wildest theories and work themselves into a state of excitement and peculiar zeal.... They claim to have "the gift of tongues" and be able to comprehend the babel. But for that reason its reports stirred the curious to come and find out what was happening. Many of them were both captivated and converted.[48]

Anderson asserted that the Azusa Mission's own publication, *The Apostolic Faith*, possibly exerted more influence than all other periodicals put together. In it Seymour declared his intention to "restore the faith once delivered to all the saints" by old-time preaching, camp meetings,

---

46. *The Apostolic Faith* 1.8 (1907).

47. Bartleman, *Azusa Street Revival*, 133.

48. *Los Angeles Times*, April 1, 1906, cited in Bartleman, *Azusa Street Revival*, 153–54.

revivals, missions, and street and prison work.[49] "We stand," he declared, "on Bible Truth without compromise."[50] More than half of each four-page monthly issue carried dozens of testimonies and information on the spread of the revival across America and the world. The summer 1907 issue of *The Apostolic Faith* wrote, "How wonderful it is that today in different parts of India, Russia, Norway, Sweden, England, Canada, Africa and America, God's Saints are enjoying the latter rain and being satisfied."[51] Azusa's large committee of workers compiled lists of all contacts and sent them the four-page monthly, free of charge. The first issue in September 1906 numbered 5,000, the second 10,000, and by the end of 1907, 40,000 copies were being printed. When the paper began to be published in 1908 from Portland, Oregon, 80,000 copies were printed each month. It was read by prominent Pentecostal leaders such as the Norwegian Methodist Thomas Ball Barratt, and J. H. King, the overseer of the Fire-Baptised Holiness Church.[52]

In addition to *The Apostolic Faith* there was a proliferation of new Pentecostal periodicals carrying news from Azusa and circulated free of charge. A. H. Argue, who received the baptism of the Holy Spirit in 1907, had 30,000 copies of the *Apostolic Messenger* distributed in that year and 70,000 in the year following. William Piper was publishing 50,000 copies of his *Latter Rain Evangel* in 1908. Anderson noted that more than fifty different Pentecostal periodicals were published during the first six years of the revival.[53]

The Azusa Street Mission commissioned a number of foreign and home missionaries, thirty-eight in all as early as October 1906. Candidates were chosen by messages in tongues and interpretation, told where to go through visions and prophecies, and assured they would be sustained and equipped by the Holy Spirit.[54] Several of the Los Angeles leaders went on preaching tours, carrying the message and experience of the revival with them. In the spring of 1907, "the indefatigable" Bartleman embarked "by faith" on a nationwide tour from California to Maine to

---

49. *The Apostolic Faith* 1.1 (1906).
50. *The Apostolic Faith* 1.4 (1906).
51. *The Apostolic Faith* 1.9 (1907).
52. Anderson, *Vision of the Disinherited*, 73.
53. Anderson, *Vision of the Disinherited*, 75.
54. Anderson, *Vision of the Disinherited*, 72.

South Carolina and back to California.[55] Bartleman then made a second tour of America beginning in March 1908,[56] and in March 1910 he set out on a world trip—which included India, Egypt, China, and Japan—to spread the message of Azusa. He wrote widely in religious journals such as *The Christian Harvester* and produced tracts about Azusa, many of which were printed and distributed in their thousands. In the first two or three years of the revival, Bartleman wrote more than 550 articles for the Christian press.[57] J. M. Pike's *Way of Faith* carried many articles on Azusa in 1906. *The Christian and Missionary Alliance*, *The Apostolic Light* (Oregon), *The Gospel Witness* (Louisville, Kentucky) and the *Herald of Light* (Indianapolis) all featured detailed information about the revival.

Notwithstanding the rise and fall in the intensity of the Azusa Street meetings the revival was soon carried across America and then on to the world beyond. On one extraordinary day, Seymour and 500 others arrived at Terminal Island, one of the beaches close to Los Angeles, where Seymour baptized 106 converts in the ocean.[58] A second service was held at the same location on September the 11th, when eighty-five people were baptized in the Ocean.[59] "Such singing, shouting and company," it was said, "Terminal Island never saw before!"[60] By the end of 1906, there were nine Pentecostal assemblies in Los Angeles, most of which were in good relationships with each other. *The Apostolic Faith* reported in January 1907 that "there is a very sweet spirit of unity among Pentecostal missions in Los Angeles and workers in suburban towns."[61] Every Monday morning the minsters and workers from these different fellowships met together for prayer and discussion. They were often joined by workers from Long Beach, Pasadena, Clearwater, Anaheim, and other more distant places.[62]

Among those in the vicinity of Azusa Street were the mission established by Bartleman at Eighth and Maple Street in August 1906,[63]

55. Anderson, *Vision of the Disinherited*, 71.
56. Bartleman, *Azusa Street Revival*, 108, chaps. 4–6.
57. Anderson, *Vision of the Disinherited*, 71.
58. Blumhofer, *Assemblies of God*, 1:108.
59. *The Apostolic Faith* 1.2 (1906).
60. *The Apostolic Faith* 1 (1906).
61. *The Apostolic Faith* 1.5 (1907). This contrasts with Hollenweger, *Pentecostals*, 23, who gives no source for his statement.
62. *The Apostolic Faith* 1.5 (1907).
63. Bartleman, *Azusa Street Revival*, 61.

the *Upper Room Mission* under the leadership of Elmer Fisher, the *New Testament Church*, and the *Alley Mission* in Pasadena.[64] At the close of 1906, *The Apostolic Faith* reported, "The waves of Pentecostal salvation are still rolling at Azusa Street Mission. From morning till late at night the meetings continue with about three altar services a day." No record was kept of the precise number of those who responded to the altar calls but a Mrs. Mary Galmond, 1106 Marengo Street, Pasadena was of the view that since Seymour's arrival "there have been more souls converted and sanctified than in all the city of Los Angeles during the last five years."[65]

As a result of the widespread publicity, preaching tours undertaken by leaders, and the enthusiasm of visitors returning from Azusa Street, the revival was carried across America and to the furthest parts of the globe. By the end of 1908, there were reports of the Pentecostal revival having reached New York City, Baltimore, Philadelphia, Washington DC, Chicago, Zion City, St. Paul, Minneapolis, Atlanta, Birmingham, Cleveland (Ohio and Tennessee), Indianapolis, Portland, Seattle, San Francisco, and Oakland; and from the British Isles, Scandinavia, Germany, Holland, Egypt, Syria, and Jerusalem; from Johannesburg and Pretoria, South Africa; and from Shanghai, Hong Kong, Ceylon, and Calcutta.[66]

The Plateauing of the Revival, Including Some Unresolved Issues

The revival probably reached its high point towards the end of 1907. After this time, several things happened which began to put the brakes on the flow of the Spirit. On the 13th of May, Seymour married Jennie Evans Moore, who had been a faithful member of his ministry. She was known for her beauty, musical talents, and spiritual sensitivity. It was she who felt the Lord was calling them to marry, she proposed, and Seymour accepted. Their union was opposed by a small influential group within the mission. One of their number, Clara Lunn, Azusa's secretary, who was also responsible for the publication of the mission's paper, *The Apostolic Faith*, left the mission possibly because she herself was in love with Seymour.[67] To make matters worse, she moved away to Portland, Oregon,

---

64. Bartleman, *Azusa Street Revival*, 56 and 84.
65. *The Apostolic Faith* 1.2 (1906).
66. Anderson, *Vision of the Disinherited*, 74.
67. Liardon, *Great Azusa Street Revival*, 49–50.

taking with her the entire national and international mailing lists. Her betrayal hugely diminished Seymour's worldwide publishing ability and outreach. When the May 1908 edition was sent out the cover appeared to be as usual but inside only the new Portland address for contributions and letters was given. When the June issue was published there was no article from Seymour and all references to Los Angeles were gone. Without this vital lifeline it was impossible for Seymour to continue publication.

Throughout 1909 and 1910, Seymour continued his ministry, but the number of attendees dropped dramatically, largely because of his losing his publishing arm, which in turn caused a serious financial shortfall. Hoping to save the day, he left the mission early in 1911 and departed for Chicago on a cross-country preaching tour. While he was away, William Durham held the hugely popular preaching meetings at Azusa, as mentioned above. On his return, Seymour found that he strongly objected to Durham's view that people could not lose their salvation even if they sinned in the flesh. Seymour took an opposing view, maintaining that a person could lose their salvation if they turned away from Christ. Indeed, he had written in *The Apostolic Faith* in 1907 that "If you get angry, or speak evil, or backbite, I care not how many tongues you may have, you have not the baptism with the Holy Spirit. You have lost your salvation."[68] When it was clear that no agreement was possible Seymour felt he had no alternative but to lock Durham out of the mission. Durham, however, soon succeeded in obtaining a large two-story building which could seat more than a thousand people. The crowds followed him and large numbers were baptized and healed while Azusa was left with only a handful of people.

While the revival continued with Durham's followers, and at other places in Los Angeles, the old Azusa Mission struggled on. Seymour remained as leader and continued to welcome any who came, though few did. He changed the schedule to one all-day service held on Sundays. Occasionally people who had experienced the glory of the early days of mission made a return visit and were welcomed. In 1921, Seymour made a last ministry campaign across America. On his return the following year he seemed fatigued and discouraged. Bartleman felt the Azusa's decline was largely due to the loss of the early freedom and spontaneity together with Seymour's increasing control. Although he attended a number of ministerial conferences, he was no longer acclaimed in the way he had

---

68. *The Apostolic Faith* (1907).

been in the past. Finally, on the 28th of September, 1922, he was taken ill with serious chest pains while at the mission and died later the same afternoon. He was fifty-two. His wife Jennie continued to pastor the mission for a further eight years. She died on the 2nd of July, 1936.

Features of the Revival

Speaking in Tongues

The most prominent feature of the revival was speaking in tongues, which came to be regarded by Seymour as the evidence of the baptism of the Holy Spirit. Many messages at the meetings were given in tongues followed by interpretation. The tongues in which people spoke were believed to be known languages. *The Apostolic Faith* stated,

> The Lord has given languages to the unlearned—Greek, Latin, Hebrew, French, Italian, Chinese, Japanese, Zulu and languages of Africa, Hindu and Bengali and dialects of India, Chippewa and other languages of the Indians, Esquimaux, the deaf-mute language, and in fact the Holy Ghost speaks all the languages of the world through his children.[69]

In the early days there was a certain amount of misunderstanding of tongues. Many felt it was a divine language given to enable the person concerned to speak to the people of the nation to whom they were being sent. Some of the early missionaries were disappointed to discover that their tongues did not enable them to communicate with the nations they had been sent to. It was then that many came to recognize that tongues were primarily a prayer language for their own use and edification. Significantly, recent psychological research has demonstrated that speaking in tongues considerably improves emotional and spiritual health and well-being.

Far from being repulsed by the sound of strange tongues, many who heard them claimed to have been converted by hearing them.[70] Many Christian leaders doubtless came to share Bartleman's experience of the Holy Spirit. He found that "the experience of the baptism of the Spirit and speaking in tongues brought a new anointing to his preaching as well as

---

69. *The Apostolic Faith* (1907).
70. Blumhofer, *Assemblies of God*, 1:103.

giving him a new revelation of the sovereignty of God."[71] Seymour was careful to stress that while tongues were an "evidential sign" of the baptism in the Holy Spirit, "your life must measure with the fruit of the Spirit."[72]

Missionary Impetus

Many of those who were baptized in the Holy Spirit felt a call to carry their newfound experience of the gospel overseas. At Azusa Street there was a strong early belief that "the gift of tongues was given as a commission to go into all the world and preach the Gospel to every creature." The outpourings at Azusa seemed to them to be a sign that they had reached the beginning of "the last days,"[73] which would herald the premillennial return of Christ. Many messages that were given in tongues were interpreted as a call to be ready for the Lord's return; "Awake! awake! The Bridegroom cometh."[74]

Healings

Healings were a significant feature of the revival, particularly in the early years. The upper room at Azusa Street was specifically kept as a place for the sick, and healings were reported every day.[75] In January 1907, *The Apostolic Faith* reported:

> The Lord is graciously healing many sick bodies. People are healed at the Mission almost every day. Requests come in for prayer from all over. They are presented in the meeting and the Spirit witnesses in many cases that prayer is answered, and when we hear from them they are healed. Handkerchiefs are sent in to be blest, and are returned to the sick and they are healed in many cases. One day nine handkerchiefs were blest, another day sixteen. A man came with a broken arm and was healed. The mission people never take medicine. They do not want it. They have taken Jesus for their healer and He always heals.[76]

---

71. Bartleman, *Azusa Street Revival*, 66.
72. *The Apostolic Faith* (1907).
73. Blumhofer, *Assemblies of God*, 1:48.
74. Blumhofer, *Assemblies of God*, 1:106.
75. *The Apostolic Faith* 1.8 (1907).
76. *The Apostolic Faith* 1.5 (1907).

Racial Equality

When the Holy Spirit was first poured out on the day of Pentecost, as described in Acts 2, on the 120 followers of Jesus and the Jerusalem Passover crowd, it was a truly multiracial occasion. There people gathered "from every nation under heaven" and most notably from Africa, Asia, Europe, and beyond. The same was true of the Pentecostal revival which was birthed at Azusa Street. Many who came to the meetings or wrote about them were impressed at the unity and love between the black and white communities and their pastors and church leaders. In fact, at Azusa there was a marked bond of love and unity among the thousands of visitors and participants who came from a spectrum of differing races and ethnicities. In the first edition of *The Apostolic Faith*, Seymour wrote, "Multitudes have come. God makes no difference in nationality."[77] A little later he added, "The meeting has been a melting time. The people are all melted together . . . made one lump, one bread, all one body in Christ Jesus. There is no Jew, or Gentile, bond or free, in the Azusa Mission. No instrument that God can use is rejected on account of colour or dress or lack of education. This is why God has built up the work. . . . The sweetest thing is loving harmony."[78] Alexander Boddy, the Anglican incumbent of All Saints Church Sunderland and a pioneer Pentecostal, wrote the following in 1912, echoing Seymour's word:

> It was something extraordinary, that white pastors from the South were eagerly prepared to go to Los Angeles to the Negroes [sic], to have fellowship with them and to receive through their prayers and intercessions the blessings of the Spirit. And it was still more wonderful that these white pastors went back to the South and reported to the members of their congregations that they had been together with negroes, that they had prayed in one Spirit and received the same blessing as they.[79]

Other Features of Note

The unity that was felt to flow from the Baptism of the Spirit led to a strong doctrine of restorationism. It seemed to many that Azusa heralded

---

77. *The Apostolic Faith* (1906).
78. *The Apostolic Faith* (1906).
79. Hollenweger, *Pentecostals*, 24.

the beginning of "the last days" when Christ would return, the millennial kingdom would come into being, and the faith once for all delivered to all the saints would be restored.

As has been noted in other revivals, women played a significant role in Azusa and in the life and worship of those churches in other parts of Los Angeles which shared Seymour's mission and teachings. He appointed twelve elders for his apostolic church. Among them were Sisters G. W. Evans, Florence Cook, and Clara Lunn, who was his first and very able administrator. He was also highly dependent on Jennie Evans Moore, who later became his wife and was a gifted musician and a faithful member of his ministry team. A number of women were sent out by the church to take the revival to other American towns and cities. They included a Mrs. Crawford who went to Oakland, Portland, and Seattle, and Florence Crawford who carried the movement to Minneapolis and St. Paul. Others went further afield. Among their number were Mrs. A. G. Carr who went to the Far East, Lucy Farrow who went to Africa, and Mrs. Hutchins and her niece, Leila McKinney, who also went to Africa.[80] In this way Azusa raised the value and status of women who came to play an important role in the many branches of Pentecostalism which followed in its wake. Mark Noll aptly stated of Azusa, "One of its most prominent features was the full participation of women in public activities."[81]

Lastly, it is clear the revival sparked a fresh interest in education and training for mission. In the years immediately following the beginning of the revival many conferences, conventions, and camps began to be organized. Anderson gives details of more than a dozen part-time Bible schools which were founded to instruct new converts and train workers for the field. In addition to these six, other longer-term Bible colleges were established.

A Worldwide Revival

Not everything at Azusa was perfection! There was theological disagreement between Seymour and Durham over the issue of sanctification. Durham insisted that a person received sanctification at the time of their conversion and that baptism in the Spirit followed as a second step. Seymour maintained that sanctification was a second step after conversion

---

80. Anderson, *Vision of the Disinherited*, 74.
81. Noll, *Old Religion in a New World*, 151.

and baptism in the Spirit was a third stage. In the early days at Azusa, much time was spent in "tarrying" for the Holy Spirit after the pattern of the first disciples who "tarried" (waited) for the outpouring of Pentecost. Later, it was recognized and acknowledged that the Holy Spirit had already been poured out for everyone. There was no need therefore to "tarry" for the outpouring of the Holy Spirit, rather his presence should simply be received as a gift which had already been given.

Some of Seymour's teachings were later tempered by denominations and churches which came out of the revival. Among these were his assertion "that every sickness is of the devil,"[82] and that Christians who divorce may not remarry.[83] There were minor jealousies and differences over the amount of singing that should take place at the meetings and the precise nature of tongues. That said, there can be no doubting that Azusa Street prompted and generated what was perhaps the greatest revival in the history of Christianity since the day of Pentecost. Before that time, most churches had taught that salvation happened when a person mentally accepted and believed that they were forgiven through Jesus' atoning death on the cross. Such teaching however had most often failed to significantly touch people's lives, emotions, and feelings at their deepest point.

The Azusa experience of the Holy Spirit was nothing less than the manifest presence of the living Jesus in people's lives experienced in strong subjective feelings of love, joy, peace, and unity, and manifested in miracles and gifts of speaking and healing. This was a salvation which was cathartic and impacted the whole person. For the people who came to Azusa Street their baptism in the Holy Spirit made Jesus' presence vivid and real. Not only did it change the face of American church life and worship, but it also spread out across the globe. The Azusa Pentecost experience led to the founding and birth of modern Pentecostalism, which has become the fastest-growing and most diverse form of Christianity in the world.[84]

Besides the growth of many thousands of independent churches already alluded to, several major Pentecostal denominations also emerged in the wake of Azusa Street. The most prominent was the Assemblies of God, which by the end of the twentieth century had nearly 12,000

---

82. *The Apostolic Faith* 1.1 (1906).

83. See Seymour's article entitled "Bible Teaching on Marriage and Divorce in *The Apostolic Faith* 1.5 (1907). See also Seymour's articles entitled "The Marriage Tie" and "The Edenic Standard of Matrimony" in *The Apostolic Faith* 1.10 (1907).

84. See Martin, *Tongues of Fire*; Dempster et al., *Globalisation of Pentecostalism*; Shaull and Cesar, *Pentecostalism and the Future*.

churches in America ministering to 2.5 million adults.[85] Several other largely African Pentecostal denominations also emerged. In 1907, a group emerged, led by Milton Ambrose Tomlinson, a colporteur of the American Bible Society. It later became known as *The Church of God*, with its headquarters in Cleveland, Tennessee. Tomlinson later separated from them and formed what became a new denomination titled *The Church of God of Prophecy*. In June 1907, a further group known as Elim, and based in Rochester, New York, was impacted by Azusa. The church became thoroughly Pentecostal and believed that the "Latter Rain" had begun to fall. A Bible training institute was established with full-time students, many of whom became active evangelists.

Azusa Street bears all the marks of a biblical revival. It magnified and uplifted Christ. In Seymour it had a leader who was humble, uncontrolling, ready to learn, and who allowed the Holy Spirit time to speak and touch people's lives. One of its great strengths was its breaking of the racial barriers in the striking way that blacks and Hispanics joined whites in the nightly meetings. The Pentecostal experience of Azusa Street began as the religion of the disinherited and marginalized, but by the second half of the twentieth century it had impacted every major denomination across the globe, including Roman Catholicism and the Orthodox Communions.

---

85. Noll, *Old Religion in the New World*, 152.

10

The Lowestoft Revival

On Monday, the 7th of March, 1921, the Rev. Douglas Brown, the minister of Ramsden Road Baptist Church in South London, arrived by train at the East Anglian fishing town of Lowestoft. He was not in the best state of health, having only just recovered from an eleven-day spell in bed with influenza. He had been invited to preach at a week of meetings at the London Road Baptist Church by the minister Hugh Ferguson. He had brought the Rev. John Edwards with him because he felt he might not be sufficiently well enough to cope. As things turned out he was able to preach with "great power" on that Monday evening and as events proved on many more days following. In fact, over a period of eighteen months he spoke at more than 1,700 occasions.[1] His preaching birthed what has thus far proved to be the last significant revival in England. Not only did it make a deep impact on the town of Lowestoft and its fishing industry, it spread to other places in both Suffolk and Norfolk.

Douglas Brown (1874–1940)

Douglas Brown was brought up in a manse, his father, the Rev. Archibald Brown, being the pastor of the East London Tabernacle. As a ten-year-old he remembered being deeply impressed as he listened to his father

---

1. Griffin, *Forgotten Revival*, 17.

preaching on Sunday mornings.[2] But he found an even greater inspiration on Friday evenings when his father was preparing his sermons. He would take off his shoes, leave his homework, tiptoe down the corridor, and peep for a few minutes through the keyhole, listening to his father humbly and intimately praying to the Lord and seeking for his wisdom and help.[3] Douglas Brown trained for the ministry and became an able preacher with a successful ministry. In fact, he wrote, "My church was filled. I loved my people, and I believe my people loved me. . . . I had never known a Sunday there for fifteen years without conversions."[4] But after twenty-six years, Brown became acutely aware that something was missing from his life. He later reflected, "Christ laid His hand on a proud minister, and told him that he had not gone far enough, that there were reservations in his surrender. . . . He nearly broke my heart while I was preaching."[5] The struggle lasted through November and December 1920 and on into the new year. Then, in February 1921, as Brown was wrestling in prayer, there came a moment when he was finally able to totally surrender his life to God. He wrote of that moment as follows.

> Then something happened, I found myself in the loving embrace of Christ forever and ever; and all power and joy and blessedness rolled like a deluge. . . . God had waited four months for a man like me; and I said: "Lord Jesus, I know what you want; You want me to go into mission work. I love Thee more than I dislike mission work. I love Thee more than I dislike that.[6]

At the beginning of the very next month Brown found himself journeying to Lowestoft to become the instrument of the revival which spread over East Anglia and reached many of the fishing ports in the northeast of Scotland. He had a very straightforward view of revival and how to achieve it. Addressing a meeting at Norwich, he said: "You cannot make a revival; but no multitude of people ever got down on its knees before Calvary, but that revival came. God bring us back to Calvary in all its simplicity. May the pierced hands of Jesus Christ rescue hundred of souls

---

2. *Yarmouth Independent*, 4 June, 2021.
3. Griffin, *Forgotten Revival*, 19.
4. Griffin, *Forgotten Revival*, 17.
5. Griffin, *Forgotten Revival*, 17.
6. Ives, "Douglas Brown and the Lowestoft Revival," para. 2.

this week. See to it that you pray. Pray in the Holy Spirit and God will answer with miracles of grace."[7]

Life and Worship in Lowestoft

As with all revivals Lowestoft's was to some extent prompted and shaped by its life, culture, and churches. It was an ancient seaport with a flourishing fishing industry. The old town was perched on the cliffs while the newer southern part was lower down with an esplanade running between two piers. The old and new towns were connected by a swing bridge across the harbor. During the peak of the herring fishing season sometimes as many as 700 Scottish drifters sailed south together with around 7,000 men. At the same time some 3,000 "fisher lassies" traveled down by train and based themselves in East Anglia. Whole families made the journey south, and their children were sent to special schools in the area.

After the First World War the fishing industry had declined somewhat due to overfishing and to the declining economy. Many ex-servicemen who had returned from the trenches found themselves without work. There was an air of despondency in the community. However, there was also evidence of spiritual life in the churches. Besides the Baptist Church where the revival began there were three Anglican churches, all of which had evangelical clergy; the Rev. John Hayes was vicar of Christ Church; the Rev. William Hardie, vicar of St John's; and the Rev. Henry Martin was rector of St Michael's Oulton.[8] The Primitive Methodists had smaller but fervent congregations in both Lowestoft and Oulton. John Rushmere, an Oulton Broad coal merchant and town councillor, was a Primitive Methodist local preacher. There was also a Fishermen's Bethel led by Peter Greasley, the port missionary, whose work included a young people's weekly Bible class with some forty or fifty members.

The Baptist Church where revival began had a large number of young people in its congregation and there were Bible classes for young men and women. The significant feature of the church's life was the weekly prayer meeting which was held on Monday evenings in the schoolroom. It was often attended by about ninety people all seeking the Lord for his transforming power in the community and beyond.[9] Many of the young

---

7. *The Christian Herald*, July 14, 1921, in Griffin, *Forgotten Revival*, 49.
8. Griffin, *Forgotten Revival*, 14.
9. Information taken from Griffin, *Forgotten Revival*, 12–14.

people who came were earnestly praying for revival. Their pastor, Hugh Ferguson, was a forthright minister who expressed his disapproval of the town council sanctioning Sunday concerts and dancing. He and the Rev. John Hayes of Christ Church resolved to pray together more specifically for a move of God. From this it becomes clear that the ground had been being prepared for the revival that was to come.

The Coming of Revival

Hugh Ferguson and his deacons distributed leaflets throughout the town advertising Douglas Brown's coming to give "a message for the times" and a notice to the same effect was also placed in the *Lowestoft Journal* on Saturday, the 5th of March. They were nevertheless apprehensive, fearing that there would not be enough people to make the planned visit worthwhile. As it happened, on Monday evening the church was well filled. Brown preached an impressive sermon, and there was a general feeling of expectancy among the people. On the following Tuesday, there was a prayer meeting at 11:00 a.m., followed by a Bible reading in the afternoon and an evangelistic sermon in the evening. There was a manifest sense of Jesus' presence and there was a feeling that Brown should have called for decisions. Ferguson declared the Wednesday morning prayer meeting as "wonderful." He described the huge impact of Brown's preaching on Thursday evening on the healing of the man at the Pool of Bethesda in John chapter 5 as momentous:

> We had the church packed in the evening. When our brother had delivered his message, he told the people he was going into the vestry and would be glad to see any who wanted help or desired to surrender themselves to Jesus Christ. I shall never forget that night as long as I live. Our brother passed through the deacons' vestry—up a little stairway and into the pastor's vestry—and had not been there many minutes when the first one came, and then another, and then another. I showed them the way into the vestry, and then I came down into the chapel. The people were singing that grand old hymn—
>
> I hear Thy welcome voice,
> That calls me, Lord, to Thee:
> For cleansing in the precious blood
> That flowed on Calvary."

> As I entered the church again and stood looking at the people, brother Edwards paused a moment and asked if there were any others coming into the inquiry room. We had been praying for "showers" that night and He gave us "a cloud-burst." They came from all parts of the building and filled the deacons' vestry. It was like waiting outside some theatre; there was one queue down this aisle and another down that. I went to Douglas Brown and said, "What are we to do? You cannot deal with these people one by one!" So, we opened the school room and in they came—fifty or sixty people to start with. Some Christians had the good sense to come with the anxious to help them. I got them together in the school room and began to speak to them in a company. I had been speaking for only a few moments, the door opened and another batch came in, and all was confusion for a few minutes. Then I tried to speak to them again; and again the door opened and another batch came in. It was a wonderful sight. We got those who had definitely surrendered to Christ to keep on one side; and those with difficulties we put into classrooms with a good Christian worker to help and deal with them. Presently there was quietness, and that night sixty and seventy of my dear young people, those we had been praying to God for—young men and women, from the ages of fifteen to twenty—some sixty or seventy of them that night passed from death to life.[10]

Astonishingly Ferguson's firsthand account proved to be the pattern of things to come. The following Thursday night, the meeting was transferred to the Fishermen's Bethel just a stone's throw from the Baptist Church. The building was packed and there was a manifest sense of the divine presence. Brown preached on the words of Peter, "If you bid me come to You on the water." After he had finished, the inquiry room was so packed within minutes that he was forced to say, "You will have to come to Christ where you are." "That night," Ferguson recalled, "the people were coming to Jesus all over the building.[11] On Friday, the meeting, which was back in the Baptist Church, was just the same as the previous night. It was now obvious that this was the start of a remarkable move of God. Douglas Brown had to return to his own church but promised to return on Monday. Before he left, Hugh Ferguson, John Hayes, Peter Greasley and the leader of Bethel met together for discussion and prayer.

---

10. Griffin, *Forgotten Revival*, 22.
11. Griffin, *Forgotten Revival*, 22, 24.

Following this they decided the moment had come to leave their carefully planned series of meetings and follow the promptings of God's Spirit.[12]

Rev. Douglas Brown[13]

Early in the second week, when Brown had returned to Lowestoft, he spotted Montague Micklewright in the congregation at one of his meetings. Micklewright had been a member of his church in London and gone

12. Griffin, *Forgotten Revival*, 24.
13. Griffin, *Forgotten Revival*, 13.

on elsewhere to become a lay pastor. He had been granted some leave and decided to come to some of the meetings for encouragement. As soon as Brown saw Micklewright he said to him, "The Lord sent you here. I want you for my curate." His new role was taking down the names and requests of those who came forward at the meetings so that they could be read out at the prayer meetings on the following morning. There were so many requests that it soon became necessary to have some in the morning, a second group at the afternoon Bible study, and a further batch in the evening. This led to a powerful foundation of daily prayer in which people literally "cried out for the salvation of the lost." Ramsden Road Baptist Church in Balham, the Metropolitan Tabernacle, and other churches joined in praying for a decisive outpouring of the Holy Spirit in Lowestoft.[14]

The Revival Grows

When Douglas Brown went back to Balham on the weekend of March 19th–21st, the same Spirit he had been experiencing in Lowestoft was immediately apparent in his own church. Scores of people young and old made open confessions of faith. After the first week the meetings in Lowestoft were expanded, with packed attendances at the afternoon's very practical Bible studies held at Christ Church. They were designed to impact everyday living. People from the seaside village of Kessingland, four miles south of Lowestoft, bused, walked, and cycled to the meetings. Tram cars were arriving full of people carrying Bibles with the conductors calling out, "Get off here for Christ Church." These Bible studies continued for three weeks, including Easter week. Among the most memorable were two sessions on "The Judgement Seat of Christ."

During the last week in March, the meetings were moved from the Baptist Church to St John's Church, whose vicar, the Rev. William Hardie, had supported the work from the beginning. The church, which was just south of the harbor, could seat 1,100. People sat everywhere: on the windowsills, round the font, on the pulpit steps, and in the aisles. It was originally planned to hold the final meeting in the Baptist Church, but because of the swelling numbers it was decided to stay with St John's. When Douglas Brown left Lowestoft on Saturday, April 2nd, crowds gathered at the station booking hall and on the platform to bid him farewell. He shook hands with as many as possible and committed them in prayer.

14. Griffin, *Forgotten Revival*, 24.

When the train reached Oulton Broad South, another group, including many converts, were on the platform to wish him well. On Monday, the 4th of April, a church business meeting was held and resolved to send a message of profound thanks to Ramsden Road Baptist Church for their support and "giving the services of your beloved Pastor, the Rev. Douglas Brown." They also expressed their conviction that "it has been a time of real revival and we trust and believe the beginning of a still greater harvest." "You will rejoice to know," their statement concluded, that we have a record of more than five-hundred converts . . . and there must be many more of whom we have not heard particulars."[15]

This wasn't yet the end of Douglas Brown's links with Lowestoft, he returned to the town during Whitsun week before going on to hold preaching missions in Ipswich, Yarmouth, Norwich, and Cambridge. Arriving on the Monday, he preached in the open air and at the Salvation Army Citadel. On Tuesday afternoon, he preached to "a large congregation"[16] at Oulton Parish Church. During the rest of the week, he preached in villages around Lowestoft. On the Thursday, he returned to St Michael's Oulton for an afternoon service which was particularly memorable for the singing of the last hymn, "When I Survey the Wondrous Cross," during which Douglas Brown, Hugh Ferguson, and the vicars of Christ Church and St John's Lowestoft and the Congregational Minister knelt together at the communion table and reconsecrated their lives to the cause of Christ. In the evening Brown preached at the Union Chapel Somerleyton and gave an invitation to any who would commit their lives to Christ. Middle-aged, the elderly, country lads and girls all responded. The publican and his wife were both converted and went back home and tipped out their barrels of beer in the marshes.[17] On the Sunday, Henry Martin, the rector of St Michael's Church, appealed for conversions at the close of the morning service and there was a good response. It was followed up by his meeting a crowd as he walked across to the church, all of them "wanting to 'get near Jesus.'"[18]

When Brown's preaching in Lowestoft came to a close, he began to preach in other towns in East Anglia and reports of his meetings appeared in the *Daily News*. It noted that during the past eleven weeks

15. Griffin, *Forgotten Revival*, 32.
16. Griffin, *Forgotten Revival*, 16.
17. Griffin, *Forgotten Revival*, 37. *Yarmouth Independent*, 4 June, 1921.
18. Griffin, *Forgotten Revival*, 37.

Brown had addressed 310 meetings and that there were over a thousand known conversions. Petitions for prayer were often close to 300 a day. The paper reported The Rev. Henry Martin's assertion that the revival "is the biggest thing I have ever seen. People have come from the whole surrounding area to attend the meetings . . . the conversions are genuine, and some of those in Lowestoft were especially striking."[19] The *Yarmouth Independent* stated,

> As remarkable as any of the services was the one which brought the Mission to a close on Friday evening. St George's was again thronged in every part. Most uplifting singing, heard far beyond the church, attracted people, and when more seats and standing room could not be had within, they crowded round the open doors. Mr Brown whose intense earnestness impresses everyone, gripped and held the great congregation with an address on Romans 12 verse 1 "Present your bodies as a living sacrifice. He said surrender of self is the way of salvation. . . . The secret of a happy useful and holy life is surrender.[20]

The *Daily News* also recounted the generosity of Christians whose giving at St John's Church following the revival had seen offerings increase by 50 percent and a debt of £600 paid off.[21]

Revival in East Anglia

On May 30th, Douglas Brown began a week at Burlington Baptist Church in Ipswich, whose minister, the Rev. Louis Parkinson, had been keen to have meetings in the town. He had enthusiastic support from both Canon Herbert Hinde, the Evangelical vicar of St John's Church, and the Rev. John Patten, minister of Tacket Street Congregational Church. No elaborate structure for the meetings had been decided upon, but the town's free church ministers had been regularly meeting each week to pray for revival. The *Daily News* reported on the first meeting as "quiet, undemonstrative with hymns of a devotional rather than a revivalist type." *The Christian* described the first meeting as "unforgettable" as 1,100 people crammed into the church to listen to Brown's sermon on revival. At the close, 250 Christians responded to the appeal to rededicate their lives to

---

19. *Daily News,* in Griffin, *Forgotten Revival,* 37.
20. *Yarmouth Independent,* 18 June, 1921.
21. *The Christian,* 30 June, 2021.

God.²² Numbers increased each evening with "char-a-bancs" packed with people coming from places in Essex. On the last night the schoolroom was filled with inquirers.

Yarmouth

Brown continued with a demanding schedule of meetings in East Anglia throughout the summer period. One of the towns which became a central focus of his preaching was Yarmouth. He began his campaign there from Monday, June 5th, to the Friday, June 9th. The organization was in the hands of the Rev. James Bevan, vicar of St George's, and the Rev. David John of Park Baptist Chapel, who were joined by Hugh Ferguson and John Hayes from Lowestoft. *The Eastern Daily News* gave detailed coverage of the first meeting, which was marked by large crowds, chairs down the aisles, and singing plenty of the old favorites from among Moody and Sankey's hymns. For the entire week St George's Church was filled beyond its normal capacity with between 1,500 and 1,600 people attending on Thursday and Friday. During the week "hundreds had indicated their commitment to Jesus Christ."²³

At the end of the week Brown moved on as planned, going to Norwich and Cambridge, and then later returned to take part in the Lowestoft Convention in September. He was, however, destined to return to Yarmouth in October where the revival was fully unleashed.

Norwich and Cambridge

Douglas Brown began two weeks of meetings in Norwich on June the 21st. The mission had been given only minimal publicity, but every building that was used was packed with men and women, with many coming to faith in Christ. During the campaign a clergyman on Norwich Station asked a porter the shortest way to the cathedral. He replied, "The Rev. Douglas Brown is preaching here. . . . I would advise you to leave the Cathedral alone and go down to St Mary's Chapel!"²⁴ The opening service was so crowded that Douglas Brown stopped the hymn "Rescue

---

22. *Daily News* and *The Christian*, in Griffin, *Forgotten Revival*, 43.

23. Griffin, *Forgotten Revival*, 48. See also reports in the *Yarmouth Independent* 4 June, 1921, and *Yarmouth Independent* 23 July, 1921.

24. Griffin, *Forgotten Revival*, 49.

the Perishing" and urged believers in the congregation to go to the school room and pray, thus enabling many of those outside to come into the building. On the Tuesday evening, so many responded to the appeal at the end of the meeting that all the ministers sitting on the platform were asked to go to the inquiry room and speak with those who were anxiously concerned about the salvation of their souls. The three largest churches in the city, which were used for the campaign, were packed every night, and twice there were overflow meetings.[25]

Douglas Brown moved on to Cambridge for the week of the 11th–15th of July. The meetings were held during a heat wave in Zion Baptist Church, pastored by the Rev. Edward Miles. Among those assisting was the evangelist Gypsy Smith. One of the services was memorable for Brown's challenge to those he sensed wanted to surrender their lives to Christ but were too fearful to walk down the aisle in testimony to the fact. He said, "If Jesus Christ isn't worth walking down the aisle for, He isn't worth having!" In just five days of mission in Cambridge some 200 people passed through the inquiry rooms and there were remarkable conversions.[26]

Early in September Brown reflected on the awakening that had been taking place in East Anglia and stated that "A momentous revival is within the reach of churches. In East Anglia it has commenced. Whether it becomes national depends upon the message and methods adopted by various churches during the coming winter."[27]

Yarmouth Again

About the time that the Lowestoft Convention was drawing to an end several thousand fishermen and fish-workers began to arrive at Lowestoft and Great Yarmouth for the herring season. The fishermen, as has been noted, came in boats with crews of nine or ten, while fisher-girls, wives, and children who attended special schools made the long journey by train.[28] The boats were met at the quayside and welcomed by Hugh Ferguson, who was himself a Scotsman. In contrast to the local fishermen, the Scots, by

---

25. Griffin, *Forgotten Revival*, 50.

26. Griffin, *Forgotten Revival*, 51–52.

27. *Norfolk News and Weekly Press*, 10 September, 1921. See also article entitled "East Anglia's Lead" in *London Daily News*, 7 September, 1921.

28. Ritchie, *Floods upon the Dry Ground*, chap. 6.

long-standing religious convictions, did not put to sea on Sundays. They went instead to the Baptist chapels and Brethren assemblies. Among the crowds who made their way south of the border to Suffolk was Jock Troup (1896–1954), a barrelmaker who hailed from Wick on the east coast of Caithness. Converted while serving in the Royal Navy during the First World War, he resumed his work but became a successful preacher, attaching himself to the Salvation Army. He had a powerful experience of the Holy Spirit at the Fishermen's Mission in Aberdeen in 1920.

On Saturdays, most Scottish vessels returned to port early in the day with their catches and then spent the rest of the day relaxing and shopping. Jock Troup seized the moment and as soon as the market stalls had closed preached the gospel in the market square. Suddenly there was an outpouring of the Holy Spirit in which "strong fishermen were thrown to the ground and cried to God for mercy."[29] It was the start of a movement which lasted many days in which large numbers committed their lives to Christ. Troup's powerful voice was captivating, and dozens of men, women, and children were literally brought to their knees as he requested them to kneel on the pavement as a sign of their commitment to Christ. A number of female fish-workers were too overcome to continue their work the following day. One convert stated, "the ground around me was like a battlefield with souls crying to God for mercy."[30] Men were also saved out at sea at the fishing ground off Happisburgh, Norfolk, and in an area known as Smith's Knoll.[31]

Douglas Brown came back to Yarmouth for the first two weeks of November, and for a brief period he and Troup were able to work together. Meetings took place in the evenings in Deneside Methodist Chapel and in St George's Church. The partnership was broken when Troup had a strong impression that he was to return to Fraserburgh as an evangelist. At the time of his departure, *The Yarmouth and Gorleston Times* described him as "an excellent advertisement for Christianity" and reported that at "every evening, and three times on Sundays, he has held open-air meetings in the Market Place or on Hall Quay. Many converts kneel down in the street each night."[32]

---

29. Mitchell, *Revival Man*, 56.

30. Ritchie, *Floods upon the Dry Ground*, chap. 3.

31. Ritchie, *Floods upon the Dry Ground*, chap. 3, in Griffin, *Forgotten Revival*, 62.

32. *Yarmouth and Gorleston Times*, in *The Christian Herald*, 24 November, 1921. See also *Yarmouth Independent*, 13 January, 1922.

The revival continued apace in Yarmouth, with Brown preaching and a number of other ministers from Yarmouth and Lowestoft and Christian workers from the Salvation Army, the Plymouth Brethren, and the Quakers assisting him. The pattern of each day was much the same as before. There were well-filled gatherings for prayer each morning in the Congregational Chapel, Bible expositions in the afternoons in Deneside Wesleyan Church, and evangelistic meetings in both Deneside and St George's Anglican Church. Perhaps importantly it was noted that petitions at the prayer gatherings were noticeably short.[33] *The Christian Herald* described the services in a lengthy article. The meetings were scheduled to start at 7:30, but by 6:30 people were flocking to both Deneside Wesleyan Church and St George's for singing and prayer, and by 7:30 "they were filled to suffocation with many standing in the aisles and sitting on the window-sills"[34] with each gathering estimated to be at least 1,500 people. Many remained in the buildings well after the official endings and people were reported to be singing and praying at eleven o'clock. The paper also observed that "fisher-lads prayed for their brothers, the fisher-girls prayed for other girls lodging in the same house. Singing, sobs and prayer prevailed in all parts of the building." The Yarmouth meetings appear to have taken on a good deal more informality compared with those of earlier days. It was reported, for instance, that a man from Stornoway stood up and said, "Lets have number 46," and in seconds Scot girls had the place ringing with "He drew me out of the horrible pit." Then a lad stood up and testified, "I gave myself to God in the fish market last week, and it has been the best week I ever had."[35] Open-air meetings continued each day in spite of blizzard conditions, with people kneeling down on the pavement in the snow and the rain to surrender their lives to Christ.

At the end of two weeks the time came for Douglas Brown to leave Yarmouth.[36] The Scottish boats set off on the northward voyage while the shoreworkers took to the trains for the long journey home. The season's herring catch had not been good compared with previous years, but many lives had been hugely changed, resulting in positive and transformed communities in the coastal ports of the east and north of Scotland.

33. Information derived from Griffin, *Forgotten Revival*, 63.
34. Griffin, *Forgotten Revival*, 31.
35. *The Christian Herald*, 1 December, 1921.
36. See "The Mission" in *Yarmouth Independent*, 12 November, 1921.

Impact of the Revival in Scotland

In November 1921, following what he took to be a vision from the Lord, Jock Troup had left Yarmouth and made his way to Fraserburgh in the north of Scotland. On his arrival there, he began preaching in the market square and soon attracted an attentive crowd. As soon as he ended his piece a bystander urged him to go to the Baptist Church and offered to go with him. Remarkably, on their arrival, they found Pastor Gilmour and his deacons just leaving a meeting at which they had agreed to invite him to come to Fraserburgh. The moment he began preaching in the church, people began weeping and seeking for salvation. It was soon apparent that what became a North Scotland revival was a continuation of what had begun in Yarmouth. At two villages south of Fraserburgh—Inverallochy and Cairnbulg—with a combined population of 1,500, nightly meetings were held in a small mission hall supplemented with four large open-air gatherings. Some 600 conversions took place in a fortnight. It was reported that "tobacco, pipes and cigarettes have been destroyed."[37]

Within a short time, the Scottish drifters began to arrive back in the coastal ports and towns with stories to tell about their salvation and life-changing experiences.

Rough and rugged sailors who had gone south to Yarmouth still with bitter memories of the Great War now returned with peace and joy in their hearts. One of their own number, David Cordiner, who had recommitted his life to Christ in Yarmouth, now became the leading speaker in Peterhead. Meetings continued every night for six weeks, and "600 seekers were registered."[38] *The Buchan Observer* stated in an article,

> Religious revival continues to spread at Peterhead. The movement has been taken up by the Salvation Army. During the past week open-airs have been held every night, and young fishermen and fisher-girls have given personal testimony to their experience of salvation. A stimulus to revival has been given through a united effort by the Congregational and United Free Churches by an Evangelist named Mr John Moor.[39]

The Glasgow Herald reported,

---

37. *The People's Journal*, 17 December, 1921, in Griffin, *Forgotten Revival*, 74.
38. Ritchie, *Floods upon the Dry Ground*, 52.
39. *The Buchan Observer*, 6 December, 1921.

> The Prairie fire of religious revival is raging along the coast from Wick to Peterhead. It was kindled by the torch lit at Yarmouth and Lowestoft. It is filling the kirks and emptying the pubs. . . . They speak affectionately of Jock and Douglas meaning their leaders. . . . The fisher folk are home from East Anglia and in every port they are spreading the message.[40]

In Wick, Jock Troup's hometown, there was a similar story to tell. A group of men from the town had come to faith in Christ through Douglas Brown's preaching. Their changed lives soon began to attract others to the meetings at the Baptist Church and the Salvation Army Hall. In the last week of November there were crowded meetings both inside the buildings and in the open air, "with tears of repentance and many surrendering their lives to Christ." The Wick Salvation Army saw "at least five hundred"[41] express concern over their salvation and many others revived in their faith. Troup returned to Wick in January and remained there, holding powerful meetings in the Rifle Hall and the open air until 1922.

There was a decided renewing of people's faith in a number of the Banffshire fishing towns, including Cullen, Portknockie, Findochty, and Gardenstown, as men, women, and in some cases whole families returned home from Yarmouth and Lowestoft. At Gardenstown, for instance, "packed meetings were held in Castle Grant Hall and it was common to hear families singing and praising God together in their homes."[42]

Among many other places in Scotland impacted by the Lowestoft and Yarmouth revival was Eyemouth, "a typical fishing village" north of Berwick-on-Tweed where on one occasion Troup preached to a gathering of "not less than three thousand."[43] There were similar accounts of other towns and villages just north of the English border being impacted by returning fisher-folk. Among them were Mussleburgh, Fisherow, Pittenweem, and Whinnyfold. The full impact of the awakening in East Anglia on Scotland will probably never be known. The city of Dundee was also stirred by the preaching of Jock Troup and David Cordiner. They were later joined by Douglas Brown in Aberdeen where there were further revival scenes.

---

40. *The Glasgow Herald*, 21 December, 1921.
41. Mitchell, *Revival Man*, 61–62.
42. "Letter from G. West" in Griffin, *Forgotten Revival*, 73.
43. Griffin, *Forgotten Revival*, 71.

The End of the Road

Most revivals tend not to last for extended periods of time, though often the positive results that flow from them endure for generations. Inevitably the significant leaders and major preachers run out of energy as they travel, attend day meetings, and give a major message each night of the week. Both Brown and Troup became exhausted on several occasions and needed to rest and take short breaks to improve their health. In an address at the 1922 Keswick Convention, Brown expressed his belief and hope that the East Anglian and Scottish awakenings might broaden into a nationwide revival, but his hopes were not realized. Part of the reason for this may have been his willingness to allow his preaching missions to be organized by a largely nonconformist committee chaired by Dr. Stuart Holden, the vicar of St Paul's Church Portman Square. In time this meant he was no longer free to go where he felt the Holy Spirit was leading and the spontaneity of his early meetings was lost. Brown felt himself weakening and was heard at a ministers' meeting pleading in tears with the words, "Pray for me, I have lost my power."[44]

That said, it must not be forgotten that Brown was one of the most influential preachers in Britain during the first half of the twentieth century. He was indeed the instrument which God had used to bring about the last significant revival in England, and one which had a major impact in both East Anglia and the north of Scotland. After the revival plateaued, he continued steadfast in the faith to preach and teach to great effect. The same was true of Jock Troup. In the years following the revival in the northern Scottish coastal ports and towns he had a powerful and effective ministry in the city of Glasgow where he became known as "the fisherman-revivalist.[45] He finally retired in 1945, ending his days as the superintendent of the famous Glasgow Tent Hall which had been built in earlier years for the American evangelist D. L. Moody.[46] His lifelong friend, Peter Connolly, wrote that "from the hour of his conversion he had a divine tongue put in his mouth, and nothing but death could silence him."[47]

---

44. Griffin, *Forgotten Revival*, 82.
45. Stewart, *Our Beloved Jock*, 4–5.
46. Ritchie, *Floods upon the Dry Ground*, chap. 15.
47. Stewart, *Our Beloved Jock*, 85.

Features of the Revival

Solid Bible Peaching

Unlike the earlier Welsh Revival, the outstanding feature of the Lowestoft outpouring was the outstanding, solid biblical preaching of Douglas Brown. His focus was on the central gospel themes of Ruin by the Fall, Redemption by the Atoning Blood, Regeneration and Renewal by the Holy Spirit, Anointing by the Holy Spirit for Service and Godly Living, and Waiting for the Return of the Lord Jesus Christ from Heaven. Hugh Ferguson stated, "Douglas Brown preaches with no uncertain sound." "You get old Bible doctrines and Apostolic preaching," he continued, "and, thank God, Apostolic results."[48] The Rev. Dr. Stuart Holden, the vicar of St Paul's Portman Square, London, wrote of Douglas Brown, "He is a teacher sent from God. His words have a power of penetration whether they be spoken or in the printed page. His subject is always Christ, and hence the Divine authentication of his words, and that has made him one of the most successful evangelists of our day."[49] The evangelist Gypsy Smith later wrote of him.

> He is a chosen vessel, God is with him, and the message comes like a "thus says the Lord." He has been thrust out—that is the word, THRUST OUT—by the Holy Ghost, with his message to the churches of our dear land. I do most earnestly ask my brethren to listen to the voice of God through him, and be willing in the day of God's power. . . . The Lord is with our dear brother. My heart bows before the power of God manifested in and through him, and my prayer will follow him.[50]

The Rev. John Hayes, the vicar of Christ Church explained to the *Daily News* reporter that "there was no emotional appeal, cheap sensationalism or manufactured revivalism in the meetings."[51] The *Eastern Daily News* gave a similar account of the first meeting held at Great Yarmouth, stating, "There is no sensationalism in style of methods, but undoubtedly a service of this character is a deep emotional experience to all taking part."[52]

---

48. Griffin, *Forgotten Revival*, 26.
49. Ritchie, *Floods upon the Dry Ground*, ch. 2.
50. *The Christian*, 28 July, 1921.
51. *Eastern Daily News*, in Griffin, *Forgotten Revival*, 39.
52. Griffin, *Forgotten Revival*, 47. See also *The Christian Herald*, 14 July, 1921.

Other leaders in the revival, such as Troup, Cordiner, and Willie Bruce, were clearly more rugged and less refined than Douglas Brown both in nature and style. Nevertheless, they preached the same gospel, focused on the centrality of the cross and the transforming presence of Jesus in the lives that were surrendered to him. They were all men whose background and experience naturally endeared and equipped them for the revival. Hugh Ferguson, as we have seen, was himself a Scot who went to the quaysides and welcomed the Scottish fishing vessels as they arrived. Douglas Brown had himself been at sea before taking up the ministry and even after his ministry had begun he signed on for occasional voyages with the White Star Line in order to improve his health. Troup, Bruce, Cordiner, and other Scottish preachers who carried the revival forward in Scotland were themselves from the sailing communities. They readily understood the lives and needs of seafaring communities. All of these men had a good basic biblical knowledge and were thoroughly familiar with Jesus' accounts of the disciples' casting their nets, catching fish, and encountering storms on the Sea of Galilee. These narratives were readily embraced by the herring fishers of northeast Scotland. They could very naturally speak in terms of Christ being their anchor or captain, of having found a safe haven or being bound to the port of heaven. *The People's Journal* noted that "at testimony meetings these weather-hardened fishermen speak of 'The Great Captain,' call Christ 'The Skipper' or of 'having the Pilot on board' because they are bound for the 'Port of Heaven.' The songs they sing are old favourites such as 'Will your anchor hold in the storms of life?' and 'When the roll is called up yonder.'"[53]

A Focus on Prayer

The East Anglian Revival was born and carried forward in prayer. Immediately following the Great War, in which Lowestoft had suffered from a German bombardment, many in the town devoted themselves to prayer. Hugh Ferguson, the Baptist minister, and John Hayes, the vicar of Christ Church, covenanted to pray for a move of God. Every Monday evening, eighty or ninety people came together in the Baptist Church schoolroom and prayer meetings were also held in St John's Parish Hall on Saturday evenings.[54] Following Douglas Brown's arrival at the beginning of the

---

53. *The People's Journal*, 1 December, 1921.
54. Griffin, *Forgotten Revival*, 102–3.

mission, prayer gatherings were held each morning. People were invited to send in requests which were read out at the meetings. Prayer was made for husbands, wives, and children who needed to be saved. When Douglas Brown moved on to Cambridge at the beginning of July, prayer meetings were held in the mornings, with large numbers attending.[55]

Unity

Hugh Ferguson was at one in the evangelical faith with the Anglican ministers of Lowestoft, John Hayes, the vicar of Christ Church, and William Hardie, the vicar of St John's Church. They worked, prayed, and shared together. Henry Martin, the rector of Oulton, wrote, "There was a happy Spirit of unity realised between evangelical churchmen and the Baptist Church. Mr Brown remarked to the writer that there were few towns where there would be a Baptist minister and four Anglican clergy so absolutely one on the great fundamentals of the Faith, the inspiration of Scripture and the hope of glory of the Lord's return."[56] Their unity undoubtedly enabled the revival to move forward in a strong and positive manner. Douglas Brown consistently stood out as a godly, gracious minister and leader. He was widely respected by his congregation in Balham and loved by the clergy and Christian leaders at Lowestoft and Yarmouth. He also worked in close harmony with Jock Troup and others. Jackie Stewart recalled the evening when Jock Troup and Douglas Brown were in the pulpit of Deneside Methodist Church, with their arms around one another, weeping as they basked in the presence of God.[57]

The Yarmouth Independent of June 18th, 1921, was also impressed by the unity among the clergy:

> Another striking feature was the Christian unity displayed among the various ministers of the town who took part in the services. . . . A sight not easily forgotten was a Salvationist, with the Anglican and Free Church ministers dealing with inquiries within the Communion rails of St George's Church. Every church in town is represented in the scores of conversions that have been recorded.[58]

55. Griffin, *Forgotten Revival*, 52. See also *The Christian*, 16 June, 1921; *The Christian Herald*, 21 June, 1921.

56. *The Churchman's Magazine*, 1921, in Griffin, *Forgotten Revival*, 109.

57. Ritchie, *Floods upon the Dry Ground*, chapter 3.

58. *Yarmouth Independent*, 18 June, 1921.

Singing

The Lowestoft Revival did not have the same dependence on singing as appears to have become the case in many more recent evangelistic campaigns, although the singing featured at all the meetings. Some of Ira Sankey's *Sacred Songs* were particularly popular and sung again and again. Favorites included "I Am Coming Lord," "Come to the Saviour Now," and "Blessed be the Fountain of Blood," which became the hymn of the revival. People reported again and again how the singing in the services could be heard in the streets of Lowestoft and Yarmouth. That said, the crowds who attended the meetings came first and foremost to hear the preacher. As they listened, people stated that they felt he was speaking to them alone.

A Revival to Inspire and Savor

As we look back on this revival there is much to inspire and reflect on which can feed our minds and stir us into hopefulness as we face the future. This was a revival born of prayer and carried forward in prayer. It was rooted in solid, dignified biblical preaching which emphasized the forgiveness which flows from the cross of Christ and his transforming presence in the lives of those who trust in him. There were times of emotion when people wept and knelt in the streets, but there was no deliberate attempt to stir people's emotions with hype or manipulative rhetoric. People's lives were manifestly improved; family life in many homes was transformed from brokenness into love and understanding. Drunkenness declined significantly in Lowestoft, with police reporting less vice to deal with as blasphemers became men and women of prayer. There can be no doubt that the churches and Christian communities of Lowestoft, Yarmouth, and other towns in East Anglia, along with the coastal ports and towns in the north and east of Scotland, were profoundly, positively, and lastingly impacted.

11

The Hebridean Revival

IN BYEGONE DAYS THE Hebridean island of Lewis had seen revival. In 1828, an awakening had taken place under the preaching of the Rev. Alexander McLeod, and since that time there had been moves of God's Spirit. Three differing Presbyterian denominational churches had faithfully stood by the Reformed Protestant faith. However, towards the end of the 1940s, after the end of the Second World War, all was not well. Many of the younger members of the population had left the island to serve in the armed forces and had returned home dispirited by what they had witnessed in the conflict. Stornoway, the island's capital, had one of the highest drinking rates in Scotland, and illegal drinking places flourished in various parts of the island.[1] There was a general air of despondency and apathy. Some secondary school pupils were even heard to liken Christian conversion to "the plague." The presbytery of Lewis noted "the lack of spiritual power from Gospel Ordinances" and the "growing carelessness toward Sabbath observance and public worship."[2] The *Stornoway Gazette and West Coast Advisor* reported a Free Church Presbyterial declaration which stated that "in certain parishes very few young people attended public worship." The "dance, the picture show and the drinking house"[3] were the institutions which now thrived in Lewis.

---

1. Woolsey, *Channel of Revival*, 112.
2. Campbell, *Revival in the Hebrides*, 1.
3. *The Stornoway Gazette and West Coast Advisor*, 9 December, 1949.

Against this background, people in the four parishes of Lewis had been praying for revival. In the parish of Barvas, two elderly women who lived in a cottage outside the main settlement took hold of God's promise, "I will pour water upon the dry ground,"[4] and began to seriously pray for a revival. Peggy Smith was eighty-four, and her younger sister, Christine, was eighty-two. Peggy was blind and Christine was almost bent double with arthritis. One night Peggy had a dream that was similar to one which the wife of their minister, the Rev. James MacKay, had had previously. It was that revival was coming to the church and that it would once again be crowded with young people. Peggy asked the minister to visit her and shared what she had received, asking him to hold meetings with the elders and deacons to wait and listen to the Lord for guidance and direction.

Duncan Campbell, who was to be the leader through whom the revival came later, reflected that the women of Barvas and the men came to recognize "four important governing principles." First, "they must be rightly related to God." This led to many prayer meetings being held in the church and in cottages, many of them lasting into the small hours of the morning. Second, it was impressed on them that God is "a covenant keeping God" who "must keep his covenant engagements." He had promised "to pour water upon him that is thirsty, and floods upon dry ground." Third, "they must be prepared for God to work in his own way and not according to his programme—God is sovereign and must act according to his sovereign purpose." Duncan was always clear that God is the God of revival, but man is the human agent through whom revival is possible. Fourth, in revival "there must be a manifestation of God." In a revival people must find themselves "bound to say, 'God did this, and it is marvellous in our eyes.'"[5]

After months of praying there was a general view that the time had come for action, and James MacKay began to plan for a mission in the forthcoming winter period. The question which then arose was: Who should be invited to preach? The answer came when MacKay unexpectedly met with Dr. Tom Fitch at a convention. Fitch informed him that Duncan Campbell, a Gaelic-speaking minister who was working with the Faith Mission, was free and able to lead missions in the Highlands. MacKay immediately sent a telegram to the Faith Mission Headquarters in Edinburgh. On his return to Lewis he was greatly surprised to hear

---

4. Woolsey, *Channel of Revival*, 114.

5. Information in this paragraph is drawn from Campbell, *Revival in the Hebrides*, 5–6.

that Peggy had dreamt that Duncan Campbell was going to be the one to lead their mission!

In one of the early prayer meetings, a young deacon stood up and read part of Psalm 24, "Who shall ascend into the hill of the Lord? Or who shall stand in His holy place? He that hath clean hands and a pure heart; who hath not lifted up his soul unto vanity, nor sworn deceitfully. He shall receive the blessing from the Lord." This man then immediately made the point that it was humbug to be waiting and praying if they themselves were not right in their own lives and in their relationship with God. He then lifted up his hands and cried out, "Oh God, are my hands clean? Is *my* heart pure?" He prayed no further but "fell prostrate on the floor."[6]

At the time he received MacKay's invitation, Duncan had planned to be at a holiday convention in Skye, an arrangement which the Headquarters staff felt to be right. Indeed, they advised him to write to MacKay stating that he was not free to visit Lewis but would do so at a later point if the invitation remained. Duncan however began to see the situation differently and felt pulled by the invitation from the people of Barvas. The Headquarters were bemused to say the least and tried their best to dissuade Duncan. However, it then emerged at a late stage that the main conference speaker was unable to go to the Skye Convention and the organizers had decided to cancel it. Duncan was thus able to inform the Faith Mission Headquarters that he would now be going to Barvas.[7] His plan was to preach at Barvas for ten days, then return to Skye after a short break in Edinburgh.

The Beginning of Revival

Duncan Campbell (1898–1972)

Duncan Campbell was born at Blackcrofts at Benderlock, in the parish of Ardchattan, in the Scottish Highlands, on the 13th of February, 1898. In December 1913, as a young man, he was playing the bagpipes at a concert and dance in aid of the Argyll Nursing Association. While listening to a song during the interval he suddenly came under a deep conviction over his own sinfulness. Such was the depth of his feelings that he got up and announced he was going home and very probably wouldn't be

---

6. Woolsey, *Channel of Revival*, 115.
7. Woolsey, *Channel of Revival*, 117.

dancing again. On reaching his home village he found the lights burning in the United Free Church. He quietly opened the door and slipped in to find that his own father, Hugh Campbell, was praying. Stunned he simply said, "I'm glad to see you here, Duncan. Mother was praying for you last night."[8] During the meeting, Mary Graham rose to her feet and quoted a verse from the book of Job and began to preach about Job 33:14, "God speaketh once, yea twice, yet man perceiveth it not."

Duncan Campbell was stunned by her words and felt himself trembling. After a few minutes he got up and left, fearing that he might create a disturbance. On the way home he knelt on the side of the road and cried out for mercy. It was 2:00 a.m. when he reached home, and he was surprised to find the lights still on and his mother still up. As she sat and listened, he poured out his story to her. His return was unexpected, and his bedroom had been taken so his mother suggested he go the barn and tell God what he told her while she prepared a bed for him in the living room. Duncan Campbell well remembered the prayer that he made that night, "Lord, I know not what to do. I know not how to come, but if you'll take me as I am, I'm coming now."[9] In that moment he was gloriously saved kneeling in the straw prepared for the horses in the morning."

When war broke out, Duncan Campbell responded to the call-up and enlisted with the Argyll and Sutherland Highlanders.[10] His experience on the battlefield taught him courage and the value of teamwork. At one point, due to heavy casualties, he found himself in charge of a platoon. Life was cheap and only two of his men survived. Later in the war he was attached to the cavalry corps and was severely injured in a charge at Amiens in April 1918.[11] Lying wounded on a horse's back, suffering loss of blood and in huge pain, Duncan summed all his effort to cry out to God in prayer. In that moment he recalled "the Holy Spirit swept through him" bringing cleansing and renewal and causing him to say, "I felt as pure as an angel."[12] Duncan Campbell sometimes spoke of this experience as the "baptism in the Holy Spirit" or an experience of "full salvation." It was his first taste of the supernatural work of the Spirit of God.[13]

8. Woolsey, *Channel of Revival*, 30.
9. Woolsey, *Channel of Revival*, 31.
10. Woolsey, *Channel of Revival*, 43.
11. Campbell, *Revival in the Hebrides*, 2; Woolsey, *Channel of Revival*, 50.
12. Woolsey, *Channel of Revival*, 51.
13. Woolsey, *Channel of Revival*, 52.

Following the end of the Great War, Duncan Campbell trained for the ministry with the Edinburgh-based Faith Mission in 1923. In 1925, he left the Mission and also married Shonah Gray. Several ministerial appointments then followed with the United Free Church, including Balintore, Easter Ross, and Falkirk. He was ordained in 1942 and rejoined the Faith Mission in 1949, which provided him with a house in Edinburgh. This led him back to ministry in Skye from where he was invited to come to Lewis by James MacKay.

Duncan Campbell duly arrived in Barvas on the evening of the 7th of December, 1949, and was met by the Rev. James MacKay (1897–1954)[14] and two of his church elders on the pier at Stornoway. As he made his way down to the jetty, he cut a strange figure wearing heavy black boots and an overly large coat. They exchanged greetings, with one of the elders inquiring, "Mr Campbell are you walking with God?" His somewhat diffident reply was, "Well at any rate, I can say that I fear God."[15] Campbell quickly recognized that his hosts were men who were living in the presence of God. As they made their way to the manse MacKay expressed his apology to him for his having experienced a long rail journey followed by the steamer crossing. He realized he must be ready for supper but wondered if he would be willing to make a brief stop and address a short and small meeting at 9:00 p.m. at the parish church.

An Unforgettable and Astonishing Night

As it happened Campbell never did get his supper. On their arrival at the church about a quarter to nine they were amazed to find about 300 people gathered. Nothing of any obvious significance happened during what Campbell called "a good meeting" in which he sensed God's Spirit was moving. He duly pronounced the benediction and began to walk out of the building. It was now about a quarter to eleven. As he did so the young deacon who had read out part of Psalm 24 at the earlier meeting stepped into the aisle and did so again. "God, you can't fail us," he prayed, and then repeated "God you can't fail us. You promised to pour water on the thirsty and floods on the dry ground. God, you can't fail

---

14. McKay trained at Glasgow Bible Training Institute, 1924–27, and Glasgow University, 1927–33. He was licensed to preach by the Church of Scotland on the 31st of March, 1933, and ordained on the 11th of May, 1933.

15. Campbell, *Revival in the Hebrides*, 35; Woolsey, *Channel of Revival*, 117.

us!" Campbell's response was, "Here is a young man who knows God in a way that perhaps I do not."[16] He then fell to his knees while Campbell continued to the door. Just before he reached it, it opened and the local blacksmith entered the church and exclaimed, "Mr Campbell, something wonderful has happened. Oh, we were praying that God would pour water on the thirsty and flood upon the dry ground and listen. He's done it!" When Campbell went outside the church "he saw a congregation of approximately 600 people—"Where had they come from?" he wrote. "I believe that very night God swept in the Pentecostal power of the Holy Ghost! And what happened in the early days of the apostles was happening now in the parish of Barvas."[17] The following lines are Campbell's own record of what proved to be an astonishing night.

> Over 100 young people were at a dance in the parish hall and they weren't thinking of God or eternity. God was not in all of their thoughts. They were there to have a good night when suddenly the power of God fell upon the dance. The music ceased and in a matter of minutes the hall was empty. They fled from the hall as a man fleeing from a plague. And they made for the church. They are now standing outside... Men and women who had gone to bed rose, dressed, and made for the church. Nothing in the way of publicity—no mention of a special effort... But God took the situation in hand—oh, he became His own publicity agent. A hunger and a thirst gripped the people. Six hundred of them now are at church standing outside. This dear man, the blacksmith, turned to me and said, "I think that we should sing a Psalm." In Lewis they do not sing hymns; they sing the Psalms of David... And they sang and they sang and they sang verse after verse. Oh what singing! What singing! And then the doors were opened and the congregation flocked back into the church.
>
> Now the church is crowded—a church to seat over 800 is now packed to capacity. It is going on towards midnight.... That meeting continued till 4 o'clock in the morning. I couldn't tell you how many were saved that night but of this I am sure and certain: that at least five young men who were saved in that church that night are today ministers in the Church of Scotland, having gone through university and college.[18]

---

16. Campbell, *Revival in the Hebrides*, 37.
17. Campbell, *Revival in the Hebrides*, 37.
18. Campbell, *Revival in the Hebrides*, 37–38.

At 4:00 a.m. MacKay and Campbell finally decided to make for the manse. Campbell had made no appeals or altar calls. His conviction was that appeals and altar calls are not necessary in times of revival. "We just leave men and women to make their way to God themselves.... God can look after his own! And when God takes a situation in hand, I tell you He does a better work."[19]

Duncan Campbell with Peggy and Christine Smith. Source unknown. Revival Library, High Street, Bishops Waltham, Hants SO32 1AA, UK.

Just as they were leaving the church a young man appeared and urged Campbell to come at once to the police station. Campbell immediately asked what was wrong. The man replied that nothing was wrong but there were "at least 400 people around the police station." There was no obvious reason why they had come there except possibly the fact that the cottage next door was where the two elderly sisters who had prayed for revival lived. As the two ministers made their way to the station they encountered four men kneeling at the roadside seeking the Lord. One of their number was saved "and he is today the parish minister." On their arrival at the police station Campbell saw something that would, in his own words, "live with me as long as I live." There was no need for any singing or preaching but "Oh, the confessions that were made!" Campbell summed up that first night as "a mighty demonstration that shook the

19. Campbell, *Revival in the Hebrides*, 38.

island." He wisely added, "Oh, let me say again, that wasn't the beginning of revival—revival began in an awareness of God. Revival began when the Holy Ghost began to grip men and that was how it began."[20]

The Revival Spreads

Following this remarkable beginning the revival immediately began to spread and the greater part of the two main islands of Lewis and Harris were soon powerfully impacted. As Woolsey delightfully put it, "News of what was happening in Barvas spread faster than the speed of gossip!"[21] Lewis was divided into four parishes—Barvas, Lochs, Stornoway, and Uig—while the smaller island of Harris to the south was a single parish. Campbell wrote in his account entitled *The Lewis Awakening, 1949-1953*.

> The Movement that began in the Parish Church of Barvas, almost immediately spread to the neighbouring parish of Ness, and it soon became evident that it was not to be confined to these two parishes. From north, south, east and west people came in buses, vans, cars and lorries, to witness the mighty movings of God and then return to their respective parishes to bear testimony to the fact that they had met the Saviour.[22]

The meetings continued with the same fervency for the next five weeks. Then there was a brief slackening for about a week after which the revival was renewed in strength, although with not quite the same degree of intensity. The churches in all the Lewis parishes and on the island of Harris continued to fill with large numbers of people seeking the Lord until 1953. During that time, Duncan Campbell carried the message of revival to other towns and cities in the British Isles but constantly returned to the Hebrides to maintain the impetus by taking part in services and meetings. A glance through the columns of the *Stornoway Gazette and West Coast Advertiser* gives glimpses of his activities. The issue of the 10th of March, 1950, for example, reported that he assisted with Communion services at Carloway and Barvas.[23] From Friday, the 26th of June, 1950, he organized and led a "Conference for the Deepening

---

20. Campbell, *Revival in the Hebrides*, 39-40.
21. Woolsey, *Channel of Revival*, 119.
22. Campbell, *Lewis Awakening*, 15.
23. *Stornoway Gazette and West Coast Advertiser*, 10 March, 1950.

of Spiritual Life in Stornoway Town Hall."[24] *The Stornoway Gazette and West Coast Advertiser* of the 19th of May, 1950, reported that Campbell would be conducting revival services on Monday the 22nd, Wednesday the 24th, Thursday the 25th, Friday the 26th, and on Sabbaths 21st and 29th at Tarbert on Harris.[25] *The Londonderry Sentinel*, in an article about Duncan Campbell's forthcoming visit to the city, gives a glimpse of one of his many journeys to Ireland. The paper reported that he "has worked all through the revival and is able to give us a first-hand account of the visitation of Divine power that has swept through the Island of Lewis, reviving the church and revolutionising the community. Mr Campbell will tell how the revival began in 1949, what it has accomplished in the lives of the people and what is happening today."[26]

In December 1950, the *Glasgow Herald* stated that "reports have been reaching Glasgow and Edinburgh for some time about the religious revival in the island of Lewis." The paper further stated that "there have been many conversions—men and women of all ages—a number of whom had showed little if any interest in religion previously."[27] Church attendances were noted "to have greatly increased with instances of whole families becoming church members."[28] In the following month, another report stated that "mission meetings are packed" and "church membership has increased rapidly in every district affected by the movement."[29] Much later, when the revival was finally beginning to draw to a close in the summer of 1953, *The Motherwell Times* noted "that the Rev. Duncan Campbell whose name is appearing in almost every Christian paper" was continuing "his wonderful work in the great revival on the island of Lewis."[30]

The revival was seen by Campbell and the parish ministers who supported and worked with him as a sovereign move of God, but they also recognized the importance of people's responses. This was seen by the way in which so many of those who came to faith in Christ at the meetings went back to their own parishes and immediately began to tell their stories. This in turn caused many others to come to the meetings to see

24. *Stornoway Gazette and West Coast Advertiser*, 26 May, 1950.
25. *Stornoway Gazette and West Coast Advertiser*, 19 May, 1950.
26. *Londonderry Sentinel*, 15 January, 1953.
27. *Glasgow Herald*, 8 December, 1950.
28. *Glasgow Herald*, 8 December, 1950.
29. *Glasgow Herald*, 26 January, 1951.
30. *Motherwell Times*, 31 July, 1953.

The Hebridean Revival

for themselves what was happening. Another important factor appears to have been transport. On one occasion Campbell counted fourteen buses and twice as many cars outside one of his morning meetings. He also told of a gamekeeper whose home was twenty-four miles from Barvas. He "was so wrought upon and burdened for the souls of others, that his van was seldom off the road and for two years, night after night, brought its loads of men and women who were seeking for Jesus."[31]

During the revival, prayer meetings were held in all the four Lewis parishes and on Harris. It became the practice that those who had surrendered their lives to Christ at the previous night would attend the mid-day prayer gathering on the following day. Duncan Campbell wrote, "At that time all work stopped for two hours—looms were silent. For two hours work stopped in the fields, and men gathered for prayer. And it was then you got to know those who had found the Saviour the previous night. You didn't need to make an appeal. They made their way to the prayer meeting to praise God for his salvation."[32] This continued for the best part of three years until both islands were deeply impacted with the message of salvation.

Campbell expressed a reluctance to count revival attendance numbers in view of the Old Testament King David being punished by God for counting the number of his people. What he did say and know was that 75 percent of those who came to faith in Christ did so before they came near a church and before they had heard any word from him or any other minister.[33]

Campbell's writings give glimpses of some of the remarkable events that took place in different parts of the two islands. He wrote that "the very air seems to be tingling with divine vitality. Everything, grass, stones, sea and sky, seems to cry out: 'God is here!' They spoke of the revival as 'a community saturated with God.'"[34] There was a heightened spiritual sensitivity with people frequently greeting one another with the words, "Have you done business with God today?"[35] In the village of Tarbert, on the Island of Harris, house meetings continued throughout the night. A master at the village school who was also a man of prayer continued

---

31. Campbell, *Lewis Awakening*, 15.
32. Campbell, *Revival in the Hebrides*, 41.
33. Campbell, *Revival in the Hebrides*, 41
34. Woolsey, *Channel of Revival*, 121.
35. Woolsey, *Channel of Revival*, 123.

for weeks with only a few hours of sleep grabbed after classes were over and before the meetings began. Groups of people gathered on the seashore, singing the praises of God and sharing their testimonies of what he had done for them. A drunkard in the village of Leurbost stood on a chair with a bottle of whisky in his hand and imitated Duncan Campbell preaching. But the next morning he awoke from his stupor with a terrible burden of sin and a fear of meeting Christ. Overcome with a fear of dying he walked across the island to the village of Arnol in the parish of Barvas. As he entered the meeting from the back door the first words he heard were, "You are here tonight because you are afraid of Christ. And the Christ you are afraid of loves you more than your mother ever did and will awaken you from the slumber of death with his loving gentle hand." On eventually reaching his home he went straight to his loom shed and surrendered his life to Christ.[36]

It was at Arnol that the people had remained aloof when Campbell began the village mission. An evening devoted to waiting on the Lord was therefore organized at which the local blacksmith stood and declared, "O God, your honour is at stake, and I now challenge you to fulfil your covenant engagement and do what you have promised to do." Many of those present witnessed that at that moment the house shook and dishes rattled in the sideboard. "A stream of blessing was released which brought salvation to many homes the following night" and the whole community became "alive with an awareness of God."[37]

During the communion season, when Presbyterians gathered for the Lord's Supper, Campbell went to the small island of Bernera, off the coast of Lewis, to assist in ministering the sacrament. He found the atmosphere to be heavy and sent word back to some of the men of Barvas to come over and assist in prayer. At one of their meetings a lad got up and said, "I see the Lamb in the midst of the Throne with the keys of death and hell at his girdle." He then began to sob and cried out, "Oh God, there is power there, let it loose!" In moments "the flood gates of heaven opened" and "the church resembled a battlefield. On one side many were prostrated over the seats weeping and sighing . . . God had come." Woolsey commented, "The spiritual impact of this visitation was felt throughout the island" and more people were "attending the weekly prayer meeting

---

36. Woolsey, *Channel of Revival*, 126–27.
37. Campbell, *Revival in the Hebrides*, 48–49; Woolsey, *Channel of Revival*, 132–33.

than attended public worship on the Sabbath before the revival."[38] Even more remarkable, that same evening "the power of God swept through the village of Crior, a small community six miles from the church." Duncan Campbell wrote, "I know it to be a fact that there wasn't a single house in the village that hadn't a soul saved in it. Not a single house!"[39]

In the village of Ness, in Barvas parish people were reported to be spilling out of a prayer meeting and singing praises to the Lord well into the night.[40] On Sunday evening, the 5th of June, he recorded, "Every available seat in the Town Hall was occupied." Stornoway became a particular focus of Campbell's concern, and he established an annual convention in the town. It was an occasion he looked forward to every year, and he took great encouragement from meeting up with his former converts. Of his ministry in Harris for most of December 1950 he wrote, "I never in all my life witnessed such crowds in the Highlands. The people came from all over the island 'walking over snow-covered roads, many of them a distance of three miles, and walking back home in the early hours of the morning.' On the last two nights the church was crowded three times between 7.00 p.m. and two o'clock in the morning."[41]

A remarkable incident took place on Easter Monday, 1952. Duncan Campbell had just ended an address at the Faith Mission in Hamilton Road Presbyterian Church in Bangor when he was suddenly overcome with a powerful conviction that he should go at once to Berneray, a small island off the coast of Harris. The Mission chairman tried to remonstrate with him as he was due to speak on the following day. Nevertheless, Campbell left the convention and flew from Belfast back to Scotland. On arrival on the island he asked a teenage boy the way to the manse. He was shocked when the lad replied that the manse was vacant and there was no minister at the present time and the elders were taking the services. Campbell then asked him to go ahead and tell them Mr. Campbell has arrived on the island. Astonishingly, the boy was back in ten minutes and informed him that the elders were expecting him and that accommodation had been booked for him and a service arranged for nine o'clock that evening.[42]

38. Woolsey, *Channel of Revival*, 134–35.
39. Campbell, *Revival in the Hebrides*, 44–45.
40. Woolsey, *Channel of Revival*, 124.
41. Peckham and Peckham, *Sounds from Heaven*, 99.
42. Campbell, *Revival in the Hebrides*, 141.

The first few services held on Berneray Island seemed to Campbell to be hard going, but one evening, as they were leaving the church, an elderly man took off his hat and pointed to the congregation who had just left in front of them and said, "Mr Campbell, see what's happening! He has come! He has come!" The Spirit of God had fallen on the people as they walked down to the main road. Many who were burdened with sin were gripped where they were and cried out to God on the hillside for mercy. Following this "the entire island was shaken into a new awareness of God and many lives were saved and transformed during the following days."[43]

Features of the Revival

Preaching

The Hebridean Revival was, above all, a revival centered and focused on solid, orthodox, biblical preaching. For Campbell, the Bible was unique, supreme, and the sole basis of salvation, life, and worship. Having said all that, Campbell was fully aware of the fact that the written word was in the last analysis the means through which men and women encounter Jesus, "the Living Word." Put another way, the Bible was simply a menu and not the meal. Knowing the Scriptures, Campbell urged, must never become a substitute for encountering the Savior. In his sermons and teaching, Campbell made frequent use of the examples taken from the changed lives of his converts, and he also quoted from Dwight L. Moody, Thomas à Kempis, George Whitefield, Henry Drummond, Oswald Chambers, and Samuel Chadwick. He also spoke of the need to see again the divine power manifested in the revivals under Edwards, Finney, and in the Welsh Revival.[44] He was an inspired, fiery preacher, and his words penetrated to the heart. Those who heard him felt he was speaking directly and personally to them. He didn't lead people to the Lord in the revival. He explained the way of salvation clearly and then left them to make their own commitment to the Lord.[45] For Duncan Campbell, the early morning hour was the most important time of the day when he spent time alone with God. He often said, "Give the best hours of the day to God."

---

43. Campbell, *Revival in the Hebrides*, 141–42.
44. Campbell, *Revival in the Hebrides*, 82.
45. Peckham and Peckham, *Sounds from Heaven*, 103.

Prayer

The Hebridean Revival was birthed and sustained by prayer. Prior to the revival a number of men and women had been praying for a spiritual awakening. The prayers of Peggy and Christine Smith had played a particular role in what took place. They had prayed together for many weeks and months that God would send revival.[46] At the same time a group of men in another part of the parish had begun to pray in a barn for an awakening.[47] Gatherings for prayer had also been taking place in many of the villages within the other three parishes. Duncan Campbell set a high value on those who gave themselves to prayer. It was their labors which held back opposition and made spiritual advance possible. "More was wrought by these men," he wrote, "than all the ministers put together, including myself."[48] On several occasions Campbell got in touch with a group of praying men in Barvas to come to other places and support him in the ministry.[49] He also always made a point of thanking those who had supported him in prayer. In a sermon entitled "The Price and Power of Revival" Campbell declared, "I think again of those people in the Hebrides. How they longed and how they prayed and how they waited and how they cried, 'Oh God, rend the heavens and come down,' and all the time God was handling them until the moment . . . the vessels are clean."[50] "It was only then," he continued, "that the miracle of revival can happen."[51] Duncan Campbell learned how to prevail in prayer, and whenever he became concerned for a district or parish, he stopped visiting and prayed throughout the day.

The Presence of God

Duncan Campbell believed that knowing the presence of God was the single most important feature of the Hebridean Revival. He quoted a Church of England clergyman who visited the islands and stated, "What I felt, apart from what I saw, convinced me that this was no ordinary

---

46. Woolsey, *Channel of Revival*, 114.
47. Woolsey, *Channel of Revival*, 114.
48. Woolsey, *Channel of Revival*, 132.
49. See for example Woolsey, *Channel of Revival*, 131.
50. Campbell, *Revival in the Hebrides*, 72.
51. Campbell, *Price and Power of Revival*, 72.

movement."[52] Campbell himself stated that he had known men out in the fields and others working at their looms so overcome by this sense of God's presence that they were found prostrate on the ground. Another person told him, "The grass beneath my feet and the rocks around me seem to cry, 'flee to Christ for refuge.'"[53] Annie MacKinnon testified "that the very fields were hallowed. Wherever people worked, they prayed. The place of solitude was precious to them."[54]

Singing

Almost all revivals have been impacted by singing, and the one in the Hebrides was no exception. Most often they sang the metrical Psalms rather than hymns. After the meetings came to an end the people would make a circle, join hands, and sing in the street. Catherine Campbell stated, "It was like heaven on earth. Everything was made new." Margaret McLeod recalled, "And the singing! It was simply glorious. It was almost supernatural, full of joy and spiritual power." And Mary Peckham testified that "when the people sang, oh the shivers chased themselves down my spine. I had never heard singing like this. The words rose to heaven in a power that could only be sensed but not described. The singing was fire! It went right through you."[55] Campbell reported that when the influence of the awakening in Lewis began to be felt in Harris "a gracious movement broke out and the centre of it was the place that singing had in the meetings." "Again and again," he wrote, "a wave of deep conviction of sin would sweep over the congregation, and men and women would be seen bending before the Lord."[56]

An Absence of Healing and Speaking in Tongues

Unlike many of the world's major revival movements the one in Lewis did not see people being healed. Campbell wrote, "Perhaps I should say this that in the Lewis revival we never saw anyone healed; that wasn't a feature of it." Equally, Campbell wrote, "We never heard anybody speaking in

---

52. Campbell, *Revival in the Hebrides*, 40.
53. Campbell, *Revival in the Hebrides*, 40.
54. Campbell, *Revival in the Hebrides*, 24.
55. Campbell, *Revival in the Hebrides*, 22.
56. Campbell, *Lewis Awakening*, 16.

tongues, in a strange language."⁵⁷ In fact Campbell stated that he had never heard anyone speak in tongues until much later in his life and that was in England. He himself asserted that "he believed in every gift mentioned in the word of God" but stressed that "it wasn't God's plan or purpose that we should be visited in this way."⁵⁸

Baptism in the Holy Spirit

Despite not speaking in tongues Campbell was a strong believer in the Baptism of the Holy Spirit as a second empowering experience. He wrote, "I hope you believe in the baptism of the Holy Ghost as a distinct experience. You may disagree, but I believe in it. I don't think that I am preaching one set of doctrine that insists upon gifts. I am not thinking of that at all because I believe that the baptism of the Holy Ghost in its final analysis is just the revelation of Jesus. It is Jesus becoming real, wonderful, powerful, and dynamic in my life . . . That is the baptism of the Holy Spirit that I believe in . . . Some of my dearest friends are among those who exercise gifts."⁵⁹

Clean Hands and a Pure Heart

From the very beginning of the Hebridean Revival there was a clear focus on the need for holiness of living. The tone was set early on by the reading of Psalm 24:3–5 on several occasions. God, it was asserted, can only manifest his presence where his people have "clean hands and a pure heart." Campbell therefore stressed not only seeking cleansing through the blood of the cross but the vital necessity of wholly surrendering to Christ every aspect of life and behavior. As he put it, "Where there is obedience and faith, this full life in God is gloriously possible."⁶⁰

---

57. Campbell, *Revival in the Hebrides*, 40.
58. Campbell, *Revival in the Hebrides*, 42.
59. Campbell, *Revival in the Hebrides*, 42.
60. Campbell, *Revival in the Hebrides*, 85.

Other Manifestations

The Hebridean Revival did however witness a number of manifestations. There were numerous occasions when people dropped to the ground in tears of repentance and called out to God for forgiveness and salvation. There were many such instances on the night of Campbell's arrival when, as we have seen, several hundred men and women had been prompted to come down to Barvas Church in the middle of the night and among the crowd who gathered outside the police station.[61] Andrew Woolsey noted that many of them fell on their knees, conscious only of the power and presence of God. Campbell also noted an occasion when seven men were discovered lying prostrate, face down behind their looms.[62] In the matter of people falling and crying out Campbell took the advice of George Whitefield and Lady Huntingdon and did not remove them from the meetings.[63] Interestingly Campbell and others noted that the Island of Harris differed from Lewis with respect to physical manifestations. While the Lewis parishes witnessed many prostrations "they were not witnessed in Harris." There was, however, an "awe-inspiring sense of the presence of God" which came over the island.[64]

A Revival to Savor

Duncan Campbell was not without his faults, and like everyone else in a fallen world he too had issues to deal with. He was constantly concerned for his wife and family. He was sometimes too ready to accept at face value reports that later proved to be exaggerated. At times he found it hard to sleep and, possibly in consequence, suffered times of spiritual darkness. His constant preaching caused damage to his vocal cords and resulted in his withdrawing from ministry for several periods of time. That said, in Duncan Campbell the inhabitants of the Hebrides had a godly and wise leader to guide them in their time of revival. He was himself a man of prayer. It was observed that some of the most powerful outpourings of the Holy Spirit came when he was asked to pray. On one occasion in a gathering at the police station, he had only uttered the word "Father" and

---

61. Campbell, *Revival in the Hebrides*, 38–40.
62. Campbell, *Revival in the Hebrides*, 41.
63. Campbell, *Revival in the Hebrides*, 41.
64. Campbell, *Lewis Awakening*, 17.

almost everyone melted into tears and there was a deep sense of God's presence among them.[65] He was careful to play down his own role in the revival. He regarded himself as an instrument through whom God brought revival and often said that revival had already come to Lewis before his arrival. Knowing well that preparation leads to expectation he was painstaking and careful in the preparation of his sermons and Bible readings. He listened carefully to the promptings of God's Spirit as to what he should teach. On one occasion, a vehicle which was taking a group of people to a meeting broke down and the passengers were fortunate in finding a boat to take them across the Loch to the church. On arrival at the meeting, Duncan, not knowing of their adventure, announced his text, "They also took shipping and came to Capernaum, seeking Jesus!"[66]

Duncan was a straightforward preacher. There was nothing complicated in his message. It was the plain truth for the plain man: biblical, solid, orthodox, and applied to everyday living. He always left his hearers with a choice between the way of life and the way of death. He focused on the love of God and the cross but was not afraid to warn of the coming judgment, particularly on those who continued to live in sinful ways. People spoke of him as "a gentleman of God" and said, "If you didn't believe in God you could no longer be an atheist after meeting him."[67]

Duncan Campbell, like other exemplary revival leaders, was humble and modest and worked in unity with other ministers on the islands. The Rev. Murdo MacLennan, the minister of Carloway, traveled many miles with his wife to assist Campbell in his ministry. In his own account of the revival, Campbell paid tribute to two Church of Scotland ministers, the Rev. Murdo McLeod of Tarbert and the Rev. Angus McKillop "who left their own parishes and threw their full weight into the movement."[68] Duncan Campbell always tried to embrace all denominations and recommended those who committed themselves to Christ at his meetings to return to their local churches. This sometimes created problems when converts were not welcomed in the way they should have been, which caused considerable anguish.

The revival had a lasting impact on many lives. Many hundreds put their faith in Christ. *The Glasgow Herald* reported "that hundreds

---

65. Woolsey, *Channel of Revival*, 134.
66. Woolsey, *Channel of Revival*, 125.
67. Woolsey, *Channel of Revival*, 163.
68. Campbell, *Revival in the Hebrides*, 14.

were converted and church membership increased in every district."[69] James McKay, the minister of Barvas, wrote of "the deep work" which had taken place in his Church of Scotland parish. "There are," he wrote, "more than one hundred souls in this parish whose hearts God has graciously touched since the movement started. God is maintaining them all; not one has gone back. . . . Many of them are staunchly upholding the cause of Christ in their own home areas; but there are some who are now scattered throughout the world."[70] A Church of Scotland minister was asked to respond to a survey on the faith of his parishioners who had been converted in the revival. He stated that "122 people found faith and I'm not talking about middle age or the old, but I'm thinking about young people. One-hundred-and-twenty-two, all of them over the age of 17. They found the Saviour during the first wave of the revival. Today, I can say that they are growing like flowers in the garden of God. There is not a single backslider among them."[71] In many areas it was reported that young people no longer danced into the early hours, many were delivered from drunkenness. There were also cases of restitution taking place following Campbell's revival services. There were reports of stolen articles, money, and even animals being returned to their rightful owners. One American visitor confessed it cost him over $10,000 to repay what he had taken by dishonest means.[72]

In short, the Hebridean Revival magnified and uplifted the name of Jesus Christ. Many hundreds of men and women of all ages, as well as children, committed themselves to him. Their lives and those of their families and communities were profoundly and lastingly changed. Duncan Campbell was a man and leader of great integrity. He made many trips to other parts of the British Isles and beyond in order to spread the message of revival further afield, but remained on the island for the most part. His solid, creedal, Protestant, and biblical preaching sustained and discipled those who had come to faith in Christ, and this resulted in their enduring faith.

---

69. *The Glasgow Herald*, in Woolsey, *Channel of Revival*, 149.
70. Woolsey, *Channel of Revival*, 149.
71. Campbell, *Revival in the Hebrides*, 53.
72. Woolsey, *Channel of Revival*, 164.

12

Inspirational Revivals

HAVING READ THE PRECEDING eleven chapters we are now hopefully able to appreciate the ways in which revivals can bring inspiration both to ourselves as individuals as well as to the wider Christian church and nation. The word "revival" speaks of bringing situations back to new life. Revivals, therefore, often occur in times of economic, social, and spiritual hardship when new life and fresh hope are particularly needed. We see this illustrated in the case of the Methodist and Primitive Methodist Revivals and in the revival in the Southern Colonies of America. In reading the accounts of revivals we are challenged to keep praying and persevering in our commitment to Christ. We are encouraged to live hopefully and expectantly as we see other people's lives and relationships transformed and renewed. What God did in the revivals of the past in and through the lives of his people he can do again in us and through today's Christian leaders and churches. Revivals in general, and the ten introduced in this book in particular, bring inspiration in five important ways which will now be considered by way of conclusion. Inevitably in the process there will be some references back to material in the previous chapters.

The Presence of a Living God

The greatest inspiration conveyed by revivals is the reminder that we have a living God. In revival movements we encounter a Jesus who is more than just a figure of the past. We experience the Jesus who is the risen

Lord, God, and Savior in ways that impact our day-to-day living. We know in our personal experience that he is not just a past-tense historical figure or a great teacher whose words we read in our Bibles or have explained to us in Sunday sermons. Revivals take us beyond a Christianity which is knowing about God to knowing him personally. In revival times Christians realize in a new way that Christianity is much more than merely giving intellectual assent to creedal doctrines; it's knowing the presence of the one on whose teachings they are based. Revivals, as we have observed in these chapters, are first and foremost about God. Revivals are about God and for God. They are times when Jesus is magnified, worshiped, and glorified. In revival, Jesus is vividly present both among his people and in the world beyond them. Revival is not about intensive human activity. It is not about crusade-style evangelism (although that may have its place). Revival is first and foremost a sovereign move of God. Indeed, a definition of revival could simply be, "God came." The revivals considered in these chapters give us glimpses of people lifted up and inspired by the manifest presence of God. In his *Narrative of Surprising Conversions* Jonathan Edwards recalled that at the height of the revival in his Congregational Massachusetts parish of Northampton "the town seemed full of the presence of God." "There were," he continued, "remarkable tokens of God's presence in almost every house."[1] Edwards, as we have noted, also remarked on the vivid presence of God in public worship and the many instances of persons coming to the town and experiencing "that shower of divine blessing which God rained down here."[2]

In the revivals that took place at Cambuslang and Kilsyth many of the people who came to receive the bread and wine at the sacramental meetings had an overwhelming sense of "the power and special presence of God."[3] In the great eighteenth-century Methodist Revival in England there was a marked focus on experiencing the Lord's presence. The heart of Whitefield and the Wesleys' mission was enabling their hearers to know God's presence through the experience of "new birth" and the "witness of God's Spirit in their hearts."[4] In November 1738, John Wesley wrote to his older brother Samuel, "I believe every Christian who has not yet received it, should pray for the witness of God's Spirit with his spirit

---

1. Edwards, *Narrative of Many Surprising Conversions*, 14.
2. Edwards, *Narrative of Many Surprising Conversions*, 15.
3. Macfarlan, *Revivals of the Eighteenth Century*, 72.
4. Wesley, *Works of John Wesley*, 6:607.

that he is a child of God."[5] Both the revival in the Southern American Colonies and the English Primitive Methodist Revival promoted camp meetings because they proved to be a powerful means by which the poor, marginalized, and rural populations encountered the presence of the living God.

Charles Finney, who was instrumental in bringing revival to many churches and communities in Upper New York State, reported cases of people experiencing the Lord's presence in unexpected ways. He wrote that men entering the town of Utica on business "felt as if God pervaded the whole atmosphere" and "some were converted without even attending the meetings."[6] When Finney visited a cotton mill at Oriskany Creek many men had such an overwhelming experience of the presence of the Lord that they "came under conviction and burst into tears." In response, the manager, a Mr. Walcott, who was a good man though not a Christian, ordered that the mill "be shut down while the men deal with their souls."[7]

This same vivid and sometimes overwhelming sense of the presence of God was seen in the Welsh Revival and in that at Azusa Street in Los Angeles. And it was also remarkably evident in the revival on the Hebridean Island of Lewis. There, on the night of the 7th of December, 1950, 600 people were awakened from sleep and directed by God's presence to go to Barvas Parish Church. A further 400 gathered around the police station at four o'clock the following morning, many of them crying out to the Lord in response to his awesome presence. Norman Campbell, who was a resident on the island of Lewis and attended many meetings, wrote that "the outstanding feature of the revival was the presence of God."[8] William MacLeod testified, "God was in the homes; God was speaking to people at their daily work. The consciousness of the divine was everywhere."[9] The Rev. John Murdo Smith of Barvas stated, "Now, if I were to tell you the outstanding features of revival it is this. There was a universal presence of God—a sense of the Lord's presence was everywhere."[10]

This powerful experience of the presence of the living God is the inspirational capstone of revival movements. As we read them and turn

---

5. Wesley, *Works of John Wesley*, 6:607.
6. Sherwood Eddy, *Spiritual Awakening*, 9.
7. Peckham and Peckham, *Sounds from Heaven*, 90.
8. Peckham and Peckham, *Sounds from Heaven*, 90.
9. Peckham and Peckham, *Sounds from Heaven*, 91.
10. Peckham and Peckham, *Sounds from Heaven*, 92.

them over in our minds, they will hopefully cause us, like the psalmist in Psalm 42, to thirst like a deer—not for water, but for the presence of the living God.[11]

The Power of Prayer

A particularly inspirational aspect of revivals is the way in which they encourage Christians to pray. They give powerful reminders of the rewards and blessings that flow from prayer, especially in times of spiritual awakening. In each of the revival movements which have been considered it is clear that prayer played a significant role both in birthing them and in sustaining their progress. Jonathan Edwards, in his account of the revival in Northampton, noted there was "an earnest application" to prayer.[12] In his account of the revival in Cambuslang, Macfarlan noted that the parish minister, William McCulloch, "spent much time in prayer." Furthermore, "he greatly encouraged private Christians to meet for social prayer, and particularly that God would revive his work everywhere."[13] The years which preceded the revival in the Southern Colonies of America were marked by "a new evangelical zeal"[14] which was led by men such as James McGready, Barton Stone, and Peter Cartwright, all of whom formed disciplined habits of prayer and study. The camp meetings which they organized had a particular focus on prayer and preaching. It was these occasions which prepared the ground for the awakening which took place in Cane Ridge, Red River, and a host of other places.

The Methodist Revival in England had its beginnings in the Oxford University Holy Club. There Whitefield, the Wesleys, and a small group of Fellows and tutors met regularly and developed a discipline of prayer which for all of them became a lifelong habit. In fact, they even recorded how much time they spent each day in prayer.[15] This later led to their organizing and setting up hundreds of societies and watchnight meetings for prayer, which then became the sustaining bedrock of the revival and impacted the culture and society of the times. Likewise, the Primitive Methodist Revival in the first half of the nineteenth century was birthed

---

11. Ps 42:1–2.
12. Edwards, *Narrative of Many Surprising Conversions*, 24.
13. Macfarlan, *Revivals of the Eighteenth Century*, 36.
14. Hudson, *Religion in America*, 146.
15. Hindmarsh, *Spirit of Early Evangelicalism*, 16–17.

through prayer; in this case "cottage meetings of a noisyish type."[16] Both Hugh Bourne and William Clowes were men of prayer; Bourne describing himself as "fitted to being a public praying labourer."[17] Clowes was also noted as "impressive"[18] in prayer.

When the focus shifts to the revivals in the 1820s under Charles Finney in Upper New York State, we are once again challenged by the priority given to prayer. As has been noted, Finney established meetings for prayer in every town and city in which he held his campaigns. In them he made particular use of women who organized and led many of the meetings. Finney urged the importance of "prevailing" or laboring in prayer until the time when those who were praying felt God had answered.[19] When that moment was reached any further prayer would amount to a lack of faith.

Prayer was therefore unmistakably at the heart of each of the ten revivals considered in this book. The Welsh Revival began in prayer meetings organized by Evan Roberts. For years there was prayer day and night at William Seymour's Azusa Street Mission and in several other centers of the Los Angeles Revival. The same emphasis was seen in the revivals at Lowestoft and in the Hebrides. At the former, Douglas Brown made sure that prayer meetings were held each morning during his ministry in the town. New converts from the previous night's meeting gave testimony to their newfound faith and requests for help and guidance were read out and prayed for. Two elderly sisters prayed for many weeks that revival would come in the Hebrides. Their prayers, along with those of other praying groups in each of the four parishes on the Island of Lewis, saw a powerful effect on the community. It lasted for three years with an impact which endured for many years thereafter.

The accounts of revival are a challenge and inspiration to God's people to pray. When we read of lives and relationships being transformed, churches revived, dishonestly taken money and goods restored, and drunkenness overcome, we will find new motivation to keep praying for revival in the present. It has been truly said that "the measure of our belief in prayer is the time we actually spend in it." The challenge is to follow the example of the two sisters in Barvas Parish on the Isle of Lewis,

---

16. Werner, *Primitive Methodist Connexion*, 180.
17. Kendall, *Origin and History*, 1:31.
18. Kendall, *Origin and History*, 1:55.
19. Finney, *Revivals of Religion*, 50, and Lecture 4: "Prevailing Prayer."

who spent long hours interceding for revival to come.[20] Griffin was surely right when he wrote, "Every revival has been prepared beforehand, as God has stirred his people to pray for it."[21]

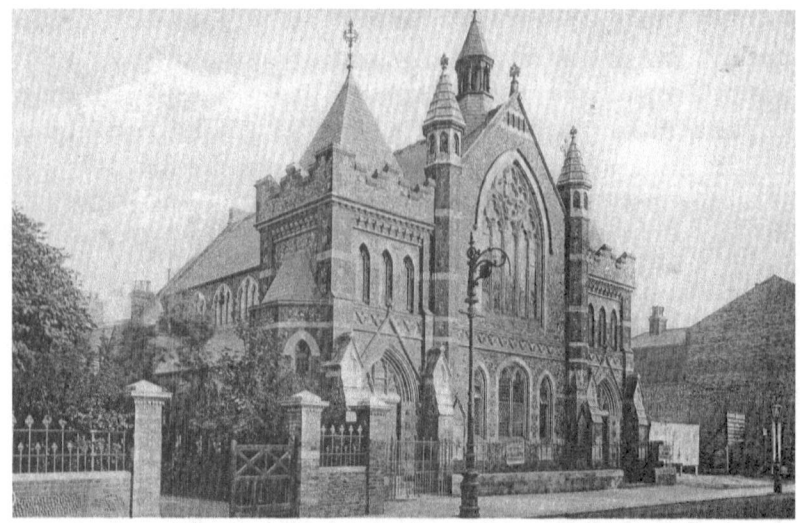

Lowestoft Baptist Church. Copyright unknown. Scanned from *A Forgotten Revival* (DayOne Publications, 1992) 21.

Christians and Churches Renewed

As well as impacting culture and society, revival embraces churches and the lives of individual Christian people. In times when the Holy Spirit is poured out there is often a strong bond of unity and love between differing denominational and independent churches. The revival in Northampton was reported to have done much to promote an "irenic ecclesiastical temper, bridging religious barriers in much the same way as it had tended to dissolve colonial boundaries by the sweeping tide of new religious life and activity."[22] This was clearly visible in the sacramental and camp meetings of the Second Great Awakening at which Methodists, Baptists, and Presbyterians all joined together for several days of prayer, worship, and preaching. When Charles Finney agreed to hold a

20. Woolsey, *Channel of Revival*, 113–14.
21. Griffin, *Forgotten Revival*, 102–3.
22. Hudson, *Religion in America*, 99–100.

campaign in a particular town or city, ensuring unity was his foremost concern. He always endeavored to secure an agreement from at least most of the churches to support his coming and to pledge to work together.[23] If possible, his aim was to hold his meetings in buildings which did not belong to one particular denomination. If that was not an option, he often arranged his meetings in several different churches. At the Azusa Street Revival, Bartleman was struck by the atmosphere of deep unity and love. He reported that people from every denomination and some from across the globe came "and seeking souls could be found under the power almost any hour, night and day." He continued, "The meeting did not depend on the human leader. God's presence became more and more wonderful in that old building."[24] All who came were given the same hospitable welcome and, even more importantly, black and white people worshiped and shared in the revival together. In the Lowestoft Revival there were similar accounts of unity and the manifest presence of God in the meetings. London Road Baptist Church and the three Church of England churches worked in perfect harmony with the clergy praying together and sharing their venues for meetings.

The vivid and powerful manifestation of God's presence in revival drives the churches' mission and evangelism forward and, in so doing, produces a growth in membership. In addition, religious life and worship are renewed and enhanced. A cursory glimpse at some of the revivals in the preceding chapters illustrates the point. For example, the revival in the Southern Colonies resulted in a huge growth in church membership, with the Presbyterians increasing by 30,000 between 1800 and 1810 and the Baptists increasing by 65,000 in the same period.[25] The eighteenth-century Methodist Revival resulted in perhaps as many as 300,000 members in 1791, the year of John Wesley's death.[26] When the Primitive Methodist Church was formed by Bourne and Clowes in 1811, it had only a handful of members, but in the 1851 Census of Religion, the number of people attending Primitive Methodist places of worship was

---

23. Finney, *Memoirs*, 195.
24. Bartleman, *Azusa Street Revival*, 52.
25. See chap. 5 of this volume, "The Revival in the Southern Colonies of America."
26. Rack, *Reasonable Enthusiast*, 438.

recorded as 266,555.[27] The Welsh Revival witnessed 100,000 converts in the first six months.[28]

In times of revival there is always a marked renewal in the worshipping life of the churches. This is seen in a desire to honor and lift up the name of Jesus, a spiritual hunger for orthodox biblical preaching of the great creedal doctrines of the faith, and a fresh delight in singing. These aspects of a sovereign move of God were evident in the revivals that have been considered. Jonathan Edwards wrote of the Northampton Revival, "Our public assemblies were then beautiful: the congregation was alive in God's service, every one earnestly intent on the public worship, every hearer eager to drink in the words of the minister as they came from his mouth."[29] Edwards also recorded a remarkable uplift in the singing and a high attendance at the sacrament.[30] In the Cambuslang Revival there was an increased delight in worship with a desire for "a daily sermon" after which "they usually spen[t] some time in exhortation, prayer and singing of psalms."[31] At Kilsyth, many services had to be held in the open air in order to cope with the large numbers attending. And at both places the people came to a new appreciation of the Lord's Supper.[32]

The renewal of singing in revival times was at its most prominent in the eighteenth-century Methodist Revival, with Charles Wesley composing more than 9,000 hymns and sacred poems.[33] His hymns demonstrate that he was a master communicator of essential Christian doctrine. They were, in the words of his brother John, "a little body of practical divinity." Many of them had refrains which those who were unable to read could memorize and then sing with exuberant joy.[34] Charles Wesley's easy melodies and frequent use of the personal pronoun, as in "my chains fell off, my heart was free," created singing that induced an experience of the presence of Christ and his Spirit.[35] Charles Finney was also very aware of the importance and value of music as a means of expressing and

27. Thompson, *Nonconformity in the Nineteenth Century*, 153.
28. Morgan, *Welsh Religious Revival*, 248.
29. Edwards, *Narrative of Many Surprising Conversions*, 14.
30. Edwards, *Narrative of Many Surprising Conversions*, 14, 16.
31. Macfarlan, *Revivals of the Eighteenth Century*, 48.
32. Fawcett, *Cambuslang Revival*, 115, 131.
33. Tyson, *Assist Me to Proclaim*, 255.
34. Tyson, *Assist Me to Proclaim*, 254.
35. Tyson, *Assist Me to Proclaim*, 255.

channeling the experience of revival. In his later years he employed Thomas Hastings to assist him with music and song.[36]

Frank Bartleman recalled the worship at Azusa Street, writing that "a heavenly atmosphere pervaded the place. Such singing as I have never heard before, the very melody of Heaven. It seemed to come direct from the throne."[37] The Welsh Revival which followed it was birthed in song which could, on occasion, be fervent. "Here Is Love Vast as the Ocean" was sung many times over in the chapels and almost became a theme song of the revival. At the majority of services traditional hymns were sung unaccompanied, and in Welsh, often with a slow impressiveness.[38] At Lowestoft, singing featured in all the revival meetings, with gospel songs from Sankey's collection being particular favorites. There were reports of people being drawn into the meetings after hearing the singing out in the streets. The Hebridean Revival was likewise marked by heartfelt singing. Duncan Campbell wrote in his account of the revival, "In Lewis they do not sing hymns; they sing the Psalms of David . . . and they sang and they sang verse after verse. Oh, what singing! What singing!"[39] Mary Peckham, who was in the heart of the revival, wrote, "Singing was a mighty instrument in the revival. They were singing the word of God and this, filled with the presence of God, made the singing mighty in the Holy Spirit. The people sang with all their hearts and meant every word they sang."[40]

The Social Impact

Although revivals are a sovereign move of God, they all necessarily have a human element which is composed of fallible, fallen people. These men and women sometimes overwork—a common fault among revival leaders—make bad decisions, and utilize unhelpful techniques. It's not indeed difficult to find human imperfections even in the greatest of revivals. There are also armchair critics and academics who down revival movements as fundamentalist enthusiasm or the product of emotionalism. However, it is much harder to explain away the social transformation which flows from revival. God-inspired revivals not only transform

36. Scotland, *Apostles of the Spirit and Fire*, 86–87.
37. Bartleman, *Azusa Street Revival*, 56.
38. Jones, *Voices from the Welsh Revival*, 71–72.
39. Campbell, *Revival in the Hebrides*, 38.
40. Peckham and Peckham, *Sounds from Heaven*, 93.

the spiritual lives of individual Christian people and churches, but they can also profoundly impact the surrounding lives and culture of the communities and places where they take place. This indeed is an inspirational aspect of revival which is hard to gainsay. It is an aspect which stands clear in the great revival text in 2 Chronicles, where in response to praying and seeking his face the Lord promises "to come and heal the land" (2 Chr 7:14).

We see this promise played out in each of the revivals considered in these pages. At Northampton, Jonathan Edwards reported that when the Spirit of God began to be so wonderfully poured out in a general way through the town, "people had soon done with their old quarrels, back-bitings and intermeddling with other men's matters. The tavern was soon left empty, and persons kept very much at home."[41] In another place Edwards wrote, "Some who before were very rough in their temper and manners seemed to be remarkably softened and sweetened." And he added, "I know of no one young person in the town who has returned to former ways of looseness and extravagance in any respect."[42] Reflecting later in a letter dated the 12th of December, 1743, Edwards wrote of "the great alteration among the youth of our town, with respect to revelry, frolicking, profane, and licentious conversation and there has been a great alteration among both old and young, with regard to tavern haunting."[43] William McCulloch wrote and published a similar testimony to the great change that came in the wake of the revival at Cambuslang:

> Such as were given to cursing and swearing have laid aside the practice, learning to speak the language of heaven, and having upon them a holy awe of God and of things divine. Such as were accustomed to frequent taverns, to drink and play cards &c., till late, or it may be the morning hours, have, for these nine years past, avoided all occasions of the kind, and kept at home, spending their evenings with their families in secret and family devotion.[44]

There were also instances of restoration of stolen money and goods being restored and of adults learning to read.[45]

---

41. Edwards, *Narrative of Many Surprising Conversions*, 23–24.
42. Edwards, *Narrative of Many Surprising Conversions*, 72.
43. Edwards, *Account of the Revival*, 148.
44. Macfarlan, *Revivals of the Eighteenth Century*, 99–100.
45. Fawcett, *Cambuslang Revival*, 176–77.

The eighteenth-century Methodist Revival, which took place under the ministries of Whitefield and the Wesleys, powerfully demonstrated the ways in which revival is able to transform society. John Wesley declared in his *Discourse on the Sermon on the Mount* that "Christianity is essentially a Social Religion" and that "it cannot subsist at all without living and conversing with other men."[46] He challenged and condemned slavery, which he termed "the execrable sum of all villainies."[47] Both the Wesleys and Whitefield took steps to improve the conditions in the prisons and visited prisoners in their cells. John Wesley was a vigorous opponent of the gin shops and urged his followers not to buy or sell spiritous liquor.[48] Frequently styling himself "God's Steward of the Poor," he wrote a tract entitled *On the Present Scarcity of Provisions* condemning the government for causing the high prices of food. He condemned gambling, opposed government public lotteries, and set up a dispensary to care for the sick. The Methodists established schools and taught reading and writing. In addition, John Wesley concerned himself with the distribution of wealth, smuggling, intemperance, and the conditions in the mines, fields, and factories. In short, the Methodist revival changed the face of England.

The nineteenth-century Primitive Methodist Revival in England replicated the same practical care for the poor and marginalized that the Wesleyan revival had demonstrated in the previous century. They founded many day and Sunday schools which taught the three Rs. They advocated temperance societies and founded benefit institutions, they championed improvements in working conditions, and Primitive Methodist local preachers formed the first mineworkers trade unions.

The revival in the Southern States of America was led by men such as Barton Stone, Peter Cartwright, and others who were strongly opposed to slavery. The awakening, which impacted the entire nation, spawned a number of educational institutions and philanthropic and missionary societies with a marked concern to promote temperance. *The American Bible Society*, *The American Sunday School Union*, and *The American Tract Society* were all founded in the wake of the revival. Winthrop Hudson was of the view that "the revival campaigns of the Second Awakening stressed a doctrine of disinterested benevolence . . . as the key to Christian

---

46. Bready, *England Before and After Wesley*, 137.
47. Wesley, *Journal*, 12 February, 1772.
48. Heaseman, *Evangelicals in Action*, 127.

responsibility." "If one's conversion was genuine," he asserted, "it would express itself in action."[49]

All the while Charles Finney was seeing outpourings of the Holy Spirit, he remained a champion of social justice. He was outspoken against slavery and refused communion to slaveholders. He was a promoter of women's rights and female education. He pioneered equal education for blacks and whites at Oberlin College. The Azusa Street Revival resulted in a remarkable coming together of black and white pastors and church members from all over the world. It played a significant role in helping to break down racism in the churches and beyond. The Welsh Revival saw a steep decline in drunkenness, and the atmosphere in the coal mines was transformed. Swearing became a thing of the past, prayer meetings were held below ground during the lunch breaks, and the pit ponies treated with kindness and respect.[50] The number of crimes committed and arrests made declined steeply, and police reported that "the taverns in many places were empty and the streets entirely quiet."[51] At Lowestoft, which had a population of 10,000 at the time of the revival, drunkenness declined and the police reported that they had fewer people to deal with from "the dens of vice in the town."[52] In the Hebrides Revival, cases of restitution frequently followed Campbell's preaching.[53] He himself noted the closure of drinking houses[54] and wrote that "Social evils were swept away as by a flood in the night."[55]

Leaders with Ability and Integrity

The main leaders through whom the revivals considered in this book came all had their weaknesses. Jonathan Edwards, for example, tried to exercise too tight a hold on his Northampton congregation, making them pledge to a rigid covenant which ultimately led to his leaving the church and town. John Wesley and George Whitefield were faithful in their marriages but were often away from their spouses for long periods and

49. Hudson, *Religion in America*, 152.
50. Jones, *Voices from the Welsh Revival*, 215.
51. Jones, *Voices from the Welsh Revival*, 218.
52. Griffin, *Forgotten Revival*, 100.
53. Woolsey, *Channel of Revival*, 162.
54. Campbell, *Revival in the Hebrides*, 49, 103.
55. Campbell, *Revival in the Hebrides*, 105.

lacked warmth and intimacy in their relationships. Some of the leaders in the Second Great Awakening placed too much emphasis on exhortation and emotion. It has been said that in some places the Welsh Revival was drowned in singing. Evan Roberts, therefore, probably needed to preach and teach more than he did. Whitefield, Charles Finney, Evan Roberts, Douglas Brown, and Duncan Campbell all overworked to a point where they had to take time out to rest and recover.

There were doubtless many other minor mistakes, misunderstandings, disagreements, and wrong emphases. That said, these leaders all stand as men of integrity who walked with the Lord, retained a discipline of worship, prayer, and the study of the Scriptures. They were individuals with a heart to know and glorify God and promote the advance of his kingdom. As we read the accounts of these and other revivals we can find and draw inspiration from their accomplishments. They were all orthodox Christians who held firmly to the doctrines of the Apostles' Creed. They loved God's word and they preached the gospel of forgiveness through the cross of Christ and new life through his resurrection and outpoured Holy Spirit. They were leaders who were prepared to take risks which included crossing new boundaries and breaking new ground in frontier states and hostile towns and cities. Above all, they were men who pursued the presence of God.

We see this, for example, in Jonathan Edwards. After graduating from Yale in 1722, he served for a brief period as an assistant minister in New York City. There he had a powerful conversion experience which led to his forming a series of *Thirty-Four Resolutions* which covered most of his personal and social life. Both the Wesleys and Whitefield experienced the new birth but continued to pursue the presence of God with disciplined prayer, worship, and attendance at the sacrament of communion. They experienced the love of God shed abroad in their own hearts. Charles Finney had an overwhelming divine encounter in which "it seemed as if I had met the Lord Jesus Christ face to face."[56] He later spoke of it as "a baptism of the Holy Spirit."[57] After prolonged days and evenings praying for God's presence in his life Evan Roberts was awakened in his sleep at one o'clock in the morning and "found myself with unspeakable joy and awe, in the very presence of Almighty God."[58] It was an experience which

---

56. Finney, *Memoirs*, 14.
57. Finney, *Memoirs*, 23–24.
58. Jones, *Voices from the Welsh Revival*, 18.

lasted for four hours and happened every day for three months.[59] Douglas Brown constantly sought to wholly surrender his life to Christ, and there came a time after he had been in ministry for many years that he "really learned the meaning of the baptism of the Holy Spirit."[60] Two weeks after his conversion, Duncan Campbell had what he described "as a mighty baptism of the Holy Spirit." He later wrote that "the baptism of the Holy Spirit in its final analysis is just the revelation of Jesus. It is Jesus becoming real, wonderful, powerful and dynamic in my life."[61]

Last Word

In conclusion, there is one thing of which we can be quite sure and that is that we need revival; our churches need revival and our nation needs revival. We need a revival that will magnify and lift the name of Jesus in our places of worship and in our nation, which is rapidly turning away both from him and his teaching. We need to turn again to the Christian democratic values which molded and shaped our country's life and constitution. So, let us follow the example of John Wesley, who once prayed, "Oh, Lord, send us a revival, without defects; but if this cannot be, send it—with all its defects. We must have the revival."[62]

---

59. Jones, *Voices from the Welsh Revival*, 18.
60. Griffin, *Forgotten Revival*, 55.
61. Campbell, *Revival in the Hebrides*, 43.
62. Hambrick-Stowe, *Charles G. Finney*, 190.

Also by Nigel Scotland

1980—*Can We Trust the Gospels?*
1981—*Methodism and the Revolt of the Field in East Anglia*
1986—*The Changing Face of RE*
1989—*Eucharistic Consecration in the First Four Centuries*
1991—*Agricultural Trade Unionism in Gloucestershire*
1991—*Going by the Book*
1993—*A Gloucestershire Gallery (editor)*
1995—*Charismatics and the Next Millennium*
1995—*Living with a Purpose*
1995—*Recovering the Ground: Towards Radical Church Planting (editor)*
1995—*The Life and Work of John Bird Sumner: Evangelical Archbishop*
2000—*Charismatics and the New Millennium*
2000—*Good and Proper Men: Lord Palmerston and the Bench of Bishops*
2000—*Sectarian Religion in Contemporary Britain*
2003—*Evangelical Anglicans in a Revolutionary Age, 1789–1851*
2005—*A Pocket Guide to Sects and New Religions*
2006—*The Baker Guide to New Religions*

2007—*Squires in the Slums: Settlements and Missions in Late Victorian London*

2009—*Apostles of the Spirit and Fire*

2011—*Rome: City of Empire, Christendom and Culture*

2014—*The Supper: Cranmer and Communion*

2015—*Jesus and Life's Four Great Questions*

2016—*The New Passover: Rethinking the Lord's Supper for Today*

2017—*Straightforward Christianity*

2019—*Questions No-one Can Avoid*

2019—*George Whitefield: The First Transatlantic Revivalist*

2021—*Joseph Cotton Wigram: Bishop of Rochester*

Bibliography

Adams, Kevin. *A Diary of Revival: The Outbreak of the 1904 Welsh Awakening*. Surrey: Crusade for World Revival, 2004.
Ambler, Rod W. *Ranters, Revivalists and Reformers*. Hull, UK: Hull University Press, 1989.
Anderson, Allan H. *An Introduction to Pentecostalism: Global Christianity*. Cambridge: Cambridge University Press, 2014.
Anderson, Robert. M. *Vision of the Disinherited: The Making of American Pentecostalism*. New York: Oxford University Press, 1979.
Anonymous. *The Book of Common Prayer and of Administration of the Sacraments*. Oxford: Oxford University Press, n.d.
———. *British Methodism and the Poor 1739–1799*. Methodist Archives, John Rylands Library, Manchester University.
Armstrong, Anthony. *The Church of England and the Methodists*. London: University of London Press, 1973.
Armstrong. John H. "Revival: What and Why?" *Reformation & Revival* 1.2 (1992) 9–21.
Asbury, Francis. *The Journals and Letters of Francis Asbury*. 3 vols. Nashville: Abingdon, 1958.
Bacon, Leonard W. *A History of American Christianity*. New York: Scribner's, 1907.
Baker, Frank. *Methodism and the Love Feast*. London: Epworth, 1956.
———. *William Grimshaw*. London: Epworth, 1956.
Bartleman. Frank. *The Azusa Street Revival: An Eyewitness Account*. Milton Keynes: Revival School, 2008.
Bewes, Richard T. *Under the Thorn Tree*. Ross-shire, UK: Christian Focus, 2017.
Blumhofer, Edith. *The Assemblies of God*. 2 vols. Springfield, MO: Gospel, 1989.
Bourne, Hugh. *History of the Primitive Methodist Church*. N.p.: Falkner, 1833.
Bradley, Ian. *The Call to Seriousness*. London: Cape, 1976.
Bready, J. Wesley. *England Before and After Wesley*. London: Hodder & Stoughton, 1938.
Briggs, Frederick W. *Bishop Asbury: A Biographical Study*. London: Wesleyan Conference Office, 1874.

Brown, Callum G. *Religion and Society in Twentieth-Century Britain*. London: Routledge, 2014.

Brown, Ford K. *Fathers of the Victorians*. Cambridge: Cambridge University Press, 1961.

Burt, Thomas. "Methodism and the Northern Miners." *The Primitive Methodist Quarterly Review* 4 (July 1882) 1–27.

Campbell, Duncan. *The Lewis Awakening, 1949–1953*. Phoenix: Evangelical Tracts, 1954.

———. *Revival in the Hebrides*. Stevens Point, WI: Kraus, 2016.

Campbell Morgan, George. *Lessons of the Welsh Revival*. Edinburgh: Cross Reach, 2017.

Cartwright, Peter. *The Backwoods Preacher: Being the Autobiography of Peter Cartwright*. London: Kelly, 1890.

Cleveland, Catherine Caroline. *The Great Revival in the West, 1797–1805*. Chicago: University Chicago Press, 1916.

Clowes, William. *Journals of William Clowes*. London: Epworth, 1951.

Conkin, Paul. *Cane Ridge America's Pentecost*. Madison: University of Wisconsin Press, 1990.

Cooper, William. "Mr. Cooper's Preface to the Reader." In *Jonathan Edwards on Revival*, 75–85. Edinburgh: The Banner of Truth Trust, 1991.

Cubberley, Ellwood P. *History of Education*. Cambridge: Houghton & Mifflin, 1948.

Currie, John. *New Testimony Unto and Further Vindication of the Extraordinary Work of God at Cambuslang, Kilsyth and Other Places in the West of Scotland*. N.p.: Smith and Hutchinson, 1743,

Cutts, William. "Presidential Address at the Primitive Methodist Conference, 1883." In *Minutes of the Primitive Methodist Conference, 1883*, 101–11. London: Ralph Fenwick, 1883.

Dallimore, Arnold. *George Whitefield: The Life and Times of the Great Evangelist of the Eighteenth-Century Revival*. 2 vols. Edinburgh: The Banner of Truth Trust, 1971.

Davenport, Frederick M. *Primitive Traits in Religious Revivals* London: Macmillan, 1905.

Davies, Rupert. *Methodism*. Harmondsworth, UK: Penguin, 1964.

Dempster, Murray W., et al., eds. *The Globalisation of Pentecostalism: A Religion Made to Travel*. Carlisle: Regnum, 1999.

Dow, Lorenzo. *Journal of the Dealings of God, Man and the Devil*. N.p.: Faulkener, 1833.

Edwards, Jonathan. *An Account of the Revival of Religion in Northampton in 1740–1742, as Communicated in a Letter to a Minister in Boston* in *Jonathan Edwards on Revival*. Edinburgh: The Banner of Truth Trust, 1991.

———. *The Distinguishing Marks of a Work of the True Spirit of God*. Edinburgh: The Banner of Truth Trust, 1991.

———. *A Narrative of Many Surprising Conversions*. Edinburgh: The Banner of Truth Trust, 1991.

Erskine, John. *An Attempt to Promote the Frequent Dispensing of the Lord's Supper*. Kilmarnock, UK: Wilson, 1749.

———. *The Signs of the Times Considered or High Probability That the Present Appearances in New England and the West of Scotland Are a Prelude of the Glorious things Promised to the Church in the Later Ages*. Edinburgh: Lumisden and Robertson, 1742.

Evans, Eifion. *The Welsh Revival of 1904*. Bangor, UK: Evangelical Press of Wales, 1974.

———. "The Welsh Revival of 1904: Problems and Blessings." *Reformation and Revival* 2 (1993) 13–28.
Fawcett, Arthur. *The Cambuslang Revival: The Scottish Evangelical Revival of the Eighteenth Century*. London: The Banner of Truth Trust, 1971.
Finney, Charles G. *An Autobiography*. London: Hodder & Stoughton, 1882.
———. *Lectures on Systematic Theology*. Grand Rapids: Eerdmans, 1953.
———. *The Memoirs of Charles G. Finney: The Complete Restored Text*. Edited by Garth M. Rosell and Richard A. G. Dupuis. Grand Rapids: Zondervan, 1989.
———. *Revivals of Religion: Lectures*. London: Oliphants, 1928.
———. *Sermons on Important Subjects*. New York: John S. Taylor, 1856.
Gillies, John. *Memoirs of the Life of the Reverend George Whitefield*. London: Dilly and Dilly, 1772.
Goforth, Jonathan. *By My Spirit*. London: Marshall, Morgan and Scott, 1957.
Goforth, Rosalind. *Goforth of China*. London: Marshall, Morgan and Scott, 1957.
Graham, Billy. *The Holy Spirit*. London: Collins, 1979.
Green, J. R. *Short History of the English People*. London: MacMillan, 1912.
Griffin, A. Rod. "Methodism and Trade Unionism in the Nottinghamshire-Derbyshire Coalfield, 1844–90." *Proceedings of the Wesley Historical Society* 37 (1969) 2–9.
Griffin, Bob. *Firestorms of Revival: How Historic Moves of God Happened and Will Happen Again*. Lake Mary, FL: Creation, 2006.
Griffin, Stanley C. *A Forgotten Revival*. Bromley, UK: Day One, 1992.
Halévy, Élie. *A History of the English People in 1815*. A History of the English People 1. 3 vols. London: Benn, 1913.
Hambrick-Stowe, Charles E. *Charles G. Finney and the Spirit of American Evangelicalism*. Grand Rapids: Eerdmans, 1996.
Harding, William H., ed. *Revivals of Religion*. Edinburgh: Oliphants, 1928.
Harrison, Everett F., ed. *Baker's Dictionary of Theology*. Grand Rapids: Baker, 1985.
Hattersley, Roy. *John Wesley: A Brand from the Burning*. London: Abacus, 2002.
Havner, Vance. *Hearts Afire*. North Charleston, SC: Independent Publishing, 2014.
Haykin, Michael A. G. *The Revived Puritan: The Spirituality of George Whitefield*. Dundas, ON: Joshua, 2004.
Heaseman, Kathleen. *Evangelicals in Action*. London: Bles, 1962.
Hindmarsh, D. Bruce. *The Spirit of Early Evangelicalism*. Oxford: Oxford University Press, 2018.
Hollenweger, Walter J. *The Pentecostals*. London: SCM, 1972.
Hopkins, Eric. *Industrialisation and Society: A Social History 1830–95*. London: Routledge, 2000.
Hudson, Winthrop S. *Religion in America*. New York: Scribner's, 1965.
Hughes, Gwilym. *Evan Roberts, Revivalist*. N.p.: Revival Library, 2013.
Hughes-Roberts, E. "Sketches from the History of Psychiatry: A French View of a Welsh Revival." *Psychiatric Bulletin* 16 (1992) 296–98.
Ives, K. "Douglas Brown and the Lowestoft Revival." https://www.keithshistories.com/moody-stuart-a-man-of-prayer/biographies-of-19th20th-church-leaders-7082.php.
Johnson, Charles A. *The Frontier Camp Meeting*. Dallas: Southern University Press, 1955.
Jones, Brynmor P. *An Instrument of Revival: The Complete Life of Evan Roberts, 1878–1951*. South Plainfield, NJ: Bridge, 1995.

———. *Voices from the Welsh Revival, 1904–1905*. Bridgend: Evangelical Press of Wales, 1995.

Jones, David Ceri, et al., eds. *The Elect Methodists: Calvinistic Methodism in England and Wales*. Cardiff: University of Wales Press, 2016.

Jones, R. B. *Rent Heavens: The Revival of 1904*. London: Pioneer Mission, 1950.

Joyner, Rick. *The Power to Change the World*. Edinburgh: Morning Star, 2010.

Kay, William K. *Pentecostalism: A Very Short Introduction*. Oxford: Oxford University Press, 2011.

Kendall, Holliday J. *The Origin and History of Primitive Methodism*. 2 vols. London: Dalton, 1906.

Kent, John. *Holding the Fort*. London: Epworth, 1978.

Lacy, Benjamin R. *Revivals in the Midst of the Years*. Hopewell, VA: Royal, 1968.

Lake, John G. *Adventures with God*. Tulsa, OK: Harrison, 1981.

Liardon, Roberts. *God's Generals: Why They Succeeded and Why Some Failed*. Tulsa, OK: Albury, 1996.

———, comp. *The Great Azusa Street Revival: The Life and Sermons of William Seymour*. New Kensington, PA: Whitaker House, 2020.

Lloyd-Jones, D. Martin. *Growing in the Spirit*. Eastbourne, UK: Kingsway, 1989.

Lowe, Karen. *Carriers of Fire: The Women of the Welsh Revival*. Llanelli, UK: Shedhead, 2004.

Macfarlan, Duncan. *The Revivals of the Eighteenth Century, Particularly at Cambuslang: With Three Sermons by the Rev George Whitefield, Taken in Shorthand*. Edinburgh; Johnstone, n.d.

Martin, David. *Tongues of Fire: The Explosion of English Protestantism in Latin America*. Oxford: Blackwell, 1993.

Matthews, David. *I Saw the Welsh Revival*. Belfast: Ambassador, 2004.

McClymond, Michael J. "Christian Revival and Renewal Movements." In *The Wiley Blackwell Companion to World Christianity*, edited by Lamin Sanneh and Michael J. McClymond, 158–254. Chichester: Wiley, 2016.

McCulloch, Robert. *Some Account of Mr McCulloch of Cambuslang, Chiefly as Furnished by His Son*. N.p.: n.p., 1793.

McDow, Malcolm, and Alvin L. Reid. *Firefall: How God Has Shaped History through Revivals*. Nashville: Broadman & Holdman, 1977.

McGready, James. "Narrative of the Revival in Logan County." *New York Missionary Magazine* 3 (1803) 192–94.

———. *The Posthumous Works of James Mc Greedy*. 2 vols. Nashville: Smith's Steam, 1831.

McLoughlin, William G. *Modern Revivalism from Charles Finney to Billy Graham*. Eugene, OR: Wipf & Stock, 2004.

Milburn, Geoffrey. *Primitive Methodism*. London: Epworth, 2013.

Mitchell, George J. *Revival Man: The Jock Troup Story*. Fearn, UK: Christian Focus, 2002.

Moorman, John R. H. *A History of the Church in England*. London: Adam and Charles Black, 1963.

Morgan, J. Vyrnmy. *The Welsh Religious Revival*. London: Chapman & Hall, 1909.

Murray, Iain. *Revival and Revivalism: The Making and Marring of American Evangelism*. Edinburgh: The Banner of Truth Trust, 1994.

Noll, Mark A. *A History of Christianity in the United States and Canada*. Grand Rapids: Eerdmans, 1992.

———. *The Old Religion in a New World*. Grand Rapids: Eerdmans, 2002.
Obelkevich, James. *Religion and Rural Society in South Lindsey, 1825–1875*. Oxford: Oxford University Press, 1976.
Orr, J. Edwin. *The Flaming Tongue: Evangelical Awakenings, 1900–*. Chicago: Moody, 1975.
Packer, James I. *God in Our Midst: Seeking and Receiving Ongoing Revival*. Reading, UK: Word, 1987.
Peckham, Colin, and Mary Peckham. *Sounds from Heaven: The Revival on the Isle of Lewis*. Ross-shire, UK: Christian Focus, 2020.
Penn-Lewis, Jesse, with Evan Roberts. *War on the Saints*. Poole, UK: The Overcomer Literature Trust, n.d.
Philip, Robert. *The Life and Times of George Whitefield*. London: George Virtue, 1938.
Piggin, Stuart. "Billy Graham in Australia, 1959—Was It a Revival?" *Evangelical History Review* 6 (1989) 2–33.
———. *Firestorm of the Lord*. Carlisle, PA: Paternoster, 2000.
Pratney, Winkie A. *Revival Principles to Change the World*. Lindale, TX: Ministry of Helps, 1984.
Rack, Henry D. *Reasonable Enthusiast*. London: Epworth, 2002.
Randall, Ian. "'The Breath of Revival': The Welsh Revival and Spurgeon's College." *Baptist Quarterly* 1 (2005) 196–205.
Rattenbury, Joseph E. *Wesley's Legacy to the World*. London: Epworth, 1928.
Reed, Andrew, and James Matheson. *A Narrative of the Visit to American Churches by the Deputies of the Congregational Union of England and Wales*. Vol. 2. 2 vols. London: Harper, 1835.
Ritchie, Jackie. *Floods upon the Dry Ground*. Peterhead, UK: Peterhead Offset, 1983. http://www.bibleteachingprogram.com/floods/floodsindex.htm.
Ritson, Joseph. *The Romance of Primitive Methodism*. London: Dalton, 1909.
Robe, James. *A Faithful Narrative of the Extraordinary Work of the Spirit of God*. London: Mason, 1742–43.
Robeck, Cecil M. *The Azusa Street Mission and Revival: The Birth of the Global Pentecostal Movement*. Edinburgh: Nelson, 2006.
Scotland, Nigel. *Apostles of the Spirit and Fire*. Milton Keynes: Paternoster, 2009.
———. *George Whitefield: The First Transatlantic Revivalist*. Oxford: Lion Hudson, 2019.
———. *Methodism and the Revolt of the Field*. Gloucester, UK: Sutton, 1981.
Semmel, Bernard. *The Methodist Revolution*. London: Heinemann, 1984.
Shaull, Richard, and Waldo Cesar, eds. *Pentecostalism and the Future of the Churches*. Grand Rapids: Eerdmans, 2000.
Sherwood Eddy, George. *A Spiritual Awakening*. Oxford: Lion, 1986.
Skevington Wood, A. *The Burning Heart: John Wesley, Evangelist*. Exeter: Paternoster, 1967.
———. *The Inextinguishable Blaze*. Grand Rapids: Eerdmans, 1968.
Southey, Robert. *The Life of John Wesley*. London: Hutchinson, 1903.
Sprague, William B. *Lectures on Revivals of Religion*. Edinburgh: The Banner of Truth Trust, 1958.
Spring, Gardiner. *Personal Reminiscences of the Life and Times of Gardiner Spring*. New York: Scribner's, 1866.
Stead, William T., and George Campbell Morgan. *The Welsh Revival*. Sun City Center, FL: Revival, 2015.

Stewart, James A. *Our Beloved Jock*. Philadelphia: Revival Literature, 1964.
Stone, Barton. *The Biography of Eld. Barton Stone, Written by Himself: with Additions and Reflections*. Cincinnati: J. A. & U. P. James, 1847.
Sykes, Norman. *Church and State in England in the Eighteenth Century*. Cambridge: Cambridge University Press, 1934.
Telford, John. *The Letters of John Wesley, Volume 3*. 8 vols. London: Epworth, 1931.
———. *The Life of John Wesley*. London: Epworth, 1969.
Thompson, David. *Nonconformity in the Nineteenth Century*. Abingdon, UK: Routledge & Kegan Paul, 1972.
Thompson, Flora. *Lark Rise to Candleford*. Harmondsworth, UK: Penguin Classics, 2008.
Tinney, James S. "In the Tradition of William J. Seymour." *Journal of the International Theological Centre* 4.1 (1976) 34–44.
Townsend, William J., et al. *A New History of Methodism*. 2 vols. London: Hodder & Stoughton, 1909.
Tyerman, Luke. *Life of the Rev George Whitefield*. 2 vols. London: Hodder & Stoughton, 1877.
Tyson, John R. *Assist Me to Proclaim: The Life and Hymns of Charles Wesley*. Grand Rapids: Eerdmans, 2007.
Wacker, Grant. *Heaven Below: Early Pentecostals and American Culture*. Cambridge: Harvard University Press, 2001.
Walford, John. *Memoirs of the Life and Labours of the Late Venerable Hugh Bourne: By a Member of the Bourne Family*. 2 vols. London: Wilkinson, 1855.
Ward, W. Reginald. *Religion and Society in England, 1790–1850*. London: Batsford, 1972.
———. "Religion of the People and the Problem of Control, 1790–1830." In *Popular Belief and Practice: Papers Read at the Ninth Summer Meeting and the Tenth Winter Meeting of the Ecclesiastical History Society*, edited by G. J. Cuming and Derek Baker, 237–57. Studies in Church History 8. Cambridge: Cambridge University Press, 1972.
Warren, Max. *Revival: An Inquiry*. London: SCM, 1954.
Watt, Eva S. *Floods on Dry Ground: Revival in the Congo*. Edinburgh: Marshall, Morgan and Scott, 1946.
Wearmouth, Robert F. *Methodism and the Common People of the Eighteenth Century*. London: Epworth, 1945.
———. *Methodism and the Working-Class Movements in England, 1800–1850*. Clifton, NJ: Kelly, 1972.
Werner, Julia. *The Primitive Methodist Connexion*. Madison: University of Wisconsin Press, 1984.
Wesley, John. *A Collection of Hymns for the People Called Methodists*. London: Wesleyan Conference, 1877.
———. *The Journal of the Rev. John Wesley*. 8 vols. Edited by N. Curnock. London: Kelly, 1909–16.
———. *Sermons on Several Occasions, First Series*. Fourth Edition. 1787. Reprint, London; Epworth, 2009.
———. *Works of John Wesley*. 13 vols. Nashville: Abingdon, 1984.
Whitefield, George. *George Whitefield's Journals: A New Edition Containing Fuller Material Than Any Hitherto Published*. London: The Banner of Truth Trust, 1965.

———. *A Short Account of God's Dealings with the Reverend George Whitefield A.B. late of Pembroke College, Oxford 1714-1736*. Carlisle, PA: The Banner of Truth Trust, 1956.

———. *The Works of the Reverend George Whitefield, Late of Pembroke College, Oxford, and Chaplain to the Rt Hon. The Countess of Huntingdon*. 1772. 6 vols. Reprint, n.p.: Forgotten, 2015.

Wilson, Linda. *Constrained by Zeal*. Carlisle: Paternoster, 2000.

Wolfe, John. *The Expansion of Evangelicalism*. Nottingham: InterVarsity, 2006.

Wood, Laurence W. "John Wesley's Mission of Spreading Scriptural Holiness: A Case Study in World Mission and Evangelism." *Asbury Journal* 73.1 (2018) 8–49. DOI: 10.7252/Journal.01.2018S.02.

Woolsey, Andrew. *Channel of Revival: A Biography of Duncan Campbell*. Edinburgh: The Faith Mission, 1982.

Select Manuscripts, Documents, and Papers Consulted

The Advance.
The Apostolic Faith.
Buchan Observer.
The Christian.
The Christian Herald.
Christian Monthly History.
Christian Register.
The Churchman's Magazine.
Durham Chronicle.
Glasgow Herald.
Glasgow Weekly History.
Keswick Week.
London Daily News.
The Londonderry Sentinel.
Los Angeles Times.
Methodist Magazine.
Metropolitan Tabernacle Pulpit.
Motherwell Times.
New York Missionary Magazine.
Norfolk News and Weekly Press.
The People's Journal.
Primitive Methodist Magazine.
The Primitive Methodist Quarterly Review (1883).
The Primitive Methodist Quarterly Review (1902).
Psychiatric Bulletin (1992).
The Revivalist.
Sentinel.
Stornoway Gazette and West Coast Advertiser.
The Western Daily Press.
Western Mail.
Yarmouth and Gorleston Times.
Yarmouth Independent.

Index

Aberdeen, 47, 193, 196
Abolition Societies, 8
Adams, 115
Africa, 172
Agape meals, 66
Age of Reason, 73
Aitken, Samuel, 121
Albany, 80
Aldersgate Street, 8, 52
Ambler, Rod, 106
America, 52, 172
American Bible Society, 181
American Colonies, 55, 221, 223–24, 227
American Tract Society, 181
A Faithful Narrative of the Extraordinary Working of the Spirit of God, 49
An Account of the Revival in Northampton in 1740-1742, 26
Andover Theological Seminary, 90
Anglesey, 148
Anglican Church, 73, 149
Antwerp, 119
anxious seat, 125
Appalachian Mountains, 73, 80
Armstrong, John, 4, 5
Arnol, 212
Asbury, Francis, 80, 84, 89
Assemblies of God, 180

Associate Presbytery, 41, 48
assurance, 52, 60, 61
Atchison, Ralph, 112
Auburn, 122
Aylesbury, 2, 105
Azusa Street, 3, 161–62, 167, 168–70, 172–75, 177–81, 223, 227, 232

Baltimore, 75, 78, 174
Bangor, 148-49
baptism in the Holy Spirit, 116, 145, 165–66, 176–77, 178–80, 217, 234
baptisms, 173
Baptists, 79, 85, 88, 148, 150, 184, 186, 195, 200, 226–27
barking exercise, 85–86
Barratt, Thomas Ball, 172
Bartleman, Frank, 162–63, 167, 169–73, 175, 227, 229
Barvas, 204, 209, 213, 215, 218, 220, 223, 225
Baxter, George, 89
Beecher, Lyman, 13, 81, 89, 125–26
Belfast, 213
Beman, Nathan, 122
Bemersley, 109
Bennet, William, 83
Benton, John, 100–102

Berneray, 213–14
Berridge, John, 67
Blackheath, 58
Boddy, Rev Alexander, 178
Book of Common Prayer, 54, 114
Bosanquet, Mary, 67
Boston, 126
Boston, Mass, 127
Bourne, Hugh, 2, 91, 94–96, 98–101, 103–4, 107–9, 225, 227
Brethren, 193
Bristol, 51, 56, 59, 63
British Temperance League, 61, 174
Broadway Tabernacle, 127–28
Brown, Douglas, 3, 182, 185–91, 193–94, 196–200, 233, 234
Buckinghamshire, 105
Buell, Samuel, 23, 27–28, 32
Bultitude, Elizabeth, 106
Burr, Aron, 89
Burt, Thomas, 111–12

Cairnbulg, 195
Cambridge, 191
Cambuslang, 1, 34–38, 41, 43–49, 222, 228, 239
camp meetings, 83–84, 96–98, 100, 102, 108–9, 171
Campbell, Duncan, 152, 157, 163, 203–5, 207–9, 211, 215–18, 220, 223, 229
Campbell, Catherine, 216
Campbell, Hugh, 205
Canada, 172
Cane Ridge, 2, 75–78, 83
Cannock Common, 101
Capper, Joseph, 111
Cardiff, 149, 156
Cardiff Baptist Tabernacle, 148
Cardiff Citizens Union, 150
Carloway, 219
Cartwright, Peter, 73, 79–82, 84–86, 88–89, 224, 231
Cennick, John, 39
Chadwick, Samuel, 214
Chambers, Oswald, 214
Charlton, George, 110
Charterhouse School, 53

Chartism, 111
Chatham Garden Theatre, 126
Chauncy, Charles, 26
Chicago, 171, 174
China, 173
Church of England, 16, 52, 71, 92, 156, 215
Church Missionary Society, 3
Church of God, 81, 181
Church of God of Prophecy, 181
Church of Scotland, 2, 41, 207, 220
Clowes, William, 2, 92, 94–99, 102–4, 108–9, 225, 227
College of New Jersey, 33
colleges, 90
colliers, see miners
Colne, 63
communicants, 20, 138
confessing Christ, 142, 147
Congleton, 96
Congregational churches 1, 16, 32, 81, 126, 189, 196
conversational preaching, 107, 114
conversions, 2, 12, 14, 20–21, 26, 46, 51–52, 77, 95, 113, 115, 130–31, 189, 193, 205, 210, 229, 225
Cooper, Thomas, 111
Cooper, William, 29
Cordiner, David, 195
Countess of Huntingdon, Selina, 58, 67, 218
Coventry, 103
Crawfoot, James, 98
Crawford, Florence, 162
Cullen, 196
Cumberland circuit, 73
Currie, John, 46
Cutts, William, 110

Daily News, 189–90
dancing, 95, 102
dancing exercise, 85
Davies, Annie, 144
Davies, Mary, 144
Day of Pentecost, see Pentecost
De Kalb, 129
Deerfield, 23
Delamotte, Elizabeth, 70

Index

Delaware, 122
Dent, Mark, 112
Dow, Lorenzo, 92–93
Dowlais, 144
Drummond, Henry, 214
drunkenness, 93, 150–51, 201–2, 232
Dundee, 37, 45
Durham, 103, 105, 112
Durham, William, 162, 171, 175, 179
Dwight, Timothy, 80

East Anglia, 103–4, 183–84, 191–92, 196–97, 201
East Dereham, 104
East London Tabernacle, 182
East Windsor, 17, 24
Eastern Daily News, 191, 198
Edinburgh, 34, 37, 45, 203, 210
Edwards, Jonathan, 1, 4, 6, 9, 17–28, 30, 32, 82, 158, 222, 228, 230, 232–33
Edwards, Timothy, 17
Enlightenment, 19
Enthusiasm, 77
Epworth, 53, 64
Erskine, Ebenezer, 48
Erskine, John, 43, 47
Evans Mills, 118–19
Evans, Florrie, 144
Evans, Eifion, 157
Evans, Owen, 159
Evans, Sidney, 139, 140, 144
Everton, 67
evening meetings, 132
Europe, 155
exhorting, 76, 83, 147

Falkirk, 206
Farrow, Lucy, 165
Female helpers, 67, 107, 135
Female preaching, 106
Ferguson, Hugh, 182, 185–86, 189, 192, 198, 209
Filey, 103
Finney, Rev Charles, 2, 116–19, 121–22, 124, 126–29, 131–32, 134–35, 223, 225–26, 229, 232
First World War, 105, 184, 193, 206

Francke, Hermann, 53
Flamborough Head, 103
Fraserburgh, 195
fruit of the Spirit, 11, 12

Gainsborough, 102
Gale, Rev George, 115, 118
Garrick, David, 56
Gasper River, 74–75
Georgia, 52, 54, 56, 88
Gilles, John, 43, 48
Glamorgan, 150
Glasgow, 1, 34–35, 37–38, 45, 197, 210
Glasgow Tent Hall, 197
Glasgow Weekly History, 42
Goreseinon, 140, 146
Gouverneur, 120
Graham, Billy, 12, 14
Greasley, Peter, 184
Great Awakening, 14, 17, 90
Great War, see First World War
Great Yarmouth, see Yarmouth
Green, Anson, 124
Griffin, Edward, 81
Grimshaw, Rev William, 66
Guyse, John, 25

Halevy, Elie, 71
halfway members, 20, 39
Halley, William, 45, 47
Hamilton, 34–35, 46, 116
Hamilton, Alexander, 89
Hanham Mount, 58
Hardie, William, 184, 188, 200
Harris, 211–13, 216, 218
Harris, Howell, 59, 61–62
Harriseahead, 94, 96, 108
Hatfield, 23
Haworth, 66
Hayes, John, 184–85
healing, 165, 168, 177, 179, 216
Hebrides, 202, 218, 225
Hebrides revival, 202, 209, 214–15, 218, 220, 229, 232
helpers, 67
Hepburn, Thomas, 112
Holden, Rev Dr Stuart, 197, 198
Holiness, 62

247

Holy Club, 41, 53, 60, 68, 71, 224
Holy Communion, 42–43, 44, 47, 54, 228
Holy Spirit, 8–9, 12, 15, 23, 27, 30–31, 37, 60, 65, 71, 74, 96, 107, 121–22, 126, 138, 141, 145, 147, 149, 153, 157, 161–62, 172, 176, 179, 193, 197, 205–7, 214, 217–18, 222, 233
Hopkey, Sophie, 54, 70
Horne, Richard, 111
Huddersfield, 63
Hull, 109
hypnosis, 87

Ilkeston, 106
impressions, 31
India, 159, 172
inquiry meetings, 121, 192
Ipswich, 189–90
Ireland, 96

James, Elizabeth, 70
Jedburgh, 48
Jefferson County, 118
Jenkins, Joseph, 137, 154
jerks / jerking, 85–87
Jones, Keri, 154
Jones, Mary, 151
Joshua, Seth, 137, 139–40, 154

Kennington Common, 56, 60, 62
Kentucky, 72–73, 79–80, 82, 89
Keswick Convention, 150, 155, 197
Key, Robert, 104
Kilsyth, 41, 44, 46, 48–49, 222, 228
King, John, 110
Kingdom of God, 8
Kingswood, 55–56, 60, 67
Kirkland, Sarah, 106
Korea, 159

labouring classes, 114
Lake, John, 170
Lane Presbyterian Seminary, 128
Latter Rain, 181
Latter Rain Evangel, 172
Law, William, 52
Le Raysville, 119

Lectures on the Revival of Religion 3, 7, 127, 133
Leicester, 101, 103
Lewis, 202, 210, 211, 216, 219, 223, 225
Lincoln College, 54
Lloyd-George, David, 148
Lloyd-Jones, Martin, 8
Lochs, 209
Locke, John, 19
Logan County, 72
London, 44, 51, 59
Lord's Supper, 29, 38–41, 44–47, 66, 75, 84, 212, 228
Los Angeles, 161, 179
Los Angeles revival, 225
Los Angeles Times, 2, 162, 169, 171–73
Loughborough, 100. 103
Loughor, 140
love feasts, 95
Lowestoft, 3. 183–84, 189, 193, 196, 200–201, 225, 232
Lowestoft Convention, 191–92
Lowestoft Revival, 189, 193, 197, 201, 227
Luddites, 103
Luther, Martin, 51
Lyle, John, 77

MacLennan, Murdo, 219
Maine, 91
Martin, Henry, 189–90
Massachusetts, 1, 16
Metropolitan Tabernacle, 150
McCulloch, William, 2, 34–36, 38, 40–42, 45, 49, 230
McGee, John, 74, 82
McGee, William, 74
McGready, James, 2, 72–73, 75, 82–83, 98, 224
McKillop, Angus, 219
McKay, James, 203, 206, 208, 220
McLauren, John, 47
McLeod, Alexander, 202
McLeod, Margaret, 216
McNemar, Richard, 82
Merthyr, 145, 151, 153
Methodism, 85, 221

Index

Methodist Episcopal Church, 88, 162, 166
Methodist Revival, 222, 224, 227–28, 231
Methodist societies, 2, 61, 68, 71
Methodists, Cavinist, 59, 71
Meyer, Frederick, 146, 147, 163
miners, mine workers, 35, 55, 60, 101, 151
Moody, Dwight, 197, 214
Moore, Jennie, 179
Moorfields, 56, 62
Morgan, Ewin, 145
mourners, 83
Mow Cop, 93, 98, 100
Murray, Grace, 70
Murray, Iain, 4, 5, 8–10, 72, 81

Narrative of Many Surprising Conversions, 6, 22, 25, 222
Neath, 147
Ness, 218
Nettleton, Asahel, 84
New Haven, 17, 81
New Quay, 137, 147
New York City, 10, 17, 91, 124, 126, 135, 174, 233
New York State, 2, 18, 124, 126, 129
Newark, 102
Newcastle-upon-Tyne, 60
Noll, Mark, 72
Norfolk, 104
Northampton, 1, 17–19, 21–23, 27, 30–31, 80, 226, 228, 230, 232
Northfield, 23
Norton-on-the Moors, 98
Norway, 172
Norwich, 102, 183, 194
Nottingham, 100, 103

Obelkevich, James, 114
Oberlin College, 124, 128–29, 232
Oglethorpe, James, 54
Ohio, 82
Oldham, 102
Olivers, Thomas, 68
Oneida County, 116, 118, 120, 129
Oriskany Creek, 121, 223
Orr, Edwin, 151

Oulton Broad, 184, 189
Oxford, 41, 54, 71
Oxford University, 53, 224
Oxtoby, Johnny, 102

Packer, James, 6
Parham, Charles, 165, 169
Parkinson, Charles, 112
Pasadena, 173
Passover, 4
Patterson, James, 123
Payson, Edward, 81
Peckham, Mary, 216, 229
Pembroke College, 55
Penn-Lewis, Jessie, 155, 156–57
Pennsylvania, 16, 91
Pentecostal denominations, 162, 179–80
Pentecostal movement, 2, 173, 181
Perronet, Vincent, 67
Philadelphia, 123–24, 132, 174
Pierpont, James, 17
Piggin, Stuart, 4, 6, 8, 13
Pisgah, 137- 140
Plymouth, 16
Portland, 82, 172, 175
Predestination, 58
prayer, 31, 35, 38, 50, 78, 81, 93, 95, 117, 120, 129–30, 137–38, 147, 169, 224
prayer meetings, 94, 203, 215
preaching, 56–57, 58, 61–63, 70, 74, 78, 82–84, 89, 101–3, 134, 145, 166, 168, 171, 182, 185, 189, 198, 214–15, 219–20, 226, 232
Presbyterians, 79, 84, 87–88, 91, 115, 121–22, 124–25, 127, 132–33, 199, 202, 226–27
Price, Peter, 153
Primitive Methodism, 2, 92, 99, 102, 105, 107–10, 112, 114, 184, 221, 223–24, 227, 231
Primitive Physic, 68
Princeton Theological Seminary, 81, 90
protracted meetings, 85
puritanism, 16

Ramsor, 102–3
Reading, 105, 132

Redruth, 63
Rees, Annie May, 144
Revival and revivals ix, 1, 2, 9–10, 15, 18, 23, 26, 37, 40, 45, 49–50, 58, 65, 71, 79, 82, 91, 99, 112–14, 136–37, 150–51, 153, 174, 211–12, 219, 221–22
Richardson, Joseph, 110
Ritson, Joseph, 102
Robe, James, 41–42, 44, 46, 48, 49
Roberts, Dan, 144, 233
Roberts, Evan, 138–40, 142–43, 146–48, 152–54, 155–57, 163, 225, 233
Rochester, New York, 124–26, 132–34, 184
Roman Catholics, 16, 34
Rome, 34, 121, 129, 131
Royal Commission on Religious Bodies in Wales, 149, 159
Rules for a Helper, 67
Russia, 155

Sabbath, 95
sacramental meetings, 74
Salvation Army, 150, 189, 193–94, 196
San Francisco, 167
Sanders, Robert, 35
Sankey, Ira, 7
Sankey's Sacred Songs and Solos, 7
Satan, 83, 107, 169, 179
Savannah, 55
Scotland, 38, 43, 59, 64, 189, 195–96, 201–2, 213
scottish drifters, 184, 195
Scougal, Henry, 53
Second Great Awakening, 2, 7, 9, 10, 72, 80–81, 226, 223
Second World War, 202
Seymour, William, 3, 161–62, 164–67, 169, 171, 174–75, 181, 225
Shaftesbury, Seventh Earl, 14
Shubotham, 92, 94
Singing, 66, 86, 144–45, 161, 207, 216, 228–29
Skevington, Thomas, 111
Smale, Joseph, 163
Smith, Christine, 203, 208, 215
Smith, Peggy, 203–4, 208, 215

Slavery, 89–90, 127
Society of Friends, 16
Somerville, Thomas, 48
South Africa, 160
South America, 160
South Carolina, 173
South Hadley, 23
speaking in tongues, 161, 165, 167–68, 176–77, 216–17
spiritual gifts, 11
Sprague, William, 3, 7, 10, 13
Spring, Gardiner, 10, 81
Spurgeon, Charles, 10, 14
St Lawrence County, 120
Stamp, John, 105
Stead, William, 153, 158
Steele, James, 99
Stockbridge, 33
Stoddard, Solomon, 17
Stone, Barton, 2, 78, 86–87, 90, 224, 231
Stornoway, 202, 209
Sunday Schools, 8, 109, 113
Sweden, 172

Tappan, Lewis, 124
Tarbert, 2, 10, 219
tarrying, 167–68, 179
taverns, 29, 36
temperance Societies, 8, 14, 89, 110, 134, 230, 232
Tennent, Gilbert, 24
Tennent, William, 24
Tennessee, 72, 79, 82, 85
Terry, Neely, 165
The American Bible Society, 91. 231
The American Society for the Promotion of Temperance, 134
The American Tract Society, 90, 231
The Apostolic Faith, 168, 170–72, 174–75, 178
The Apostolic Light, 193
The British Temperance League, 111
The Buchan Observer, 195
The Christian Harvester, 173
The Christian Herald, 194
The Distinguishing Marks of a Work of the Spirit of God, 29–30, 32
The Evening Lights, 165

The Female Missionary Society of the Western District of New York, 118
The Glasgow Herald, 194, 195, 210, 219
The Lancet, 145
The Last Call, 167
The Lewis Awakening, 209
The New York Evangelist, 133, 136
The Oberlin Evangelist, 133, 137
The Peoples Journal, 199
The Primitive Methodist Magazine, 109
The Revivalist, 130
The Sheffield Iris, 112
The Stornoway Gazette and West Coast Advisor, 202, 209, 210
The Troy Review, 122
The Western Mail, 141, 146
Thompson, Flora, 108
Tolland, John 19
Tomlinson, Milton, 181
Toronto, 13
total abstinence, 110
trade Unions, 113
Trevecca College 67
Troup, Jock, 193, 195–98
Troy, 122, 131
Tulip, John, 112
Tunstall Non-Mission Law, 100
Turner, Richard, 110
Tyson, John, 65

Upper New York State, 136, 223, 225
Upton-All-Saints, 104
Utica, 121 223

Virginia, 73, 82, 88

Wales, 140, 148–49, 151, 158–59
Walford, John, 97
Wapping, 64
War on the Saints, 155, 158–59
War of Independence, 73

Warren, Max, 3, 5
Warrington, 98
Washington DC, 174
Washington College, 89
Webster, Alexander, 41, 43
Wedgewood Pottery, 92–93
Wedgewood Pottery, 92, 93
Welsh Revival, 2, 6, 8, 137, 139, 163, 198, 214, 223, 225, 228, 232–33
Wesley, Charles, 2, 6, 8, 14, 53, 65, 67, 70, 84, 158, 222, 228, 230, 233
Wesley, John, 2, 8, 14, 52–54, 59–61, 64, 67, 70, 84, 92, 158, 222, 227, 230, 232, 233
Wesley, Samuel Junior, 70, 222
Wesley, Samuel Senior, 53
Wesley, Susannah, 53
Wesley's Hymns, 6
Wesleyan Methodism, 66, 92, 98, 103, 104, 149
Wesleyan Methodist Conference, 92
Whitefield, George, 26, 32, 36–42, 44, 66–70, 82, 84, 214, 218, 222, 230, 232–33
Wick, 196
Wigtown, 34
Wilberforce, William, 8
Williams, Nantlais, 154
Willison, John, 37
witches, 108
women's roles, 135, 147, 179, 232
Woolsey, Andrew, 218

Yale College, 17, 81, 90, 233
Yarmouth, 189, 191, 194–96, 198, 200–201
Yarmouth and Gorlestone Times, 193
Yarmouth Independent Standard, 190, 200
Yorkshire, 52, 105–6

www.ingramcontent.com/pod-product-compliance
Lightning Source LLC
Chambersburg PA
CBHW022004220426
43663CB00007B/960